"Seventy Sevens Are Decreed"

Journal of Theological Interpretation Supplements

MURRAY RAE
University of Otago, New Zealand
Editor-in-Chief

1. Thomas Holsinger-Friesen, *Irenaeus and Genesis: A Study of Competition in Early Christian Hermeneutics*
2. Douglas S. Earl, *Reading Joshua as Christian Scripture*
3. Joshua N. Moon, *Jeremiah's New Covenant: An Augustinian Reading*
4. Csilla Saysell, *"According to the Law": Reading Ezra 9–10 as Christian Scripture*
5. Joshua Marshall Strahan, *The Limits of a Text: Luke 23:34a as a Case Study in Theological Interpretation*
6. Seth B. Tarrer, *Reading with the Faithful: Interpretation of True and False Prophecy in the Book of Jeremiah from Ancient Times to Modern*
7. Zoltán S. Schwáb, *Toward an Interpretation of the Book of Proverbs: Selfishness and Secularity Reconsidered*
8. Steven Joe Koskie, Jr., *Reading the Way to Heaven: A Wesleyan Theological Hermeneutic of Scripture*
9. Hubert James Keener, *A Canonical Exegesis of the Eighth Psalm: Y*HWH*'s Maintenance of the Created Order through Divine Intervention*
10. Vincent K. H. Ooi, *Scripture and Its Readers: Readings of Israel's Story in Nehemiah 9, Ezekiel 20, and Acts 7*
11. Andrea D. Saner, *"Too Much to Grasp": Exodus 3:13–15 and the Reality of God*
12. Jonathan Douglas Hicks, *Trinity, Economy, and Scripture: Recovering Didymus the Blind*
13. Dru Johnson, *Knowledge by Ritual: A Biblical Prolegomenon to Sacramental Theology*
14. Ryan S. Peterson, *The* Imago Dei *as Human Identity: A Theological Interpretation*
15. Ron Haydon, *"Seventy Sevens Are Decreed": A Canonical Approach to Daniel 9:24–27*
16. Kit Barker, *Imprecation as Divine Discourse: Speech Act Theory, Dual Authorship, and Theological Interpretation*

"Seventy Sevens Are Decreed"

A Canonical Approach to Daniel 9:24–27

Ron Haydon

Winona Lake, Indiana
Eisenbrauns
2016

Copyright © 2016 Eisenbrauns
All rights reserved.

Printed in the United States of America

www.eisenbrauns.com

Library of Congress Cataloging-in-Publication Data

Names: Haydon, Ronald, author.
Title: Seventy sevens are decreed : a canonical approach to Daniel 9:24–27 / Ronald Haydon.
Description: Winona Lake, Indiana : Eisenbrauns, [2016] | Series: Journal of theological interpretation supplements ; volume 15 | Includes bibliographical references and index.
Identifiers: LCCN 2016027092 (print) | LCCN 2016027812 (ebook) | ISBN 9781575064352 (pbk. : alk. paper) | ISBN 9781575064369 (pdf)
Subjects: LCSH: Bible. Daniel, IX, 24–27—Criticism, interpretation, etc.
Classification: LCC BS1555.52 .H395 2016 (print) | LCC BS1555.52 (ebook) | DDC 224/.506—dc23
LC record available at https://lccn.loc.gov/2016027092

The paper used in this publication meets the minimum requirements of the American National Standard for Information Sciences—Permanence of Paper for Printed Library Materials, ANSI Z39.48-1984.♾™

Table of Contents

Acknowledgements ix
Abbreviations x
1. The Role of a Canonical Approach 1
   1. Introduction 1
      1.1. A Brief Outline of the Study 2
      1.2. Current Approaches to Daniel 4
   2. Literary Approaches to Daniel 9;24-27 4
   3. Daniel 9:24-27 in Light of Qumran 5
   4. Cultic Motifs as an Interpretive Method for Reading Daniel 9:24-27 6
   5. Canonical-Intertextual and Inner-Biblical Readings of
      Daniel 9:24-27 7
2. A Canonical Approach 10
   1. Canonics: The Historical Reconstruction of Canon 11
      1.1. Canonical-Intertextual Methods 15
   2. A Non-Material Unity of Canon 16
   3. Features of a Canonical Approach 18
      3.1. History, "Artifact" and the Final Form 18
      3.2. Unity and the Historical-Theological Shape of the Text 22
      3.3. Textual Characteristics of the Canonical Shape 22
      3.4. Textual Association within the Canonical Shape 22
      3.5. The Role of Intertextuality 23
      3.6. Inner-Biblical Exegesis 26
      3.7. The "Law and the Prophets" 28
      3.8. Bi-Partite vs. Tri-Partite 29

A Canonical Approach to Daniel

    4. Conclusion 31

3. The "Law and the Prophets" in Daniel 9:3-19 32

    1. Daniel 9:2–The Beginning of a Framework 33

        1.1. "The Books" 33

    2. Daniel 9:3-19 35

        2.1. Prayer for Revelation 35

        2.2 Prayer of Confession 37

        2.3. The "Law and the Prophets" in Daniel 9:3-19 38

        2.4. "Law of Moses" and the Pentateuch (Dan 9:11,13) 40

        2.5. Leviticus and the Pentateuch 41

        2.6. "Servants the Prophets" and the Prophetic Corpus

            (Dan 9:6,10) 45

        2.7. Jeremiah and the Major Prophet in Daniel 9:3-19 46

        2.8. The Bond Between Leviticus and Jeremiah 50

        2.9. Leviticus and Jeremiah as "Braided Texts" 52

    3. Daniel the "Servant" and the Outpouring of a Tradition 54

    4. The Seams Between the Torah-Prophets and Daniel 9:3-19 58

    5. The Deuteronomistic Editor as Main Interlocutor? 61

    6. Conclusion to 9:3-19 and Transition in 9:20-23 65

        6.1. Conclusion to 9:3-19 65

        6.2. Daniel 9;20-23: Transition to Interpretation (9:24-27) 66

4. Daniel 9:24-27 67

    1. The Seventy Sevens 67

        1.1. Past Research on the Seventy Sevens 67

        1.2. Lexical and Semantic Characteristics of the Seventy Sevens 69

        1.3. "Seventy Sevens" and Sabbath-Heptadic Themes in Interim

            Period Literature 73

        1.4. Jubilees and Daniel 9:24-27 73

        1.5. Enochic Texts and Daniel 9:24-27 75

        1.6. Other Scrolls and Daniel 9:24-27 75

    1.7. The Seventy Sevens as a Time Image 82

  2. Daniel 9:24-25: Introduction to the Kingdom Pattern 86

    2.1. Daniel 9:24 86

    2.2. The Most Holy? 87

    2.3. Daniel 9:25 93

    2.4. Various Breakdowns of the Heptadic Units 95

    2.5. To "Know and Understand" the Word Going Forth 99

    2.6. Identifying the "Anointed" Figures 102

    2.7. Ambiguity Within the Heptadic Units: "Seven and Sixty-Two Weeks" 104

  3. Daniel 9:26-27: The Conclusion to the Kingdom Pattern 107

    3.1. Daniel 9:26 107

    3.2. Daniel 9:27 110

    3.3. The Rise of the Desolating Force 112

    3.4. The Decreed End of the Desolating Force 116

  4. Conclusion 120

5. Ambiguity and Space 122

  1. The Biblical Theological Dimension of Daniel 9:24-27 122

    1.1. Daniel's Expansion of Meaning: Preface to a Biblical-Theological Reading 123

    1.2. Prediction and Prophecy 124

    1.3. Apocalyptic and the Openness of the Text 125

    1.4. The Importance of History 127

    1.5. Creating Space and the Reception of Daniel 9:24-27 130

  2. Daniel 9:24-27 in the Olivet Discourse 131

    2.1. Persecution of the Faithful Saints 132

    2.2. The Mantle of Wisdom 133

    2.3. The "Abomination of Desolation" 135

    2.4. Discontinuities Between Daniel 9:24-27 and Matthew 24-25 136

  3. Daniel 9:24-27 and the Character of Two-Testament Scripture 138

  4. Daniel 9:24-27 and the Rule of Faith 140
6. Conclusion 143
  1. Daniel 9:24-27 as Christian Scripture 143
    1.1. Space Enough for the Reader 143
    1.2. "Wisdom and Discernment" from the Reader 145
  2. Conclusion 147
Appendix. The Dual-Location of the Book of Daniel 150
Bibliography 153
Index of Authors 174
Index of Scripture 178

Acknowledgments

I thank Julie for her love, resolve and hard work—without her, there would not even be a proposal. I would like to thank Dr. VanGemeren, for his encouragement, wisdom and resolute dedication to the strangeness of my thesis. God's faithfulness navigated me through this project. He has allowed me to glimpse but a hint of His mystery. Lastly, I acknowledge the notion of ambiguity, a topic humbly presented not only in content but also in form.

Abbreviations

BTONT	*Biblical Theology of the Old and New Testament*
IOTS	*Introduction to the Old Testament as Scripture*
LP	The Law and the Prophets
TrinJ	*Trinity Journal*

CHAPTER 1
The Role of a Canonical Approach

1. Introduction

Daniel 9:24-27 has long been fertile ground for various interpretive practices, prophecies and political illustrations. Unfortunately, as more and more interpretations have mounted, this fertile ground has come to be, according to James Montgomery, a "trackless waste of assumptions and theories."[1] Though we need not share Montgomery's bleak outlook, it is striking that so many interpretive possibilities (and positions) exist. This small, but pregnant, section of text has generated, and continues to generate, a broad tradition of timelines and predictions.[2] Is such a high volume of interpretations purely an issue of genre?

In its use of time and imagery, Daniel 9 is unlike any other text in the Old Testament. There are odd combinations of numbers, a confession that appears out of place (9:3-19) and even mysterious, unnamed figures that move in and out of sequence of the passage (9:25-26). Combining imagery with earlier texts and Daniel's unique style of ambiguity leaves a number of questions open to the reader. We tend to forget that Daniel is both a revelation (2:47; 7:16; 9:23) *and* a "sealed" text (8:26; 12:4, 9). Such tension makes it difficult to adjudicate between a valid interpretation and an invalid interpretation that oversteps the boundaries of context. Unfortunately, few ask what are the hermeneutical forces surrounding Dan 9:24-27 that cause so many chronologies and historical-allusions to break down or achieve meager success. By focusing on Daniel's associative techniques (e.g., Jer 25:10-12, 29:10; Lev 26:34-35), we add a new angle of interpretation to an old discussion. A careful approach to the text is necessary: one that entails attention to methodology, an expansion of our notions of history and tradition building, healthy theological discernment and a keen, hermeneutical sensitivity.

---

[1] James Montgomery, *A Critical and Exegetical Commentary on the Book of Daniel*, 3rd ed. (Edinburgh: T&T Clark, 1959), 390.

[2] Oddly enough, the popular readings of Daniel 9 tend to also be the most extreme: one interpreter sees the "covenant" (9:27) as an attempt to settle the current Arab-Israeli controversy (David Jeremiah, *What in the World is Going On? 10 Prophetic Clues You Cannot Afford to Ignore* [Nashville: Thomas Nelson, 2008], 66); see also Hal Lindsey, *The Late, Great Planet Earth* [Grand Rapids: Zondervan, 1970], 54-57).

What does this new angle of interpretation submit? I suggest Dan 9:24-27 forms an interpretive space in which communities locate themselves and shift their expectations from rest and sin-debt (Lev 26:34-35 and Jer 25:10-12, 29:10-14) to Daniel's vision of complete rest stresses the restoration and trials of the saints (cf. Dan 7:21-22) amid oppressive human regimes, envisioning an exile that spans over all epochs and finalizing in the "end of sin" itself (9:24). Two arguments support this claim; a) the text of Daniel 9 patterns itself after the images, motifs and themes of Lev 26:34-40 and Jer 25:10-12, 29:10, building from the Sabbath-heptadic traditions, into a large-scale pattern of seventy sevens; b) at the same time, the author ambiguates key historical details in 9:24-27 in order to make room for more than one possible readership. In the end, Daniel's notion of completion focuses on the wise saints who indwell the text of 9:24-27.

1.1 A Brief Outline of the Study

We begin with the images, motifs and patterns of textual association found in Lev 26:27-40 and Jer 25:8-14, 29:10 and trace back the roots of the Sabbath-heptadic tradition.[3] Images constituting these patterns include, but are not limited to, time-imagery (hnv, obv, tbv, owbv) and cultic imagery (vdqm, Mmv, ovp, tatj, Xwqv). Indeed, Daniel scholarship recognizes the influence of Jeremiah and the Pentateuch on Daniel 9. Yet only a fraction of studies attempts an in-depth analysis as to why Daniel chooses these associations. These links are interwoven patterns from which Daniel weaves a larger pattern (e.g. seven, weeks, desolation, iniquity, Sabbath, rest, restoration, end, completion). To produce this pattern, Daniel inherits a narrative that begins in the Pentateuch, continues (primarily) through the work of Jeremiah, and reaches a canonical *dénoument* in ch. 9. Along the way, the narrative widens in scope. This development in organic and a natural result of interpreting the "theological grammar" of the Law and the Prophets (LP).[4] The pattern results in an exploration of the seventy sevens (v. 24), wherein empires rise and fall, followed by the finalization of this time-image "in disguise" or behind a veil (vv. 26-27).

Additional associations will also come from selected extra-biblical texts. These associations sharpen the argument for "sabbatical patterning" acquainting us with both the similarities and divergences in canonical and extra-canonical language. Extra-biblical texts also reveal that the seventy sevens image is anything but homogeneous. Webs of imagery (obv, tbv, owbv, Ktj,

---

[3] These central texts do not preclude a study of related texts which may contain components of the "sabbatical-cycle" pattern: Lev 25:8-12; Jer 27:17-22.

[4] Stephen Chapman, *The Law and the Prophets: A Study in Old Testament Canon Formation* (FAT 27; Tübingen: Mohr Siebeck, 2000). Chapman's work provides guidelines for an evaluation of "the Law and the Prophets" in Daniel 9 (esp. vv. 3-19). Two "related scriptural traditions" stitch together the final form of Daniel 9 with seemingly "deuteronomic language and ideas" (146).

Mmv) and prominent word-clusters (e.g. seventy//sabbath, weeks//jubilee, temple//iniquity) are starting points. This constellation of apocalyptic texts is what, in part, informs Daniel's *Vorbild* and the book's reception in later Judaism. In examining these extra-canonical sources, we can also compare associative techniques involving the seventy sevens or variations on the Sabbath-heptadic tradition.[5] Comparing these extra-canonical interpretations of a heptadic oracle to the techniques in Daniel 9 will shed light on the chapter's multifaceted, intertextual strategy. Are these authors – both canonical and extra-canonical—using the Sabbath-heptadic tradition to encourage the community in light of dire predictions (cf. CD III, 20-IV, 4) or to accentuate the triumph of the righteous at the end of time (cf. 1QM XI, 5-7; 4Q174 III, 18-IV, 4)?

Given the scale of this sabbatical patterning, who takes on the role of audience? It is here that ambiguity in 9:24-27 plays an integral part. Sadly, the obscurity of the text is not a common feature in studies on Dan 9:24-27. Scholars fixate on a particular historical reality behind the text; this preoccupation tends to neglect the puzzling nature of Daniel's imagery. Forming a hard, historical structure(s) behind Daniel 7-12 short-circuits the canonical force of the book, as Childs rightly claims, and fails to recognize how the meaning of Dan 9:24-27 is not readily available.[6] Daniel's intent to hide the meaning of certain texts hints at the author's goal to broaden the base of potential readers of 9:24-27. Most think of "gapping" information as indicative of ambiguity, but Daniel also forms ambiguities in word-choices (MyIoVbIv MyIoUbDv) omission of key terms (e.g. the term hînDv), open-ended syntax (e.g. punctuation in 9:25) and broad phrasing (e.g. Owl NyEaϑw [9:26]).

The final section moves into the biblical theological dimension of Dan 9:24-27. Ambiguity transitions into the creation of interpretive and confessional space. Within the space left by Daniel's style, the faithful community is able to locate itself within the theological message of the text. From this vantage point, the faithful community of the NT (cf. Matthew 24-25; Mark 13-14; Luke 21) and, it follows, the contemporary "two-testament" community find themselves in accordance with the canonical shape of the text.

To conclude this brief sketch, we are tracking how Daniel shifts the "rest" of Lev 26:34-35 into completeness (cf. 9:24-27) through the images, motifs, patterns and traditions of Leviticus and Jeremiah. A pattern of loss, hardship and imperial upheaval enters into the tradition of rest and anticipated comfort. Restoration and exile grow larger in Daniel 9, expanding to arch over all time. Through his ambiguation of the text, the scale of reception becomes equally expansive, and includes a multitude of faithful readerships. Restoration, ac-

---

[5] Cf. Divorah Dimant, "The Seventy Weeks Chronology (Dan 9,24-27) in the Light of New Qumranic Texts," in *The Book of Daniel in the Light of New Findings* (ed. A.S. van der Woude; BETL 106; Leuven: Leuven University Press, 1993), 57-76. This study is an excellent paradigm outlining the role of interim period writings in studying Dan 9:24-27.

[6] Childs, *Introduction to the Old Testament as Scripture* (Philadelphia: Fortress, 1979) 613-17.

cording to Daniel's depiction, pertains less to the land (Lev 26:2, 11, 31; Dan 8:11-14, 9:17), and more to Yahweh's people who suffer in expectation of His kingdom.

1.2. Current Approaches to Daniel

To engage the size and complexity of Dan 9:24-27, we require sources that not only offer exegetical conclusions on the unit, but also consider how the passage's compositional logic, shape, themes, associations and tradition-history inform these conclusions. Unfortunately, many studies pit one camp of scholarship against another when divulging their sources (e.g. early versus late dating). The following selection, however, attempts to free the interpreter from choosing sides—rather, the intricacies of the approach obligate us to search for voices outside of two artificial extremes.[7] Without a balance of canonical, contextual and exegetical questions, these two poles fall victim to the same result: (1) an isolated and myopic reconstruction of events outside the text and (2) and a highly exclusive method of textual association. With this in mind, we turn to contributions that counter this problem to various degrees and are able to add points, clarify discussion or apply a necessary pressure to my proposal.

2. Literary Approaches to Daniel 9:24-27

Literary approaches to the book attempt to navigate between a conservative view and the "older critical view." Goldingay, for example, considers a "reconstructed critical view."[8] An overtly historical approach, according to Goldingay, "centers on a topic on which the text does not overtly focus, it

---

[7] Viewing the study of the book's context as a *web* of interrelated issues seems best (not just the assertion of a particular date or chronology). For most, the genre of the book is a product of its apocalyptic setting, which *in turn* sets a second century date for the book, which *in turn* affirms the book's diverse authorship, which *in turn* views prediction as part of the historical bedrock, which situates the messianic figures and hopes (e.g. 9:24-27) within the Antiochene crisis, which *in turn* speaks to the "end of prophecy," which *in turn* places the book in the Writings (MT), and so on. For others, a Babylonian date gives way to a single author, which *in turn* avoids charges of pseudonymity, which *in turn* reaffirms the authority of the prophetic oracles, whereby the predictions are no longer *vaticinum ex eventu*, which *in turn* allows for a Christotelic/messianic interpretation of certain passages (e.g. 9:24-27), which *in turn* confirms the genre as prophecy, and *in turn* sets Daniel into the corpus of Prophets (LXX) and so on. These two models represent large swaths of Daniel scholarship, but are by no means the only options. Questions of context—viewed in networks—can create a healthy variation. For example, an interpreter does not require a Babylonian date for the book of Daniel in order to affirm a Christotelic prediction of Dan 9:24-27 (cf. Hippolytus) or for Daniel 9 as a whole (cf. Jerome).

[8] Goldingay, "Story, Vision, Interpretation: Literary Approaches to Daniel," in *The Book of Daniel in the Light of New Findings*, 297.

misses the text's specific burden and thus misfocuses the interpretive task."⁹ This conviction plays out in his comments on Daniel 9: Goldingay emphasizes the interplay between Dan 9 and Leviticus/Jeremiah while effectively departing from the standard rendering of 9:24 and the seventy sevens.¹⁰ He also argues for multiple, prophetic voices in Dan 9:24-27 (cf. Ezek 28:2, 8, 14, 17; Isa 10:22-23).

3. Daniel 9:24-27 in Light of Qumran

Some interpreters compare Dan 9:24-27 to Qumran texts. Another way to describe this comparison, of course, would be a culturally and exegetically "genetic relationship."¹¹ Michael Knibb reads Daniel as "crisis literature" and argues that the canonical form "stems from the circles of those described in the book as 'the wise' (משכילים; 11:33, 35; 12:3, 10)."¹² Much of the language within these circles is part of a shared vocabulary functioning between Daniel and the sectarian texts.¹³ These studies shed light on the reception history of Daniel and add interpretive possibilities by way of language, socio-cultural background, and our textual-historical understanding of Dan 9.

Aside from the exegetical comparisons, evaluating the associative techniques of both text-types (canonical and non-canonical) is critical. James Vanderkam, Hanna Vanonen, and Moshe Bernstein examine these techniques within the scrolls themselves as well as Daniel apocalypses, compiling various taxonomies of intertextuality.¹⁴ In addition to the comparative research done

---

⁹ Ibid.

¹⁰ Ibid., *Daniel* (WBC 30; Nashville, Tenn.: Thomas Nelson, 1989), 228-29.

¹¹ Stefan Beferle, "The Book of Daniel and Its Social Setting," in *The Book of Daniel: Composition and Reception, Vol. 1*, 207. Some move beyond shared motifs and vocabulary to locating possible sectarian sources for Daniel (cf. Esther Eshel, "Possible Sources of Daniel," in *The Book of Daniel: Composition and Reception, Vol. 2*, 387-94).

¹² Knibb, "The Book of Daniel in Its Context," in *The Book of Daniel: Composition and Reception, Vol. 1*, (ed. John J. Collins and Peter W. Flint; Leiden: Brill, 2001), 18.

¹³ Ibid., "'You are Indeed Wiser than Daniel': Reflections on the Character of the Book of Daniel," in *The Book of Daniel in the Light of New Findings* (ed. A.S. van der Woude; BETL 106; Leuven: Leuven University Press, 1993), 399-411; Koch, "Die mysteriösen Zahlen der judäischen Könige und die apokalyptischen Jahrwochen," *VT* 28 (1978) 433-41; Dimant, "The Seventy Weeks," 57-76.

¹⁴ Vanderkam, "To What End? Functions of Scriptural Interpretation in Qumran Texts," in *From Revelation to Canon: Studies in the Hebrew Bible and Second Temple Literature* (ed. James Vanderkam; Leiden: Brill, 2002), 302-20; Vanonen, "The Textual Connections Between 1QM 1 and the Book of Daniel," in *Changes in Scripture: Rewriting and Interpreting Authoritative Traditions in the Second Temple Period* (eds. Hanne von Weissenberg and Juha Pakkala; Berlin/New Yorks: De Gruyter, 2011); Moshe Bernstein, "Scriptures: Quotations and Use," in *The Encyclopedia of the Dead Sea Scrolls* (ed. L.H. Schiffman and J.C. Vanderkam; Oxford: Oxford University Press, 2000), 839-42; see also Peter Flint, "Daniel and Qumran," in *The Book of Daniel: Composition and Reception Vol. 2*, 329-67.

in Qumran and Dan 9:24-27, we will also interact with select studies relating Dan 9:3-19 and the extra-canonical material—these insights provide valuable context for the canonical shape in and around 9:24-27.[15]

4. Cultic Motifs in Daniel 9:24-27

Emphasis on temple, priesthood and the sacrificial system of Israel create another avenue of Daniel study. Winfried Vogel, in his work *The Cultic Motif in the Book of Daniel*, believes Dan 9:24-27 is a window into the cultic backdrop of the book.[16] The temple is central to Vogel ("cultic space"), arguing that the surrounding time-imagery (9:2, 24) represents "cultic time." He also makes close connections to biblical numbers and their respective Levitical institutions—his primary interest lies in researching the cultic use of these numbers in the Hebrew canon.

Though cultic motifs are not central to her work, Amy Willis' *Dissonance and the Drama of Divine Sovereignty in the Book of Daniel*, considers the cognitive upheaval Israel experiences through the defilement and destruction of her cultic elements, particularly the temple space.[17] Like Vogel, Willis focuses on the cultic vocabulary of Dan 9, which aligns the crushing blow of temple defilement with God's apparent "hiddenness." Daniel 9 expands upon the looser narrative of chs. 7-8, Willis argues, but remains a "discontinuous" part of the theme and, therefore, "provides a complementary response to the profound dissonance evident in ch. 8."[18] As for the construction of Dan 9, Willis summarizes her findings with special attention to the interplay between "divine relationality," a deuteronomistic prayer and notes of mantic historiography.[19] Coupled with this larger work, Willis' 2011 SBL paper, "The Plans of God in Jeremiah and Daniel," effectively demonstrates the manner in which the breadth of Daniel's exegetical program is *at least* partially informed by Jeremianic material.[20]

---

[15] See Daniel Falk, "Qumran Prayer Texts and the Temple," in *Sapiential, Liturgical and Poetical Texts from Qumran - Oslo, 1998* (Leiden: Brill, 2000), 106-26; also "Scriptural Inspiration for Penitential Prayer in the Dead Sea Scrolls," in *Seeking the Favor of God, Vol.2: The Development of Penitential Prayer in Second Temple Judaism* (ed. Mark Boda and Daniel Falk; Atlanta: SBL, 2007), 127-57.

[16] Vogel, *The Cultic Motif in the Book of Daniel* (New York: Peter Lang, 2010).

[17] Willis *Dissonance and the Drama of Divine Sovereignty in the Book of Daniel* (OTS 520; New York: T&T Clark, 2010).

[18] Ibid., 124. Central to the chapter is the prayer, which, to Willis, finds its roots in Leviticus 26—"the prayer's narrative of the desolate city and sanctuary" (130).

[19] Ibid., 124.

[20] Ibid., "The Plans of God in Jeremiah and Daniel" (SBL Consultation, "The Book of Daniel," 2011).

5. Canonical-Intertextual and Inner-Biblical Readings of Daniel 9:24-27

Through few in number, these studies focus on methods of association within the Hebrew canon and capitalize upon the connectivity of vocabulary, morphology, semantic structure and the like. In a recent work by Jordan Scheetz, *The Concept of Canonical Intertextuality and the Book of Daniel*, we find a study devoted to the intersection between canonical method, intertextuality and Daniel.[21] The term "canonical," in Scheetz's sense, "speaks of the reality that certain texts have been intentionally placed together" to fill a "particular collection of literature."[22] "Intertextuality" speaks to "the dialogue inherent in the canonical text because of the canon and canonical process."[23] Scheetz's canonical-intertextual interpretation of Dan 9:24-27 highlights his method through the varied divisions of synchronic and diachronic analysis. To illustrate, his closing remarks on Dan 9 pertain to the relationship between chs. 7-12 and the four "kingdoms" throughout (ch. 7 = kingdom 1; ch. 8 = kingdom 2; ch. 9 = kingdom 3; ch. 11 = kingdom 4).

Klaus Koch approaches the book of Daniel with a different set of "canonical" categories: form criticism, editorial stages and conflicting levels of compilation. Koch provides a collection of learned studies on the interpretation of and circumstances generating the text of Dan 9:24-27, and its "stage" within the book's development.[24] The passage, according to Koch, is not "eine beliebig herausgegriffene Zahl von Jahren für die Endzeit der Welt darbietet, auch nicht das Resultat eine spontanen visionären Eingebung" but is rather "das Ergebnis gelehrter und überkommener apokalyptischer Forschung und Exegese ist."[25] The use of the term "seventy sevens," according to Koch, is a convention or "apokalyptische Einteilung der Weltchronologie."[26] Little ties this convention to the sort of canonical method that looks to organic growth out of earlier biblical tradents (Fishbane) or shapes the text into a final form

---

[21] Jordan Scheetz, *The Concept of Canonical Intertextuality and the Book of Daniel* (Eugene: Pickwick, 2011).

[22] Ibid., 32.

[23] Ibid., 33. Scheetz draws from Julia Kristeva to flesh out the "intertextual" dimension. He follows her argument that "any text is constructed as a mosaic of quotations; any is the absorption and transformation of another" (Kristeva, *Revolution in Poetic Language* [trans. Margaret Waller; New York: Columbia University Press, 1984], 60).

[24] Koch, *Das Buch Daniel* (EdF 144; Darmstadt: Wissenschaftliche Buchgesellschaft, 1980), 155; "Stages in the Canonization of the Book of Daniel," in *The Book of Daniel: Composition and Reception, Vol. 2*, 421-46; "Sabbatstruktur der Geschichte," ZAW 95 (1983) 403-30; *The Rediscovery of Apocalyptic* (trans. Margaret Kohl, *Studies in Biblical Theology* Second Series 22; Naperville, Ill.: Alec R. Allenson, 1972).

[25] "... a randomly picked number of years depicting the end of the world, nor the result of a spontaneously, inspired vision" rather "it is a result of apocalyptic research and exegesis that is scholarly and traditional (Ibid., *Das Buch Daniel*, 154).

[26] Ibid., 152.

by incorporating associations to Leviticus, Deuteronomy and Jeremiah (Childs). "Canonical," in this case, is quite different from Childs's canonical approach; indeed, the exegetical conclusion that Koch reaches reflects his own redefinition of the term.[27]

Michael Fishbane studies Dan 9 within the context of inner-biblical exegesis.[28] The chapter, to Fishbane, expresses an "exegetical consciousness" that emits an awareness of prior text-sources and their influence on (or generation of) an exegetical program. For this reason, Daniel presents "an imposing concatenation of prophetic authorities."[29] Fishbane alludes to, at least in part, to a pressure exerted by the Prophets as a whole upon the text (9:2; vv. 3-19; vv. 20-23; vv. 24-27).

Interpreting the seventy sevens as a type of "sabbatical pattern" makes sense of the textual links to Lev 25 and other extra-biblical material.[30] In Fishbane's estimation, Daniel respecifies Jeremiah's 'seventy-year' oracle, a prophecy ending in failure, so that the author might transplant the number into "seventy sabbatical cycles" or a prolonged period of time. Adding, omitting and shaping earlier texts to fit and speak through new contexts is the essence of this "transformative exegesis." The exegetical task in vv. 24-27 reiterates the authority of God's decrees in spite of a failed prediction, Fishbane believes, and points to the links between 9:24-27, Jer 25:10-12, Zech 1:12 and 2 Chr 36:21. Lying behind the relationship between Jeremiah and Dan 9, Fishbane adds another component about which the author of Daniel 9 was "perfectly aware": the prayer (9:3-19) functions in response to the protatic nature of Lev 26:24-27. The same text and message is also taken up by the author of 2 Chr 36:21.[31] Fishbane writes, "the whole of Lev 26:27-45 has thus been exegetically reworked through a recontextualization of its contents, and cast

---

[27]Koch devotes an entire section to his disagreements with Childs's canonical approach to the book of Daniel ("Is Daniel also Among the Prophets?," *Int* 39 [1985] 117-130). Koch concedes that "the process of canonization must be taken into account in exegesis" (128), but for "correct understanding" of the text, an interpreter requires "new modes of interpretation exterior to the text" (129). Moreover, he finds it "dangerous to speak of a canonical shape of writing" since there is no evidence of "exact meanings intended by the canonizers" (129). Koch, in response to Childs's approach, notes how Childs dismisses the order of canonical books preceding Daniel ("The sequence of books ... had little significance" in *IOTS*, 503) as well as Daniel's role as prophet (618). Koch seems to define "canonical" as a theological afterthought to be applied over the pure text, much like a layer of paint. It follows, in this analogy, that various communities paint with various colors.

[28] Fishbane, *Biblical Interpretation in Ancient Israel* (Oxford: Clarendon, 1985). See also Knibb's article where he points to "the importance of inner-biblical exegesis in the formation of Daniel 7-12" and the "essentially scholarly character of this material" ("The Book of Daniel in Its Context," 17).

[29] Fishbane, 492.

[30] Ibid., 483.

[31] Ibid., 488.

as a prophecy of doom and hope for which Dan 9 is the fulfillment and antidote."[32] Daniel 9, therefore resolves the tension created by the negative outcome of Jer 25:9-12 and the potential for a positive outcome in Lev 26:40 by plotting these situations on a revealed "timetable of divine historical activity."[33]

We conclude the review with Brevard Childs' contribution. Childs believes we need "to reassess the book from a canonical perspective."[34] As the architect of the canonical approach, his works include a short study of the book of Daniel as it appears in its final form and theological shape. Childs, therefore, outlines a reading of Dan 7-12 that is both unique and noteworthy.[35] For Childs, Daniel is not creating a "new prophecy."[36] Rather, Daniel makes a series of interpretive moves and "combines the prophecy of Jeremiah with the punishment of disobedience which the Law of Moses (Dan 9:11) had threatened."[37] A duality of revelation and confession is forged in conjunction with the dual-authority of "the prophecy of Jeremiah" and the "law of Moses."[38] The governing question embedded within a canonical reading of Dan 9 is, Childs Asks, how a message set in the Babylonian Exile is to be read by a Maccabean audience (and subsequent audiences thereafter)? This reading of Dan 9 fuels a major claim of the following study: Dan 9 forms an interpretive space in which future generations may locate themselves. Emphasis shifts from the cult and temple to the well-being of the people; the author of Dan 9 is indeed "interested in history only in so far as it has significance for his own people."[39]

---

[32] Ibid., 489.

[33] Ibid.

[34] Childs, *IOTS*, 613.

[35] See also Childs' article, "Midrash and the Old Testament," in *Understanding the Sacred Text: Essays in honor of Morton S. Enslin on the Hebrew Bible and Christian Beginnings*, ed. John Reumann (Valley Forge: Judson, 1972), 47-59.

[36] Ibid., 616.

[37] Ibid., 617.

[38] In terms of biblical source-material, Daniel associates his text closely to Jeremiah, utilizing the text of the prophet in such a way that "the old prophetic text is adjusted to the new situation, but the new is still understood by means of the old text" (Childs, "Midrash," 55).

[39] C.C. Cargounis, "History and Supra-History: Daniel and the Four Empires," in *The Book of Daniel in Light of New Findings*, 395.

CHAPTER 2
A Canonical Approach

Before applying a canonical approach to Dan 9, we must clarify which "canonical" approach we are implementing. This approach depends, in large measure, upon Childs' canonical model.[1] His contribution has since become a well-forged field of inquiry and debate. Therefore, by comparing and contrasting the approach with similar methodologies, we will better illuminate the features at work in our study. In so doing, we will learn Childs' approach occupies a position between two notions of the term "canonical."[2] The first position fuses the *function* of canon with the form of the canon. This position, along with its field of study, has been termed "canonics."[3] The second position focuses almost entirely on the non-material aspects of canonical "unity." Proponents of the non-material position do not abandon the physical features of canon or the value of its historical development, but tend to look at the canon *from outside* the canon and through the lens of theological (and a theocentric) unity. Most of the recent proposals fall into one of these patterns. And though

---

[1] Childs, *IOTS*, 58-59. Many confuse this aim with James Sanders' own "canon criticism," which fails to see canonical development as anything more than "a search for identity in times of crisis" (*Torah and Canon* [Philadelphia: Augsburg/Fortress, 1972]); for a recent treatment of this idea by Sanders, see "What's Up Now? Renewal of an Important Investigation," in *Jewish and Christian Scriptures: The Function of 'Canonical' and 'Non-Canonical' Religious Texts* (London: T&T Clark, 2010), 1-7.

[2] Just within the last ten years, we can see a notable increase in "canonical" proposals: Frank Thielman, *Theology of the New Testament: A Canonical and Synthetic Approach* (Grand Rapids, Zondervan, 2011); Charles J. Scalise, *Hermeneutics as Theological Prolegomena: A Canonical Approach* (Macon, Ga.: Mercer University Press, 1994); Bruce K. Waltke, *An Old Testament Theology: An Exegetical, Canonical and Thematic Approach* (Grand Rapids: Zondervan, 2011); Scott Hahn, *Kinship by Covenant: A Canonical Approach to the Fulfillment of God's Saving Promises* (New Haven, Conn.: Yale University Press, 2009); Kevin J. Vanhoozer, *The Drama Of Doctrine: A Canonical-Linguistic Approach To Christian Theology* (Louisville: Westminster John Knox, 2005). Other works filling the category within the last 15-20 years include the following: John Sailhamer, *Introduction to Old Testament Theology: A Canonical Approach* (Grand Rapids: Zondervan, 1995); "Biblical Theology and the Composition of the Hebrew Bible," in *Biblical Theology: Retrospect & Prospect* (ed. Scott J. Hafemann; Grand Rapids: IVP, 2002), 25-36.

[3] Stephen Dempster, "An Extraordinary Fact: Torah and Temple and the Contours of the Hebrew Canon, Part 1," in *TynBul* 48/1 (1997): 23-56, here 24.

battle lines are usually drawn between biblical and theological studies, the *nature* of canon remains some strange, neutral ground upon which two warring factions are forced to make camp while ignoring the others' tents.

Once we explore these groupings, we will move to the final point: the collective merits of a middle approach. The canonical approach, as pioneered by Childs, positions itself between these spheres of "canonical" methodology and, by way of response, demonstrates the inextricable link bonding canonical shape to theological reflection. A traditional canonical approach, we will find, circumnavigates the pitfalls of these two notions while taking seriously the concerns of both.

1. Canonics: Historical Reconstruction of Canon

In 2002, the flagship volume on canonics–*The Canon Debate* edited by Lee McDonald–collectively defined how this particular sphere of scholarship views "canon" and "canonical."[4] Within this work, Eugene Ulrich accurately represents the assumption underlying canonics: on one side, there are historians who study the canon and its compilation, and on the other side, are "pastoral apologists" who plant "today's beliefs" in "yesterday's evidence."[5] To explore the full significance of this dichotomy and how it interacts with a canonical approach, I divide the section on canonics into two sections: development criticism and socio-political studies.

Within the vanguard of development criticism, Ulrich himself remains one of the most audible voices in the debate over the definition of "canon" and "canonical" texts. He calls canonical development a "journey," bringing together works of literature that are "somehow authoritative" in their nascent form and achieve closure through an "endorsement process."[6] The notion of a biblical canon, according to Ulrich, is a Christian construct of standardization borrowed by Judaism. Fixity and closure function as indicators of authority, popularity, textual sophistication and connectivity with the literature of other cultures.[7] A critical distinction grows from this model: canon as an authorita-

---

[4] *The Canon Debate: On the Origins and the Formation of the Bible* (ed. Lee McDonald; Peabody, Mass.: Hendrickson, 2002). The volume is quite one-sided in its contributions. Absent are portrayals of canon that promote the givenness or reception of God's word to His church; see a similar collection edited by J.M. Auwers and H.J. De Jonge (*The Biblical Canons* [Leuven: Leuven University Press, 2003]).

[5] Eugene Ulrich, "The Notion and Definition of Canon," in *The Canon Debate* (ed. Lee McDonald; Peabody, Mass.: Hendrickson, 2002), 21-35. Ulrich also provides a recent interpretation of the "canonical" development of the Hebrew Bible ("The Evolutionary Composition of the Hebrew Bible," in *Editing the Bible: Assessing the Task Past and Present* [ed. John Kloppenborg and Judith Newman; Atlanta: SBL, 2012], 23-40).

[6] Ulrich, "Notion and Definition," 30.

[7] See McDonald, *The Formation of the Christian Biblical Canon* (Peabody: MA: Hendrickson, 1995). McDonald writes "canon ... denotes a fixed standing or collection of writings" (20).

tive collection of books or *a collection of authoritative books*.⁸ In canonics, this remains less of a decision and more of a sequence. A seal of community approval is applied on completion of the canon (as late as the fourth century CE) which itself reflects a message conducive to the community's self-interest.

Functioning as the basis for most models in development criticism is Herbert E. Ryle's proposal. Ryle argues that the tri-partite canon of the Hebrew Bible began with the Torah which (closing in c.400 BCE), followed by "the Prophets" in the Maccabean era (c.200 BCE), confirmed by the exclusion of the book of Daniel, and concluded with the Writings, which were closed at the rabbinic council of Jamnia (90 CE).⁹ Each corpus allegedly underwent "discrete acts of canonization" and were supplied, filled and "closed" in a sequential manner.¹⁰ Canon, in this case, is a collection of authoritative books crystallized around the end of the first century. Though many insightful and conclusive studies question this nineteenth-century view, the majority of canon scholars still operate within the parameters of Ryle's model.¹¹

In contrast, a small group within canonics *minimizes* the role of fixity and closure in favor of an "open canon" wherein canonical texts are equivalent to authoritative scripture.¹² Canonicity is, therefore, an early development – naturally, the line between "canon" and "scripture" begins to blur. These two groups form the frontlines of what is called "the canon debate." As a number of writers point out, the disagreement consists of one fundamental question: is the canon *early* or *late*? Do all of these corpora of scripture need to be closed and fixed before the whole unit can be declared "canon" (late)? Or is "canon"

---

⁸ See Bruce M. Metzger, *The Canon of the New Testament: Its Origin, Development, and Significance* (Oxford: Oxford University Press, 1997), 283; Ulrich, "Notion and Definition," 33; Sidnie Crawford, "Understanding the Textual History of the Hebrew Bible: A New Proposal," in *The Hebrew Bible in Light of the Dead Sea Scrolls* (ed. Nóra Dávid and Armin Lange; Göttingen: Vandenhoeck & Ruprecht, 2012), 60-69.

⁹ Also A.C. Sundberg, *The Old Testament of the Early Church* (HTS 20; Cambridge: Oxford University Press/ Harvard University Press, 1964); cf. Frants Buhl, *Canon and Text of the Old Testament* (Edinburgh: T&T Clark, 1892); cf. Gerritt Wildeboer, *The Origin of the Canon of the Old Testament: An Historico-Critical Enquiry* (London: Luzac, 1895). For a redefinition of the council's purpose, see Sid Leiman, *The Canonization of the Hebrew Scriptures: The Talmudic and Midrashic Evidence* (Hamden: Archon Books, 1976), 126; cf. Stephen Chapman, "The Old Testament Canon and its Authority for the Christian Church," in *Ex Auditu* 19 (2003) 125-148; cf. E. Earle Ellis, *The Old Testament in Early Christianity: Canon and Interpretation in the Light of Modern Research* (Eugene: Wipf and Stock, 2003).

¹⁰ Chapman, *Law and the Prophets*, 4.

¹¹ *The Canon of the Old Testament: An Essay on the Gradual Growth and Formation of the Hebrew Canon of Scripture* (2d ed.; London: Macmillan and Co., 1904). Ryle organizes his work by the "first," "second," and "third" canons.

¹² Cf. John Barton, "Modern Exegesis and the Literary Conventions of Ancient Israel," in *Intertextuality in Ugarit and Israel* (ed. Johannes de Moor; Leiden: Brill, 1998), 6; Benjamin Sommer, "The Scroll of Isaiah as Jewish Scripture, Or, Why Jews Don't Read Books," in *SBL 1996 Seminar Papers* (Atlanta: Scholars Press, 1996), 225-242.

equivalent to "scripture," in which case the origins of canon and the origin of authoritative texts are indistinguishable (early)?[13] My point in introducing the dynamics of the debate is two-fold. First, it is critical to demonstrate how the definitions of "canon" and "canonical" matter. Both sides of the debate posit different timelines, and yet, rely on the *same* essential definition of canon: a closed list imposed by a community of faith at a certain point in history. We require a different set of questions. Secondly, when we confine the definition of canon to these terms and disregard the theological contours and shaping process of the canonical form, studies in Dan 9 become monochromatic and, in the end, reductionistic (more anon).

Composition criticism, our next sub-discipline within canonics, emphasizes the *socio-political* background of a text as the central feature. This area grows increasingly popular.[14]

David Carr's work *The Formation of the Hebrew Bible* is one of the newest examples of such a study.[15] He argues the Hasmonean monarchy (164 – 64 BCE) is responsible for the formation of the Hebrew canon by "initially defining the contours" of the text for the purpose of political preservation and the promotion of national identity.[16] Developing within the Hellenistic Period (333 – 64

---

[13] At this point, we must address the issue of Childs and "canon criticism." Labeling Childs' approach "canonical criticism" is incorrect, yet remains a common misnomer among critics. Childs is on record, saying, "I have always objected to the term 'canon(ical) criticism' as a suitable description of my approach" ("An Interview with Brevard S. Childs [1923-2007]," www.philosophy-religion.org/bible/childs-interview.htm, February 1, 2014).

[14] Cf. Konrad Schmid, *The Old Testament: A Literary History* (trans. Linda Maloney; Minneapolis: Fortress, 2012); Carr, *Writing*; Stefan Scholz, "Kanones in Theologie, Literaturwissenschaften und Kulturwissenschaften. Einführende Bemerkungen zur Kanonforschung der Neuzeit und Moderne," in *Kanon in Konstruktion und Dekonstruktion: Kanonisierungsprozesse religiöser Texte von der Antike bis zur Gegenwart, Ein Handbuch* (ed. Eve Becker and Stefan Scholz; Berlin/Boston: De Gruyter, 2012), 33-38. For an example of how this methodology unfolds in Daniel studies, see Rodney Werline, "Prayer, Politics, and Social Vision in Daniel 9," in *Seeking the Favor of God, Volume 2: The Development of Penitential Prayer in Second Temple Judaism* (ed. Mark Boda and Daniel Falk; Atlanta: SBL, 2007), 17-32. Differing from Carr or Schmid, Anathea Portier-Young exposes the political context exclusively in Daniel (*Apocalypse Against Empire: Theologies of Resistance in Early Judaism* [Grand Rapids: Eerdmans, 2011]). Critical of some of the premises of these studies, Robert Wilson prefers a *multitude* of possible socio-political leanings "behind" the biblical texts ("The Persian Period and the Shaping of the Prophetic Literature," in *Focusing Biblical Studies: The Crucial Nature of the Persian and Hellenistic Periods: Essays in Honor of Douglas A. Knight* [ed. Jon Berquist and Alice Hunt; London: T&T Clark, 2012], 107-20).

[15] *The Formation of the Hebrew Bible: A New Reconstruction* (Oxford: Oxford University Press, 2011).

[16] Carr, *Formation*, 156. See also Philip Davies, "The Jewish Scriptural Canon in Cultural Perspective," in *The Canon Debate*, 36-52. For Davies, the Hasmonean dynasty was

BCE), the Hasmoneans were influenced by Greek thought, particularly the textual culture of the Greeks.[17] According to Carr's account, the Jewish leadership believed the canonical techniques of Greek textuality (compilation, fixity, closure and revision) afforded the Hasmoneans a degree of political and cultural power. Canonical, in this case, means the inclusion of a text that sufficiently reflects the socio-political struggles of the day.

Expressing the main struggle – how to sustain covenant-obedience and nationhood under foreign rule – legitimates the goals and, as Carr argues, the overall architecture of the Hebrew canon. Priest, scribes and monarchs were the best equipped among the Jewish institutions to "enforce textual standardization and delimitation of a corpus of approved books" in a campaign to gain cultural recognition.[18] With an eye toward Homer's epic of twenty-four canonical books, the monarchy solidified the Hebrew corpus, utilizing the same alphabetic numbering and expanding the authority of earlier traditions.[19] Following this logic, canonical formation is no different from cataloguing authoritative texts precious to *ancient* communities. Entrees into canonical activity after this period, according to Carr, are merely the soundings of a Christian faith-community tailoring its own Bible. Rather, interpreting canon as "cultural capital" is preferable to canonics, always maintaining a platform that is historically pure and universally available. There are no "metaphysics" of canon and no "transcendent divine action generating or guiding canonization."[20] In the end, proposing a canonical method for communities *today* is a task for theology and (oddly) outside the purview of canon studies.

---

responsible for the final form of the Hebrew canon. He notes that the presence of Daniel in the list "suggests that the rise of this dynasty is the *terminus a quo*" (50).

[17] See 1 Macc. 14:25-49, this may be an account of the Hasmoneans rallying support from and making concessions to their Hellenistic overseers.

[18] Ibid., 163.

[19] Ibid., 165. This section of Carr's analysis is important because it hints at his definition of "canonical." When he treats the "final shaping of the Hebrew Torah-Prophets corpus," Carr expects to detect "intentional shifts present in the Masoretic text that might link to interest and concerns of the Hasmoneans as surveyed in...the profile of Hasmonean texts" (167). Preservation becomes the key component, not necessarily a canonical shape with future generations in mind. His conclusion is clear: "If this overall hypothesis is sound, it would suggest that the Hasmoneans were the last to have a chance to adjust the contents of the Hebrew Torah-Prophets corpus they promoted. Since the value of the time was on antiquity, they could not make large changes. Ostensively, the Torah-Prophets Scriptural corpus was being protected and restored, not created" (166). In this analysis, the term "canonical" is grounded in Greek culture while separated from the *scriptural* aspect of Israel's treasured texts. All too often, recourse to historical-allusions is the interpretive linchpin for studies in canonics.

[20] John Webster, *Word and Church: Essays in Church Dogmatics* (Edinburgh/New York: Continuum, 2001), 13.

1.1 Canonical-Intertextual Methods

A small cottage industry within canonics bases most of its method on intertextuality. These methods commonly reflect a material view of canon that results in a theological claim.[21] Some bind intertextuality and canonical methods so close together they appear interchangeable. Sailhamer, in a 2002 conference paper, reiterates his three-fold canonical model for biblical theology, positioning "canonical shaping" at the second, intertextual stage, between "composition" of the text and "consolidation" within the community.[22] Georg Steins is another example—he argues for a *"kanonisch-intertextuellen Lektüre,"* preferring a textual "anamnesis" for the purpose of generating a hard, reproducible method.[23] Similarly, Julius Steinberg highlights textual associations at the macro- and micro-structural levels of canon.[24] Steinberg's model (*strukturell-kanonischen Methode*) uses the term *"kanonisch"* to mean *"die*

---

[21] Cf. Carr, "The Many Uses of Intertextuality in Biblical Studies: Actual and Potential," in *Congress Volume: Helsinki 2010* (VTSup 148; Leiden: Brill, 505-36; Richard Schultz, "Intertextuality, Canon, and 'Undecidability': Understanding Isaiah's 'New Heavens and New Earth' (Isaiah 65:17-25)," *BBR* 20 (2010): 19-38; Timothy Stone, "The Compilational History of the Megilloth: Canon, Contoured Intertextuality and Meaning in the Writings" (Ph.D. diss., St. Andrews University, 2010); Georg Steins, "Kanonisch-intertextuelle Bibellektüre—My Way," in *Intertextualität: Perspektiven auf ein interdisziplinäres Arbeitsfeld* (ed. Karin Herrmann and Sanra Hübenthal; Aacken: Shaker, 2007), 55-68; Craig Broyles, "Traditions, Intertextuality and Canon," in *Interpreting the Old Testament: A Guide for Exegesis* (ed. Craig Broyles; Grand Rapids: Baker, 2001), 157-75; Fishbane, "Types of Biblical Intertextuality," in *Congress Volume: Oslo 1998* (ed. A. Lemaire and M. Sæbø; VTSup 80; Leiden: Brill, 2000), 39-44. Some of these intertextual methods have roots in exegetical reinterpretation, arising primarily from a "consciousness of canon" (*Kanonbewußtein*). See comments by Chapman (*Law and Prophets*, 47); for the foundation study of "canon-consciousness," see I.L. Seeligman, "Voraussetzungen des Midraschexegese," *SVT* 1 (1953): 150-1. For the Jewish OT scholar Michael Fishbane, intertextuality "is the core of the canonical imagination" ("Types of Intertextuality," 39).

[22] Sailhamer, "Biblical Theology." The basic outline is in his *Introduction to Old Testament Theology*.

[23] See primarily Steins, "Kanonisch-intertextuelle Bibellektüre," 55-68; "Kanon und Anamnese: Auf dem Weg zu einer Neuen Biblischen Theologie," in *Der Bibelkanon in der Bibelauslegung: Methodenreflexionen und Beispielexegesen* (ed. Egbert Ballhorn and Georg Steins; Stuttgart: Kohlhammer, 2007), 129.

[24] Steinberg, *Die Ketuvim—ihr Aufbau und ihre Botschaft* (BBB 152; Hamburg: Philo, 2006), 75-82. When comparing the two canonical-intertextual models, Steinberg's model works on many of the same principles and techniques as Sailhamer's model—the main comparison is a commitment to a single, canonical order (*Introduction*, 222-23). Sailhamer is unique in that he does not appeal to a concrete list, but an allegedly visible pressure or phenomenon "felt in the textual shape of the OT" (223). Furthermore, it is striking Sailhamer labels his method, an "approach" (222-23), while he calls Childs's approach, a *method* ("canonical criticism," 97)!

Gesamtbotschaft" of the Hebrew Scriptures which is "*synchron*," focusing on "*der vorliegenden Endgestalt.*"[25]

2. A Non-Material Unity of Canon

Standing opposite canonics are those who argue for a canonical unity outside of the canon's material form. Nicholas Wolterstorff captures the tone well: "For...the unity of the text *as a work* is a mode of unity that lies *behind* the text."[26] This and other "philosophical-theological perspectives" on canonical unity (including an unlikely alliance with James Barr!) make up a collection of essays entitled *One Scripture or Many*. These scholars explore the transhistorical nature of canon.[27] Pinning history to biblical unity, as Francis Watson explains, is to misapprehend canon: "Integral to the concept of the scriptural canon is the idea of its 'unity' or 'coherence.' A canon is not an anthology," since "an anthology cannot be held accountable for the unity or coherence of its contents."[28] Intriguing here is the potential for meaning in Watson's terms, "unity" and "coherence"—can *divine* coherence and *textual* coherence meet? If so, how? If not, why? This division reveals itself in a later work, edited by John Barton and Michael Wolter, with the telling title, *Die Einheit der Schrift und die Vielfalt des Kanons*.[29]

Consider an extended example: Kevin Vanhoozer's canonical-linguistic approach orients the normative role of the biblical canon around the role of "ecclesial culture."[30] For Vanhoozer, the canon displays a number of functions. It is the "church's authoritative script," active within the divine theo-drama, working "as an authoritative and binding witness to the fact, and the terms, of

---

[25] "The overall message of the Hebrew Bible should correspond synchronically with the final, extant shape/stage of the individual books ...." (Steinberg, 75); cf. Hendrik Koorevaar, *A Structural Canonical Approach for a Theology of the Old Testament*, Version 3.2 [Leuven: Evangelische Theologische Faculteit, 2000]).

[26] Wolterstorff, "The Unity Behind the Canon," in *One Scripture or Many? Canon from Biblical, Theological and Philosophical Perspectives* (Oxford: Oxford University Press, 2004), 228.

[27] The volume edited by Christine Helmer and Christof Landmesser collects multiple disciplines, including theology, for a discussion on canonical unity (*One Scripture or Many? Canon from Biblical, Theological and Philosophical Perspectives* [Oxford: Oxford University Press, 2004]); cf. Wolterstorff, *Divine Discourse: Philosophical Reflections on the Claim that God Speaks* [Cambridge: Cambridge University Press, 1995]; cf. Kit Barker, "Speech Act Theory, Dual Authorship, and Canonical Hermeneutics: Making Sense of Sensus Plenior," *JTI* 3.2 [2009]: 227-239).

[28] Watson, "Gospel and Scripture: Rethinking Canonical Unity," *TynBul* 52.2 (2001) 161.

[29] *Die Einheit der Schrift und die Vielfalt des Kanons* (ed. John Barton and Michael Wolter; Berlin: DeGruyter, 2003).

[30] *Drama*, 16.

the covenant relationship" between God and man.³¹ It is a "playbook" that conveys "patterns of speech and action" as well as "a response to an *evangelical exigence.*"³² As for the nature of "canonical" texts, the shift in nuance is simple enough to detect. We no longer encounter terms commonly associated with canon—shape, corpus, connection, editing, association, history—but instead find "covenant," "action" and "practice." This distinction makes sense in light of Vanhoozer's differentiation between "a purely textual entity" and "a phenomenon of discourse."³³ Coupling textual unity with speech-act theory, scholars take this same definition further, deeming the entire venture "canonical hermeneutics."³⁴

In a surprising use of the phrase, Vanhoozer calls the canon, "the final form of 'Holy Scripture.'"³⁵ This tag is intriguing since it is certainly not the same "final form" outlined by Childs. Vanhoozer's meaning is not entirely clear, but it's fair to say he does not mean the final shape of the biblical text; rather, he means the *final form that the Bible takes on within the divine economy, that is, the form of a covenant document*. The distinction is key: the primary ingredient in this "final form" is application. After all, "[T]o speak of a canonical-linguistic approach to theology is to make sure that what get passed on to future generations are the dominical and apostolic *practices* embodied and preserved in the canonical Scriptures."³⁶ Vanhoozer's interest lies in "the continuity that transcends and transfigures" the readers of the biblical canon."³⁷ Such a distinction exposes a critical difference between Childs' approach and a non-material approach to canonical unity.

Daniel Treier also opts for a "canonical" alternative that emphasizes "a more coherent way of understanding the text's authority and unity."³⁸ The canonical approach, according to Treier, requires a "clearer doctrine of biblical inspiration."³⁹ To be sure, Treier recognizes the virtues of the canonical approach as being "church-centered, somewhat hermeneutically and method-

---

³¹ Ibid., 116, 139.
³² Ibid., 145, 216 (italics original).
³³ Ibid., 217.
³⁴ Cf. Barker, "Speech," 227.
³⁵ Vanhoozer, *Drama*, 141.
³⁶ Ibid., 121 (italics mine).
³⁷ Ibid., 119.
³⁸ Treier, *Introducing Theological Interpretation of Scripture: Recovering Christian Practice* (Grand Rapids: Baker Academic, 2008), 116. Treier echoes the criticism leveled by Paul Noble (*The Canonical Approach: A Critical Reconstruction of the Hermeneutics of Brevard S. Childs* [Leiden: Brill, 1995]).
³⁹ Treier, *Introducing*, 116. To be fair, Treier acknowledges how the shortcomings of the canonical approach are a natural result of working within such a wide scope of biblical interpretation. Treier balances his criticisms with insights from Seitz's article, "The Canonical Approach and Theological Interpretation" (*Canon and Biblical Interpretation* [SHS 7; ed. Craig Bartholomew; Grand Rapids: Zondervan, 2006], 62-65).

ologically flexible, and creedally orthodox."⁴⁰ But, ultimately, Treier faults Childs for adhering to certain convictions regarding historical presentation and compares Childs' thoughts on history with the ideals of "evangelical 'progressive revelation.'"⁴¹

3. Features of a Canonical Approach

Turning to the specific features of the approach, we will elaborate on (1) the final form of the text and its historical underpinnings, (2) the unity of the text in a canonical approach and, finally, (3) the textual characteristics of the approach such as (a) the type of associative activity occurring in the canonical shape of the text, (b) the dual-corpora of Law and Prophets (LP), and (c) the dynamics of a tri-partite Hebrew canon.

3.1. History, "Artifact" and the Final Form

No shortage of criticism is leveled at the canonical approach,⁴² but it is in the area of *historical inquiry* about which opponents remain most critical. Concerned with historical reference and the canon's chronological growth, it should come as no surprise that the main criticism aimed at the canonical approach by canonics is that it functions *a-historically*. Seitz, in compiling the nine most popular arguments against the canonical approach, finds this concern at the forefront: "insufficient attention to the 'facts of history' as constitutive of any serious theological approach."⁴³ A canonical approach, according to this claim, is no more than an interpretive gloss one applies to the rough textures of the canon.⁴⁴

---

⁴⁰ Treier, *Introducing*, 115.

⁴¹ Ibid., 116.

⁴² Recent articles devote considerable energy these criticisms: Iain Provan, "Canons to the Left of Him: Brevard Childs, His Critics, and the Future of Old Testament Theology," *SJT* 50 (1997): 1-38; Stephen Dempster, "Canons to the Right and Canons on the Left: Finding a Resolution in the Canon Debate," *JETS* 52.1 (2009): 47-77. Christopher Seitz addresses why this scope exists: "Rarely is it said that it seeks to do too much and is disqualified by virtue of its ambition. As noted above, it is this desire for comprehenisiveness which I shall argue is the hallmark of the canonical approach and its legacy for our day...that this is not singled out as a fault is worth keeping in mind," ("Canonical Approach," 62). For an extensive treatment of criticisms and responses, including from German scholarship, see Daniel Driver, *Brevard Childs*. Arguments that the canonical approach neglects history have not gone unanswered.

⁴³ Seitz, "Canonical Approach," 62.

⁴⁴ In the end, the culprit behind this interpretive gloss is theological "dogmatics"—an attribute of the canonical approach, according to detractors (James Barr, *The Concept of Biblical Theology: An Old Testament Perspective* [Minneapolis: Augsburg Fortress, 1999], 401). John Barton also criticizes Childs for smoothing over the historical textures of the canonical witness, but he does so on linguistic grounds, calling the canonical approach

Historical inquiry, even the canon's *Enstehungsgeschichte*, is necessary for any biblical method. However, a canonical approach rightly chastens a critical mindset that divorces the ancient text from its theological shape or reduces the text to an historical artifact. At issue within much of historical-critical scholarship is its propensity to surgically remove the theological element from an otherwise robust and multi-layered historical landscape. This problem is addressed in what I consider to be an oblique counter to MacDonald's *Canon Debate* volume, that is, the seventh installment of the Scripture and Hermeneutics Series, *Canon and Biblical Interpretation*. In the 2006 SHS volume, canon is seen as "a guarantee that the biblical materials have not been collected for antiquarian reasons," but to constitute "an eternal Word of God."[45] The concept of "history" then takes on different guises when we read along canonical lines, revealing history to be more than a report of events.

Also troubling to Childs is an historical model undergirded by socio-political agendas. These construals of canonical method go "very wide of the mark" by fixating on "the minds of the canonical editors."[46] Amplifying the social and political psychology *behind* the text runs counter to the theological presentation *of* the text. Rather, a canonical approach "serves to focus attention on the theological forces at work" not a "process largely controlled by general laws of folklore, by socio-political factors, or by scribal conventions."[47] If we distill the canonical process to a pursuit of "standardization," to take Carr's example, we fail to address the logic of shaping books to convey a theological, and sometimes self-effacing message.

But how does the canonical approach locate itself within the same, hisorical arena as canonics? Childs makes two moves. First, instead of appealing to

---

"a form of structuralism" (*Reading the Old Testament: Method in Biblical Study* [Louisville: John Knox, 1984], 133).

[45] Childs, "The Canonical Shape of the Prophetic Literature," *Int* 32.1 (1978): 46-55, here 48.

[46] "Response to Reviewers of Introduction to the Old Testament as Scripture," *JSOT* 16 (1980) 52-60, here 56. A strong socio-political framework also invites a community-centered picture of canon and canonical models. Admittedly, the role of the community is a salient feature of the canonical approach as well as a point of misunderstanding. The "reflection" on God's given Word to the community of faith is often mistaken for the generation of the same word or, at the very least, the conflation of "canon" and "community." Likewise, Webster sees a connection between those who make ecclesiology "*the* basic doctrine" and the "moral distortions found in nineteenth-century theologies of moral community" (*Word and Church*, 18).

[47] Childs, *Biblical Theology of the Old and New Testaments: Theological Reflection on the Christian Bible* (Minneapolis: Fortress, 1992), 71. After this, I will refer to this work as BTONT.

either an "early" or "late" canon, Childs transforms what "canonical" and "canon" means.[48] Note the following summary of Childs' approach:

> The authoritative Word gave the community its form and content in obedience to the divine imperative, yet con-versely the reception of the authoritative tradition by its hearers gave shape to the same writings through a historical and theological process of selecting, collecting, and ordering. The formation of the canon was not a late extrinsic validation of a corpus of writings, but involved a series of decisions deeply affecting the shape of the books.[49]

For Childs, to call a text "canonical" is not to refer to the book's secured location within an authoritative group of canonical books, but is an acknowledgement of the canon as "a cipher" that encompasses "the various and diverse factors involved in the formation of the literature."[50] The canon is not a theological gloss or an isolated literary convention—rather, it took shape through a complex, textual history guided and super-intended by God's divine hand. For his second move, Childs argues that the canon houses "an internal logic of faith within the framework of the confession." Reading canonically is to read *confessionally* to some degree. As Childs personally affirms, "I cannot act as if I were living at the beginning of Israel's history, but as one who already knows the story, and who has entered into the middle of an activity of faith long in progress."[51]

With these two points combined, we have a picture of the *final form*. Oftentimes, readers mistake the "final form" of the biblical text for the "only form," or the "only interpretation of the text."[52] Canonics tends to ask what a 'final form' reading achieves besides distracting the reader from clearly understanding the parts of the whole? For these scholars, the final shape is "the *ad extra* brought to the biblical text in order for it to make theological sense or encour-

---

[48] Other scholars also call for an alternative to the terms of the "canon debate": Stephen Chapman, "The Canon Debate: What It Is and Why It Matters," *JTI* 4.2 (2010): 273-294; cf. Stephen Dempster, "Canons on the Right," 50-51.

[49] Childs, *IOTS*, 58-59.

[50] Ibid., *BTONT*, 70.

[51] Ibid., *Old Testament Theology in a Canonical Context* (Philadelphia: Fortress, 1985), 29.

[52] Cf. William John Lyons, *Canon and Exegesis: Canonical Praxis and the Sodom Narrative* [JSOTSup 352; Sheffield: Sheffield Academic, 2002], 37). Even those unsympathetic to Childs's approach realize that "canon implies the attempt to impose a definitive shape and meaning on the [biblical] tradition as it comes to expression in the texts" (Joseph Blenkinsopp, *Prophecy and Canon: A Contribution to the Study of Jewish Origins* [Notre Dame: University of Notre Dame Press, 1977], ix-xi).

age virtues or habits of various kinds."[53] Conversely, the final form, according to Childs, is the "essential element."[54] Attending to the final form means attending to scripture "in its own integrity."[55] Readers of scripture are, after all, subject to a basic truth, elucidated by the final form: the layers of textual history are not completely accessible. Attempts to map out the sedimentary levels of redaction and source material are precisely the historical-critical moves about which Childs and others are skeptical. Still, appealing to the final form of the text by no means ignores possible sources, editorial markers, diverse literary conventions or theological tensions. On the contrary, reading the final form of the text *welcomes* such developments and demonstrates how the presentation of the text supports multiple voices while projecting them into the hearing range of future generations. A final shape indeed "directs the reader's attention to the sacred writings rather than to their editors."[56] Childs cautions, however, that although "it is possible to distinguish between different phases within the canonical process—the term canonization would then be reserved for the final fixing of the limits of scripture—the earlier decisions were not qualitatively different from the later."[57]

To offer an alternative to the philosophy of canonics is not to abandon or even circumvent historicity. Instead, we can appeal to an approach that upholds a text referring "realistically to the world."[58] Relating historicity to the theological forces responsible for the text's canonical shape is not like mixing "oil and water." By form, content, and figuration, the biblical canon points to the ultimate subject matter—the Living Word—within reality and not solely in metaphor. On the other hand, minimizing canon to an *artifact* provides one assurance: without recognizing the theological shape of the historical canon, the function of the Hebrew and Christian scriptures are beholden to the historical reconstructions underneath the text. They will no longer be a theological witness, but an echo chamber fitted for a single occupant. Historical context, therefore, in a canonical framework, means "to be pointed to our God who has made himself known, is making himself known, and will make himself known."[59]

---

[53] Seitz, "Prophetic Associations," in *Thus Says the Lord: Essays on the Former and Latter Prophets in Honor of Robert R. Wilson* (ed. John J. Ahn and Stephen Cook; London: T&T Clark, 2009), 160.

[54] Childs, *IOTS*, 59.

[55] Ibid., 73.

[56] Ibid., 59.

[57] Childs, *IOTS*, 59.

[58] Seitz, *The Character of Christian Scripture: The Significance of a Two-Testament Bible* (Grand Rapids: Baker, 2011), 37. Julius Steinberg identifies this careful balance in Childs's work.

[59] Childs, *BTONT*, 28.

3.2. Unity and the Historical-Theological Shape of the Text

Just as we cannot remove the theological element from its historical cradle neither can we replace the canon's historical complexity with a theological coherence *in abstractum*. Seitz tracks this, noticing a problem with the "level of abstraction" on offer.[60] For Seitz, the silence is a "deeply historical" problem that says "practically nothing at all about the constitutive, historically, real, indeed 'elected and providentially chosen' manner" by which Scripture developed.[61] Unity in the canon, therefore, is not without its embodied character. We quickly find that separating textual coherence from spiritual coherence is an unrealistic division of labor. Such is the "fruit" and the "toil" of canonical interpretation.

In our discussion of canonical unity, we would do well to remember the tension facing biblical interpreters at all times, that "although historically the decision of the church actively shaped the canon, the Church itself envisioned its task as one of acknowledging what God had given as a gracious gift in Christ for the nourishing of the continuing life of faith."[62] The community of faith shapes the canon while simultaneously *receiving* the canon the church is tasked to shape. In this way, the reception of God's Word or "givenness" to the church is in lockstep with Scripture's theological and *textual* reality.[63]

3.3. Textual Characteristics of the Canonical Approach

With an approach that navigates between the two types of canonical methodologies discussed above, one anticipates a series of defining features that allows us to clarify and enhance our study of the text. This section describes three formal characteristics of a canonical approach: (a) the type of associative activity occurring in the canonical shape of the text, (b) the dual-corpora of Law and Prophets (LP), and (c) the dynamics of a tri-partite Hebrew canon.

3.4. Textual Association within the Canonical Shape

Textual association is such a vast field of study, we require three subsections in order to pinpoint areas relevant to this approach: (i) a response to recent canonical-intertextual methods; (ii) the role of intertextuality within a canonical approach and (iii) the use of inner-biblical exegesis. First, we address the aforementioned canonical-intertextual methods. A clear distinction arises between Childs' approach and these models. Under scrutiny, many of these

---

[60] Seitz, *Character*, 80. Here, Seitz has in mind recent proposals in the theological interpretation of scripture, but specifically the contribution of Speech-Act Theory. Likewise, in Childs' final article, Childs is skeptical of of such proposals and their place in biblical studies ("Speech-Act Theory and Biblical Interpretation," in *SJT* 58.4 (2005): 375-392, here 385-87).

[61] Seitz, *Character*, 80.

[62] Childs, *Biblical Theology in Crisis*, 64.

[63] Chapman, "Canon Debate," 289.

methods could operate "intertextually" without any canonical arch or final form. Little of the descriptor—*canonical*—is necessary, apart from a fixed collection of texts meant to connect with one another. A canonical approach, rather, re-prioritizes intertextuality and the role of canon. It assigns "a *function* to the literature as a whole" which transcends its parts, a function that moves beyond marking intertexts.[64]

In this way, Childs does not ignore intertextuality, but sets it within a wider, textual economy. In his critique of recent methods, Childs writes, "the role of intertextuality served as a means by which the coherence of the developing canonical corpus was sustained" and "once the canonical corpus reached its relative stability, the text as religious Scripture continued to generate new intertextual relationships, but the distinction between text and figuration was maintained, at least in principle."[65]

3.5. The Role of Intertextuality

Intertextuality *is* a feature of the canonical approach, as Seitz echoes, but a feature that manages "to keep the model of association capable of accounting for more than one thing at once," since the final form is "far more than a kind of redactional accounting for seams and disjunctures."[66] To begin, we must consider the types of textual association in play.[67] Beyond verse-to-verse associations, there are two other components inherent to associative activity: the locative component and the group/cluster component.

An association can be enhanced by *location*. We find this association at three levels: the level of the passage, the level of the book and the level of the corpus. All of these levels of textual association function in service to the theological shape of the canon. On the level of the immediate text, verbal repetition and shared themes that join Dan 9:1-2 (introduction), 9:3-19 (body) and especially 9:24-27 (conclusion) are the means of associating the disparate parts of Dan 9. Reference to the heptad (v.2 // v.24) and the "word" (v.2 // v.25) are

---

[64] Childs, *OT Theology*, 22.

[65] Ibid., "Critique," 177. Also, without the canonical shape to manage textual associations, it is difficult to determine whether or not an author is introducing a "course-correction." This is not to say later authors attempted to correct the mistakes of earlier, "naïve" authors. But authors did take the relevant themes, expressions, images and messages in new directions– such is the reality of God's unfolding plan through scripture.

[66] Seitz, "Prophetic Associations," 164.

[67] In terms of definition, Fishbane's tactic in speaking of intertextuality and allusion is identifying them as one in the same; see Fishbane, "Types of Biblical Intertextuality," in *Congress Volume: Oslo 1998* (ed. A. Lemaire and M. Sæbø; VTSup 80; Leiden: Brill, 2000), 39-44. I use the term *association* to reflect this point. The benefit of using "association" is having the freedom to hold in tension instances where it is difficult to differentiate between textual dependence (e.g. a repeated expression, continuity of tradition) and textual independence (e.g. a break in tradition, modification of stock language).

parts of an envelope structure in Dan 9, for example, forging associations by way of location. At the book-level and corpora-level, the author registers allusions, shared motifs and stylistic similarities and, again, a locative sense—referring to *key phrases from key locations* within the Hebrew corpora. The writer weaves these types of association into a patterns, for example, firmly planted along the trajectory of Lev 26:34-35 and Jer 25:10-12, 29:10. Again, associations are not reducible to a one-to-one lexical connection, but can be fitted with enhancements like location and grouping.[68]

Still, we have to exercise caution. Sensitivity to the canonical form, both at the level of the book and the level of the corpus, does not give us license to acknowledge textual associations *in any place* and *without qualification*. To demonstrate, the repetition of a common phrase (e.g. the Law of Moses) throughout Dan 9 does not oblige the interpreter to conclude that the author is citing the Pentateuch. But if such phrases occur at key locations between corpora—particularly locations that are advantageous for constructing summaries—the likelihood of an association increases.

The *group* association is the second, critical characteristic. It is indeed possible to compare only one or two catchwords. Some scholars who pursue a definition of the seventy sevens (Dan 9:24) argue on this basis. But associating groups of words and configuring them with other groups is far more useful. Evaluating associations requires a "synoptic vision" to discern how the parts cohere.[69] Texts within the canonical form are evidence of this vision or "conjunction of associations," connecting multiple authors, multiple text-units and multiple contexts.[70] However, "synoptic" is not the same as "totally harmonious." These conjunctions can substitute anticipated language, vary in morphology or engage in any number of meaningful transformations. *Divergences* are equally possible. These divergences (and conjunctions) within a word-

---

[68] James Nogalski expands the definition of "intertextuality" to include the strength of an allusion and the significance of location when evaluating a textual association ("Intertextuality and the Twelve," in *Forming Prophetic Literature: Essays on Isaiah and the Twelve in Honor of John D.W. Watts* [JSOTSup 235; ed. J.W. Watts and Paul House; Sheffield: Sheffield Academic, 1996], 109-11). Timothy Stone takes Nogalski's contribution and re-forms them into five guidelines for identifying textual associations: (1) quotation of a phrase, sentence or paragraph; (2) an association to another text "for a specific purpose"; (3) catchwords (*Stichworte*) linking books together at the seams; (4) themes and motifs; (5) "framing devices" at the beginning and conclusion of a group of books (e.g. the Twelve) or corpora ("Compilational History," 18-20).

[69] Willem VanGemeren, "Our Missional God: Redemptive-Historical Preaching and the *Missio Dei*" (Trinity Evangelical Divinity School, 2010; forthcoming), 6; cf. Kevin Vanhoozer, "Lost in Interpretation: Truth, Scripture, and Hermeneutics," in *Whatever Happened to Truth?* (ed. Andreas Köstenberger; Wheaton: Crossway, 2005), 121.

[70] Seitz, "Prophetic Associations," 165. G.K. Beale calls these groups, "allusive clusters" (*The Use of Daniel in Jewish Apocalyptic Literature and in the Revelation of St. John* [Lanham: University Press of America, 1984], 285).

group, motif or pattern are the "rough textures" signaling the reader to recognize a theological movement in the passage.

In accounting for locative and group associations within a canonical shape, we uncover hints of a larger, coordinated intentionality, not mindless connections originating with a single scribe or an inventory of stock language.[71] To be sure, without a canonical framework, an interpreter could not recognize the compositional basis for an allusion or intertext.[72] We would risk reducing textual associations to their relationship to influence (e.g. Carr) or some other species of comparison.[73] By way of illustration, Fishbane, in broad agreement with Childs' view on intertextuality, fixes this associative activity to "the core of the canonical imagination."[74] Canonical imagination resides in the textual culture that shapes (and is shaped by) an authoritative collection of scripture. Two points mark Fishbane's "exegetical culture": (1) "the fact that all interpretation takes place *within* the canon and presupposes that *all* its texts may be compared or in some way correlated"; (2) and "the assumption of the omnicoherence of Scripture in all its details."[75] Though I disagree with some aspects

---

[71] Barton insinuates these random links explain the presence of biblical intertextuality: "Any text within Scripture can illuminate any other text, not because the texts form a rhetorical unity, but because Scripture forms a kind of compendium or thesaurus of terms and turns of phrase and word associations" ("Intertextuality," 35).

[72] In debates over allusion and intertexts, a great deal of energy goes into defining intertextuality and allusion/influence. Julia Kristeva is a major voice behind the distinction (*Desire in Language: A Semiotic Approach to Literature and Art* [trans. Thomas Gora; New York: Columbia University Press, 1980], 66); she moved from intertextuality to "transposition" (*Revolution in Poetic Language*, 59-60). Whereas "influence" is identified with a specific literary canon (plays, novels, poems, etc.), "intertextuality" possesses a non-canonical focus and draws from any and all levels of composition. Potential intertexts, in this model, can be literary or non-literary, written or non-written, and generally without conscious "allusion" to prior work (see Thaïs Morgan, "The Space of Intertextuality," in *Intertextuality and Contemporary American Fiction* [ed. Patrick O'Donnell and Robert Con Davis; Baltimore, MD: John Hopkins University Press, 1989], 30-38; Timothy Beal, "Intertextuality," in *Handbook of Postmodern Biblical Interpretation* [ed. Andrew K.M. Adam; St. Louis, Mo.: Chalice, 2000], 128-30).

[73] Carr, "The Many Uses of Intertextuality in Biblical Studies: Actual and Potential," in *Congress Volume: Helsinki 2010* (VTSup 148; Leiden: Brill, 505-36).

[74] Fishbane, "Types of Intertextuality," 39. See also "Law to Canon: Some Ideal-Typical Stages of Development," in *Minḥah Le-Naḥum: Biblical and Other Studies Presented to Nahum M. Sarna in Honour of His 70th Birthday* (ed. Marc Zvi Brettler and Michael Fishbane; London: Continuum International Publishing Group, 1993), 65-86. Carr levels his argument mainly at Fishbane, who describes intertextuality within the context of canonical development ("Many Uses," 505-6).

[75] Fishbane, "Types of Intertextuality," 43 (italics original). Moving in the opposite direction, Pieter Venter divides the classifications of association into *sub-groups* of sub-groups ("Daniel 9: A Penitential Prayer in Apocalyptic Garb," in *Seeking the Favor of God: The Development of Penitential Prayer in Second Temple Judaism, Vol. 2* [ed. Mark J. Boda, Daniel K. Falk, and Rodney Alan Werline; Society of Biblical Literature, 2007], 33-34).

of Fishbane's model of canonical compilation, he rightly situates intertexts within the shaping process of canon and the traditions therein.[76] Also, Fishbane's definition is no less aware of the creativity inherent to intertextuality, despite Carr's argument for a "literary" version of intertextuality.[77] Unlike Carr, Fishbane insists the defining characteristic of intertextuality is "tradition-building" and constitute a wider textual significance.[78] A canonical approach, therefore, includes intertextuality and recruits it for its own purposes. However, minimizing intertexts to a literary convention keeps intertextuality from speaking to the theological reality of the canonical shape.[79]

3.6. Inner-Biblical Exegesis

Thorough studies of Dan 9 provide at least a passing comment on inner-biblical exegesis.[80] This activity traces the "interbranching network of relationships that connects distant texts and binds them to one another."[81] After evidence is presented, practitioners of IBE usually produce a taxonomy of reasons for the exegesis. These reasons range from "pious revisions" to "theological addenda" for resolving discrepancies.[82] Such options are the answers to Benjamin Sommer's fundamental IBE question: *how* and *why* do biblical writers use texts from other biblical writers?[83]

But we must first establish the appropriate framework for this method. Even in IBE, the canon was "the major factor in this process of reinterpretation."[84] Exegetical reinterpretation arose primarily from a "consciousness of canon" (*Kanonbewußtein*), rather than, for example, a drive to make biblical texts relevant.[85] This framework does not discount the careful and learned insights regarding streams of tradition (*traditum*) and the textual activity shap-

---

Venter's initial attempt at categorizing these terms is in "Intertekstualiteit, Kontekstualiteit en Daniël 9," *IDS* 31 (1997): 338-43. These sorts of micro-divisions are necessary if we attempt to classify the textual associations of Dan 9 *outside* of a canonical shape.

[76] "Types of Intertextuality," 42.

[77] "[I]ntertextuality is a form that literary creativity takes when innovation is grounded in tradition" (Fishbane, "Types of Intertextuality," 39).

[78] Ibid., 40.

[79] Also, without the canonical shape to house textual associations, it is difficult to determine whether or not an author is introducing a "course-correction."

[80] Daniel 9 is the premiere case study for IBE in Fishbane's work (*Biblical Interpretation*, 443-65).

[81] Yair Zakovitch, "Inner-biblical Interpretation," in *A Companion to Biblical Interpretation in Early Judaism* (ed. Matthias Henze; Grand Rapids: Eerdmans, 2011), 27.

[82] Ibid., 66-77.

[83] Sommer, "Inner-biblical Interpretation," in *Jewish Study Bible: Tanakh Translation* (ed. Marc Zvi Brettler and Adele Berlin; Oxford: Oxford University Press, 2004), 1819.

[84] Chapman, *Law and the Prophets*, 47.

[85] Ibid. For the foundation study of "canon-consciousness," see Seeligman, 150-1.

ing them (*traditio*). Childs writes that "such exegetical activity grew out of a concept of the canon as an established body of sacred writings, it is a derivative phenomenon which does not represent the constitutive form lying behind the actual canonical process."[86] However, to express the methodology of this study, we must distinguish between a canonical approach and the canonical method inherent to IBE—in so doing, we create an order of operation. A canonical approach exceeds the boundaries of IBE by housing a "component which was a theological extension" of scripture's "primary meaning."[87] Inner-biblical exegesis, for example, does not concern itself with the wider implications of the final form of the text.[88] Such a tool works under the arch of the canonical approach and is a sub-routine for "rendering the material theologically," offering "countless different compositional techniques by means of which the tradition was actualized."[89] The findings of IBE, based on the points above, cannot be overlooked and or go unnoticed within a canonical framework.

Similarly, IBE cannot be mistaken for intertextuality. Exegesis within scripture enables an assortment of textual connections and should not be restricted to, what is usually considered, a task for semiotics.[90] Textual association within a canonical shape is larger than this—it incorporates intertextuality, allusion and quotation. On the other hand, we must not blur

---

[86] Childs, *IOTS*, 60.

[87] Ibid., *BTONT*, 71. Eslinger boldly claims that the traditional sense of inner-biblical exegesis and allusion is beset with difficulties and is "problematic" since critical scholars "are not as open to assumptions like inspiration, divine authorship, or typological engineering of history" ("Inner-Biblical Exegesis and Inner-Biblical Allusion: The Question of Category," *VT* 42.1 [1992] 48).

[88] As with a final form reading, "inner-biblical exegesis starts with the received Scripture and moves forward to the interpretations based on it" (Fishbane, *Biblical Interpretation*, 7). Fishbane confirms Childs' response in his sequencing of the *traditum* and *traditio*: "the *traditum* dominates the *traditio* and conditions its operations. And to the extent that the scribal *traditio* makes the *traditum* lexically more accessible, theologically more palatable, or materially more comprehensive, its operations are intended to reinforce the authority of the *traditum* in their attempts to provide alternatives to it" (86-87). For Childs, canonical shaping *and* authority overlaps—there is canonical shaping in its *literary* development and canonical shaping in its *textual* development (*IOTS*, 95). See also Sommer, "Psalm 1 and the Canonical Shape of Jewish Scripture," in *Jewish Bible Theology: Perspectives and Case Studies* (ed. Isaac Kalimi; Winona Lake, IN.: Eisenbrauns, 2012), 199-221. Sommer misunderstands certain aspects of a "final form" reading, mistaking the final shape for an exclusive interpretation of the text (*A Prophet Reads Scripture: Allusion in Isaiah 40-66* [Stanford: Stanford University Press, 1998], 4, emphasis mine).

[89] Childs, *BTONT*, 70.

[90] Daniel Boyarin draws from Michael Riffaterre's terms of "dual-signs" (*Semiotics of Poetry* [Bloomington: Indiana University Press, 1978], 82) and the inherent ambiguity present in the dialogue between texts. Boyarin labels the union, "inner-biblical ambiguity" ("Inner Biblical Ambiguity, Intertextuality and the Dialectic of Midrash: The Waters of Marah," *Prooftexts* 10 [1990]: 29-48).

the lines of IBE and intertextuality so that they bleed into one another and absorb the significance of the other. Often "intertextuality" is the term used when a scholar means two or more texts connecting to one another without regard for intent, peculiarity, context or theological effect. Inner-biblical exegesis reminds us that an impetus existed for association and texts do not associate with one another in a vacuum. Real events and traditions occurred and required interpretation.

3.7. The "Law and the Prophets"

Owing much to Childs' work, we find a contingent of scholars generating renewed interest in the arrangement of the tri-partite Hebrew canon, particularly the bonds between the LP.[91] This interest encourages a fresh look at the mutual interpretation of biblical books inside and outside of their corpus. The dual-authority of the LP is of special importance to a study of Dan 9:24-27—it is a prolific source of exegetical insight (cf. Dan 9:3-19) and a theological mainstay for Daniel's reflection.

For these proponents, the LP make up more than a "core canon." This dual-authority is a "theological grammar" that generates theological reflection. Seitz defines the "grammar" this way: "this literary conjunction is the means (rule and syntax) by which the language of Israel's scriptures makes its voice most fundamentally heard, and hearing that rightly is unaffected by the existence of additional writings."[92] Recourse to this grammar was formative for the Writings and certainly a productive theological construct for the NT writers. In the full shape of the canon, it is not difficult to see how this dual-authority "comprised equal and complementary voices within a single divine economy."[93]

Alongside Seitz, Chapman uses the phrase "theological grammar" to describe the interpretive force of the LP.[94] The grammar is "an explicitly *theological* interpretation of Israel's traditions, in which both 'Law' and 'Prophets'—as developing collections of *scripture*—function as joint witnesses to the one will

---

[91] Among others, Seitz, *The Goodly Fellowship of the Prophets: The Achievement of Association in Canon Formation* (Grand Rapids: Baker, 2009); *Prophecy and Hermeneutics: Toward a New Introduction to the Prophets* (Grand Rapids: Baker, 2007); Chapman, *Law and Prophets*; Dempster, "Torah, Torah, Torah: The Emergence of the Tripartite Canon," in *Exploring the Origins of the Bible: Canon Formation in Historical, Literary, and Theological Perspective* (ed. Craig Evans and Emanuel Tov; Grand Rapids: Baker, 2008); "The Prophets, the Canon and a Canonical Approach," in *Canon and Biblical Interpretation*, 293-329; Rolf Rendtorff, *The Canonical Hebrew Bible: A Theology of the Old Testament* (Leiden: DEO, 2005). Others recognize a "core canon" as well, albeit with varying degrees of significance: Donn Morgan, *Between Text and Community: The "Writings" in Canonical Interpretation* (Minneapolis: Fortress, 2000); Steinberg, *Die Ketuvim*.

[92] Seitz, *Goodly Fellowship*, 4.

[93] Chapman, *Law and Prophets*, 52.

[94] Ibid., 110;

A Canonical Approach 29

of Israel's one god."[95] In Chapman's estimation, the Law-Prophets-Writings unit is a "literary and conceptual framework for Scriptures."[96] Interpreters can identify full patterns of association by means of this grammar, and safeguard against reducing these associations to a word-to-word relationship.

Childs speaks to the links between the LP briefly: "[T]he canonical process should not be conceived of as a closed section of Law to which the Prophets were joined only secondarily. At an early date the two collections, Law and Prophets, were joined and both experienced expansion. By the first century BCE both sections of the canon were regarded as normative scripture."[97] Childs is intentionally vague about the growth of the corpora, but quite clear about the theological force expressed in the grammar's shape and expansion. Therefore, it is necessary that we explore the manner in which Daniel cherishes, interprets and expands select traditions from the LP.

3.8. Bi-Partite vs. Tri-Partite

When speaking of the LP, we must also acknowledge how the relationship affects the Writings; after all, there is evidence that "the third division defers to that and works alongside it in its own special way."[98] The tri-partite model of the Hebrew Bible, however, is by no means uncontested. Certain voices propose variations on a *bi-partite* construction—the Law (Torah) and "the Prophets" (non-Torah books). This model of Torah and non-Torah books ignores the achievement of LP as well as this achievement's ability to function as a "grammar."

As early as 1970, T.N. Swanson concluded that the Writings developed alongside the Prophets as a secondary, canonical sub-division.[99] Swanson argues the essential canon is the "Law and the Prophets," whereas the "tri-

---

[95] Ibid., 118 (italics original).

[96] Ibid., 110; also Gerald Sheppard, "Canonization: Hearing the Voice of the Same God Through Historically Dissimilar Traditions," *Int* 36 (1982): 21-33.

[97] Childs, *IOTS*, 65. See also Clements, *Prophecy*. For Clements, these groups of books "subsequently underwent a good deal of expansion and further editorial development" (55).

[98] Seitz, *Goodly Fellowship*. Aside from the logic of a tri-partite structure, there is also historical evidence: The Wisdom of Ben Sira (c. 180 BCE) refers to the entire shape of the Hebrew scriptures (46.1-49.13); likewise, in the *Prologue of Ben Sira* (130 BCE), we read about "the Law and the Prophets and the others that followed him." Josephus (cf. *Ant.* 3:38; 4:302-4; 5:61) also enumerates a tri-partite structure (AD 93-95); however, the order does not originate with either the MT or Greek lists, but is "historically arranged" (Childs, *BTONT*, 58). By this time, reference to the Minor Prophets as a recognized unit—the *Twelve*—is further evidence for a prophetic corpus that exhibits firm (but not crystallized) bounds; also see Qumran literature for "the Law and the Prophets" and "Moses and the Prophets" (1QS 1:2-3; 8:15-16; CD 7:15-17).

[99] T.N. Swanson, "The Closing of the Collection of Holy Scripture: A Study in the History of the Canonization of the Old Testament" (Ph.D. diss., Vanderbilt University, 1970).

partite" structure is a late, rabbinic development. Another sketch of the bi-partite/tri-partite forms, according to Blenkinsopp, shows the Torah to be a closed unit without any need of additional books; from this point, the prophets were added to recast the Law in a different light. Likewise, the prophetic corpus underwent transformation by means of the Writings attached to it. Blenkinsopp argues that legalism (Torah *alone*) and eschatological radicalism (Prophets *alone*) are held in tension. Beyond the books that are clearly prophetic we find those works "divinely inspired in general, aside from the Torah."[100] Many of these reconstructions reflect this basic framework of fixity and closure. The third division, according to this proposal, is part of a general group of "non-Mosaic" books. However, the cost of mislabeling these books cannot be overstated. The sequence and contribution of both Torah and Prophets are necessary, leading up to the role of the Writings—a theological lens upon the corpora before it.

Does it follow that the MT (tri-partite structure) deserves a privileged position? Though the MT and its early forms convey a unique picture of the "lived life" of God's people, the tri-partite model does not restrict our field of study to the MT. Understanding the theological value of other orders is much like a "search," or to use Childs' full term, "the church's ongoing *search* for the Christian Bible."[101] Echoing Childs' concern, Seitz writes "the Christian church 'searches' for the Bible because the variety of listings that exist in its long life are the consequence of translation, custom, habit, innocent reordering, and the like."[102]

Seitz reflects upon the crucial role of canon and its mobility: If the theological significance of the tripartite structure– what Childs called the lens only through which to understand the 'canonical text'—is appreciated, *then divergences from it can be accepted for what they are*, and the major contribution of a

---

[100] Carr, *Formation*, 159. Strangely, Carr, Seitz and Chapman agree on this: the distinct "end of prophecy" is not accurate and somewhat misleading. However, these scholars differ on how the corpora of the Hebrew canon mature throughout the shaping process. Where Seitz and Chapman see an organic and generative effect running from the LP (being a unit), Carr sees a fluid and disheveled space that includes "non-Torah" texts.

[101] Childs, *BTONT*, 67. By this, Childs does not mean an "open canon" or confusion as to what text the Church should appropriate for its praxis. He rebuts Sundberg's thesis and proposes, rather, that a rich *Kanonbewußtein* is at work in the Old Testament (see Childs, "Biblische Theologie und christlicher Kanon," in *Zum Problem des biblischen Kanons* [ed. Ingo Baldermann et al.; JBTh 3; Neukirchen-Vluyn: Neukirchener, 1988], 14). Such an observation leaves room for a "mystery of Israel" that is in continuity (figurally, not traditionally) with the christological shape of the NT. This juxtaposition of the Testaments is not discontinuous, but maintains a delicate balance and is careful not to fall into a "*Christuszeugnis* of the Old Testament" (Driver, 194). Childs's concern is to recognize the value of the MT as the most informative vantage point from which to see Israel's deposit of faith *without ignoring alternative compositions*.

[102] Seitz, *Goodly Fellowship*, 47-48.

Law, Prophets, and Writings achievement can remain untouched and theologically significant.[103]

Setting the MT in a central position, therefore, does not detract from other orders, but reorients them according to their compilational and theological contributions.

4. The Conclusion

The canonical approach, I suggest, framed (and reframes) the entire discussion of what "canon" and "canonical" means. But without posing the fundamental questions of the text-*rez* relationship or a canonical shape of scripture, canonical methods—in their hyper- and non-material patterns—remain half-full and brittle to the touch. It is certainly true: we are now aware that although canonical treatments of the last decade have benefitted from the boon of scholarly hindsight, it is not possible to reconstruct a history of canon and add a scaffolding of theological tidbits after the fact. Neither can we build a theological hermeneutic or method and then subpoena the notion of canon from a few historical studies, again, after the fact. Committing to either of these processes is to misappropriate the canonical shape and devalue the grand architecture of the inspired text. In Chapman's words, implementing a canonical approach will always require that theological and historical attention be paid to the text "all-the-way-down."[104]

---

[103] Ibid., 57, italics mine. Dempster notes the benefits to wrestling with these configurations since they "suggest different hermeneutical understandings of the Law and the Prophets and their relationship to each other" ("The Prophets, the Canon, and a Canonical Approach," in *Canon and Biblical Interpretation*, 303).

[104] Chapman, "Imaginative Readings of Scripture and Theological Interpretation," in *Out of Egypt: Biblical Theology and Biblical Interpretation* (ed. Craig Bartholomew; SHS 5; Grand Rapids: Zondervan, 2006), 411.

CHAPTER 3
The "Law and the Prophets" in Daniel 9:3-19

A canonical approach to Dan 9:24-27 requires that we consider the shape of the entire chapter.[1] Studying the broader context not only reveals elements discussed in the methodology, but also entails a number of coordinating factors leading into 9:24-27. First, we will determine the contextual significance of Dan 9:2 and how it introduces Daniel's source material—not only Jeremiah and the Prophets, but also Jeremiah's own source material (e.g. Leviticus) and the surrounding Torah. Rather than sift for quotations, we will gather around major points of interest that best reflect the mechanics and logic of the passage's canonical shaping. Daniel 9:2 also contains the number of years by which the author interprets the seventy sevens, creating an identifiable frame around the chapter (9:1-2/ 9:24-27). Second, the penitential prayer in 9:3-19 bridges the two edges of the chapter's frame. Here, we encounter the canonical "prologue" (9:2) to Daniel's interpretation and the features of a long tradition of Sabbath rest throughout the theological grammar of the Hebrew Scriptures. Daniel 9 recovers the same narrative we read in key texts such as Leviticus and Jeremiah, transforming its depth and scope.

Two matters derived from our analysis of the prayer include (a) the role of Daniel as "servant" and (b) the importance of the seams connecting the Law, Prophets and Writings (Deut 34:10-12; Mal 4:4-6 [3:22-24]). These components are equally significant for determining the canonical shape of 9:24-27. We notice a family resemblance between the charge of Moses and the charge of Daniel. Running between these figures is language relating to "servant," "proph-

---

[1] Some studies take a holistic interpretation to varying degrees: Barbara Schlenke, "Verantwortung angesichts des Endes Das Gebet des Daniel in Dan 9,4-20," in *Juda und Jerusalem in der Seleukidenzeit* (ed. Ulrich Dahmen and Johannes Schnocks; Göttingen: Bonn University Press, 2010), 105-123; Werline, "Prayer, Politics, and Social Vision"; Paul Redditt, "Daniel 9: Its Structure and Meaning," *CBQ* 62 (2000) 236-49; Kindalee Pfremmer De Long, "Daniel and the Narrative Integrity of His Prayer in Chapter 9," in *A Teacher for All Generations: Essays in Honor of James C. VanderKam, Vol. 1* (ed. Eric Mason et al.; Leiden: Brill, 2012), 219-49; John Bergsma, "The Persian Period as Penitential Era: The 'Exegetical Logic' of Daniel 9.1-27," in *Exile and Restoration Revisited: Essays in Memory of Peter R. Ackroyd* (ed. G. Knoppers and Lester Grabbe; LSTS 73; London: T&T Clark, 2009), 50-64.

et," "sin-bearing" and the like, developing into an image familiar to post-exilic readers. Next, the texts placed at the seams of the canon strengthen the bonds between the corpora. We find these junctures within Dan 9, "self-indicating" their importance and function as a shorthand form of reference to the Hebrew corpora. To summarize: the factors that impact our reading of 9:24-27 inform and dictate how a canonical approach might proceed organically through the text, slowly building to a crescendo in 9:24-27.

1. Daniel 9:2–The Beginning of a Framework

Daniel 9:2 is the access point through which the reader understands the numerical logic of 9:24-27. It also mentions the author's source material. Daniel "interprets" (בין) the "seventy years" (שבעים שנה) of Jeremiah which leads to a call to "consider" (בין) the "seventy sevens" (שבעים שבעים) in the latter verses.[2] Put another way, Dan 9:2 starts the passage, offering a summary of the discussion, whereas 9:24-27 provides a re-summary of its own.[3]

1.1. "The Books"

Although 9:2 precedes the prayer, this verse mentions the source-material responsible for engineering the chapter: the "books" (ספרים) from which Daniel understands (בין) the number of years (מספר השנים) in question. It is noteworthy that although Daniel refers to Jeremiah and the "books" (ספרים; 9:2), he does not direct the reader to any clear text. The reference to "seventy years" (9:2) may narrow the field of texts to Jer 25:1-12; 29:10-15. Still, Daniel's prayer is not constrained by Jeremiah's letters or even the divisions in Jeremiah where the "books" supposedly begin and end (29:1-23, 24-32).[4] Is Daniel pointing to large portions of scripture? Or a trustworthy exegetical resource? Interpreters tend to agree that Daniel is referring to a collection of Israel's scriptures. Precise labels may vary but given our inability to locate either a clear quotation or boundaries suggests the "books" are a text-source with a wide scope.[5] Collins sees the literature as "the Prophets," albeit in an open and un-

---

[2] The syntactical location in these texts may play a important role in uniting the chapter: 9:2 ends with שבעים שנה in an asyndetotic construction, possibly as a collective product of Daniel's interpretation (9:2a)—"according to the word of Jeremiah the prophet, *must pass before the end of the desolations of Jerusalem—seventy years*"(שנה שבעים ירושלם לחרבות למלאות), while the parallel construct is fronted in 9:24—"*Seventy sevens are decreed*...." (שבעים שבעים נחתך).

[3] According to Vern Poythress, the relationship is one of "analogy," not "pure identity" ("Hermeneutical Factors in Determining the Beginning of the Seventy Weeks [Daniel 9:25]," *TrinJ* 6 NS [1985]: 131-49, here 143.

[4] Gerald Wilson provides the most notable work on the "letters" (ספרים) of Jeremiah, the books of Dan 9:2, and Dan 9:5-19 ("The Prayer of Daniel 9: Reflection on Jeremiah 29," *JSOT* 48 [1990] 91-99).

[5] The *Prologue* to Ben Sira (132 BCE) and related texts contain a similar designation for "books": "the *books* of our fathers" (πατριων βιβλιων; 1:10); the "rest of the *books*"

fixed sense[6] while Mark Boda narrows the sense to "the Prophets as authoritative inscripturated tradition."[7] Childs himself writes how Dan 9:2 offers evidence of some sort of fixed collection of prophetic writings."[8]

Some scholars narrow the search to Jeremiah. Wilson believes the prayer is more intelligible when Jeremiah is read as an active source.[9] According to Wilson, the "books" (ספרים) in Dan 9:2 may be the "letters" (ספרים) in Jer 29 (cf. 51:60-63). Jeremiah 29:12-14 becomes the impetus for Daniel's prayer; specifically, as a protasis from which Dan 9:5-19 unfolds. However, it is disappointing no remarks are made of Lev 26, Deut 30:2-3, Torah (as a whole), or the significance of Jeremiah's Deuteronomic background.

Others believe the most fitting designation for Daniel's "books" is the LP in one, *mostly* coherent collection. The "books," therefore, reveal "the existence of an identifiable collection of authoritative religious writings" that resembles the "Torah and Prophets" of the tri-partite construction found in the MT and proto-MT models.[10] For Chapman, the "books" (9:2) are a "new appellation for a canon of scripture" or "a traditional designation for pro-phetic scripture ('the word of the LORD to the prophet Jeremiah,' cf. Jer 1:1-4 and *passim*)."[11] Daniel, therefore, recognizes the LP as a "*union* of two roles and traditions."[12] Those less committed to a material collection expand the usage to include a variation of "the Scriptures."[13]

In sum, there is a consensus among Daniel interpreters: the most conservative estimates include one or more large divisions of scriptural source-material.[14] As further evidence, the standing authority of the "Law of Moses" (9:11, 13) and the "prophets" (9:6, 10) later in the passage is a determinative

---

(τα λοιπα των βιβλιων; 1:25); also the singular designation of the Pentateuch, "the book of Moses" (τη Μωυσεως βιβλω; 1 Esdras 5:49, 7:6, 9; cf. 1:33, 42).

[6] John J. Collins, *Daniel* (Minneapolis: Fortress, 1993), 360; for a reference to "prophetic books" see Fishbane, *Biblical Interpretation*, 482.

[7] Mark Boda, "Biblical Theology and the Old Testament," in *Hearing the Old Testament*, Grand Rapids: Erdmans, 2012), 132.

[8] Childs, *IOTS*, 65.

[9] Wilson, "Prayer of Daniel 9," 92; also Willis, "The Plans of God in Jeremiah and Daniel."

[10] Goldingay, *Daniel*, 240. It is not a requirement, as Goldingay argues, to have a complete, material form of the LP. Instead, the prayer may be composed by "someone who knew this tradition well" (234).

[11] Ibid., 239.

[12] Chapman, *Law and the Prophets*, 151.

[13] Maurice Gilbert, "La Prière de Daniel: Dn 9, 4-19," *RTL* 3 (1972) 284-310, esp 288; Schmid, "Deuteronomistic," n48. Lacoque, *The Book of Daniel* (trans. David Pellauer; Atlanta: John Knox, 1979), 179. He notes this usage is the first instance of such a term designating a constrained body of "scriptures."

[14] The summary-form "Law and Prophets" and its variations are well attested within writings related to Dan 9: Sir 1:1, 20; Josephus's construction in *Ag. Ap.* 1.38-40; *2 Macc* 15:9; *4 Macc* 18:10; see also CD VII, 15-17; 4QMMT[a], 9-11; 2Q25; 1QS I, 2-3.

complement to our designation of "the books" and imply Daniel is relying on these texts to refer to the authority, traditions and histories of the dual-corpora in shorthand.[15]

2. Daniel 9:3-19

Daniel 9:3-19 challenges interpreters on multiple levels. The prayer appears as a smattering of motifs and phrases from the Pentateuch, mixed at random with wording from the Former Prophets, and attached to Jeremiah only by name.[16] Is this prayer a confession? A plea for revelation? Is it a Deuteronomic insert functioning as a stamp of authority? Once the reader solves the problem of form, how then does the prayer contribute to the whole chapter (9:1-2, 20-27)? Though many treat the prayer as secondary or a separate subject altogether, this confession is critical for how we understand 9:24-27.[17]

2.1. Prayer for Revelation

Investigating the *nature* of the prayer is a worthwhile starting point. Despite minor differences in word and nuance, interpretations of 9:3-19 usually fall into one of two categories: a request for further revelation or a prayer based on confession. The wording that the prayer and the interpretation stitch together discloses the unity of Dan 9. The revealed material (9:24-27) is intimately connected to 9:3-19.[18]

---

[15] In the case of Jer 25-30, commentators note breaks or indicators in textual development of the book of Jeremiah, particularly breaks that mark where text-sets or scrolls begin and end. Jeremiah 25:14 functions as a conclusion (completion of seventy years; cf. 25:11-14) while 30:1-2 is an introduction to chs. 30-33. Between these larger sources sits Jer 29 (a short letter, in comparison). This same letter is an extended treatment of the promises comporting with the fullness of "seventy years" (29:10) and an uncertain end (v.28). Much of the context, vocabulary and themes circulating between Dan 9 and Jeremiah are present at the boundaries highlighting the outline of texts and may, therefore, indicate texts from which Daniel studied.

[16] H.C. Ginsberg popularized the two-part sequence of the chapter, setting apart 9:1-3 and 9:21-27 as Part 1 while Part 2 is the "genuine Hebrew text" (*Studies in Daniel* [New York: Jewish Theological Seminary of America, 1948], 41). A canonical approach to the prayer and the framing texts insists on recognizing a "literary development" and a "textual development," though not in a distinct sequence (Childs, *IOTS*, 95-96). Transposing this reading onto Dan 9:3-19, we find, for example, the submission and response to the Law and the Prophets (literary development) and, by way of a second example, the preservation of Yahweh's name (hwhy) exclusively in Dan 9:3-20.

[17] Goldingay adds another interpretive dimension to the 9:3-19, namely, how "the passage of scripture fulfills the role of the symbolic vision in chaps. 7 and 8, the prayer takes the structural place occupied by the symbolic vision there" (*Daniel*, 236).

[18] Note the network of connections associating the prayer with the rest of the chapter: "poured out" (9:11; תתך) with the decreed end "poured out" (9:27; תתך); the

In considering the revelation option, we must ask what exactly is being revealed. The object of revelation is far from settled.[19] Also, this text is hardly the "revelation of the vision" (8:19-27) we read earlier. Is Daniel "interpreting" Jeremiah's text or performing some other action? Werline proposes Daniel is "seeking" by through an underlying and undisclosed question—the answer is "the interpretation of the prophetic prediction."[20] In like manner, Lacocque concludes that the passage is a revelatory "prerequisite" from Jer 1:12: "the Lord keeps watch (שקד) over the accomplishment of His Word" (cf. Dan 9:14).[21] The prayer becomes "a kind of initiation rite...for receiving divine secrets."[22] Fishbane clears a better path, tying exegetical development to revelation directly; for Fishbane, Dan 9 is the *key example* of how exegesis can be wed to a means of revelation.[23]

Henze, on the other hand, feels that Daniel knew perfectly well what Jeremiah was communicating—"I, Daniel, *understood* (בין; cf. 10:1, 14) in the books the number of years."[24] It is because of Jeremiah's "promise of restoration" (Jer 29:10-14) that Daniel responds to the prayer. In an illuminating discussion that focuses on Dan 9:2-4, Henze proceeds to level a criticism at Fishbane's alternative classification of "mantological exegesis," based on the introduction to the prayer.[25] Daniel 9 is a poor example of mantic reinterpretation, according to

---

phrase "not obeying your voice" (9:10-11, 14; ולא שמענו בקול), refers back to Jer. 25:8; the people are "to gain insight" (9:13; להשכיל) and Daniel gains insight (9:22; להשכילך); also, the need for Daniel to "understand" (9:22; בין) may allude to Jer 30:24; the Lord "watches over" (9:14; שקד) calamity (cf. Jer 23:20-30.24); the people and the temple are left "desolate" (9:17-18; שממתינו/שממה) just as the ultimate "desolation/desolator" (9:27; שמם/משמם); also, the "supplication" (תחנון) of 9:17 repeats in 9:23. Volume and proximity alone corroborates the link between these sections, but, as mentioned above, these associations also reach beyond Daniel 9.

[19] Cf. Matthias Henze, "The Use of Scripture in the Book of Daniel," in *A Companion to Biblical Interpretation in Early Judaism* (ed. Matthias Henze; Grand Rapids: Eerdmans, 2011), 299-301.

[20] Werline, "Prayer," 23.

[21] Lacocque, *Daniel*, 179.

[22] Ibid., 121. Koch also appeals to Daniel's supra-prophetic authority, stating "in this book the prophetic word always is taken as a riddle ...." ("Is Daniel Among the Prophets?" 125)

[23] Fishbane, *Biblical Interpretation*, 487-88. Although Dan 9 shows how exegesis transitions into written revelation, Fishbane still argues for a "cognitive dissonance" between person and text (509-10).

[24] Henze, 301. Much hinges on the rendering of בין. Hansjörg Rigger, in considering the exegetical possibilities, notes how the references to time in 9:2 may be separate images depending on how we read twbrjl and —instead of "to bring the desolations of Jerusalem, namely, 70 years" (ESV), we may have a softer connection, "*die Zahl der Jahre...(beträgt) siebzig Jahre*" (*Siebzig Siebener: Die 'Jahrwochenprophetie' in Dan 9* [TTS 57; Trier: Paulinus, 1997], 53). The "number of years" in Daniel's interpretation may *contain*, and not be equivalent to "70 years."

[25] Cf. Fishbane, *Biblical Interpretation*, 474-524.

Henze, because Daniel comprehended (בינתי) Jeremiah's prophecy and "seeks" with a penitent heart. Fishbane, arguing for an exegetical context, sees Daniel "searching" (בינתי) within Jeremiah's books. Daniel is unable to understand the full meaning of the prophecy on his own.[26]

Is Daniel, therefore, searching for the truth of Jeremiah's "seventy years," having assumed the restoration of 538 BCE failed? Neither the form of the prayer or the precise identity of what Daniel "seeks" (9:3) is clear. Is Daniel seeking "the Lord" (את יהוה; Jer 50:4; Hos 3:5, 5:6; Zeph 2:3; Zech 8:21), seeking "a word of the Lord" (את דבר יהוה; Amos 8:12) or seeking the correct "prayer and supplication" (תפלה ותחנונים; 9:3)? None of the standard terminology appears; instead Daniel acts by "speaking" (מדבר), "praying" (מתפלל), "confessing" (מתודה) and "offering supplication" (מפיל תחנה; 9:20). Fishbane is correct in his notion of exegesis (9:2) evident by the carefully chosen textual resources. But Henze is also correct in substituting mantology for *penitence*. Daniel endeavors to interpret the material surrounding this numerical image and, at the same time, to honor the admonitions of Leviticus and the forewarnings of Jeremiah. More terms encircle the notion of penitence than revelation, but a revelation component is still present.

2.2. Prayer of Confession

Having weighed the merits of the revelation option, we must ask if branding the prayer "confession" is a satisfactory alternative? Goldingay puts the matter simply and, in my estimation, successfully: "In the prayer, then, Daniel is seeking the fulfillment of the prophecy referred to in the narrative opening, by offering the response that *opens up the possibility of its fulfillment*."[27] It is not (only) a call to confess Israel's sins in Daniel's contemporary situation and it is not a new revelation detached from the preceding narrative. Rather, the prayer "opens up" and carries forward prior traditions and narrative plots. It is "an act of praise" in response to "the justice of the judgment of God."[28] Unlike the tone of despair and resignation we hear in Josh 7:20-21, 2 Sam 12:13a and the Deuteronomic background, Daniel pleads for mercy in the midst of Israel's shortcomings (cf. Judg 10:15; 1 Sam 15:24-25; Ps 106).[29] In this way, Daniel repurposes the prayer to argue for a time of completion—Israel will not perpetually serve a sentence for violating God's commands.

Flashes of a reversal appear to the reader: the emphatic particle ועתה in 9:15 could be an "element ... of forgiveness and restoration," leading the audience through 9:16-19 with a sense of optimism.[30] After Daniel seeks to "understand" (*Qal* בין) Jeremiah's text (9:2), the reader does not expect the angelic messenger—a messenger sent to respond—to make Daniel "understand" (*Hiphil*

---

[26] Fishbane, 487-88.
[27] Goldingay, 236 (italics mine).
[28] Ibid., 233.
[29] Ibid. Goldingay also contrasts Daniel's appeal with the tone of Ezra 9.
[30] Cf. André Laurentin, "Weattah-Kainun," *Bib* 45 (1964) 190-97.

בין) additional levels of interpretation (9:22). This development is difficult for both types of prayer. Merging the two types of prayer into a hybrid may ease some of the difficulty; however, it is more accurate to view the prayer as a unique mixture with its own mechanisms. Canonical shape and genre mix together and solidify in accordance with the theological goal of the final form. Possibly, the prayer is an amalgam that includes confession and a plea for revelation. It is also a housing for the discrete voice of the LP. Many readings liken the prayer to an equation from which we receive a result, namely the revelation of 9:24-27, but 9:3-19 is also an outworking of 9:2, what is "understood in the books." Regardless, the text quickly reminds us (9:20-24), that a rudimentary tag such as "confession based on Leviticus 26" will not suffice and that the result of seventy sevens demands a closer, canonical reading of the prayer.

2.3. The 'Law and the Prophets' in 9:3-19

We have noted the problems with the popular labels for 9:3-19 (revelation and confession), mostly their inability to capture the beginning of the conceptual shift from the expectations of Lev 26:34-35 and Jer 25:10-14 to Daniel's own vision of "complete" rest (9:24-27). Few models centralizing the confessional element are willing to comment on, for example, the framed role of Jeremiah (9:2, 24). For this reason, interpreting not just the associations with Leviticus in the Torah, but also associations with Jeremiah and the Prophets redefines the nature of the prayer and its transition into 9:24-27. A bond between Dan 9 and the LP seems to be the most sensible platform for understanding the connections in and purpose for 9:3-19.[31]

The LP are invaluable when reading Dan 9:3-19, 24-27 because they contain "the prophetic oracles and narratives about the prophets that present their understandings of the reasons for Israel's suffering and the future restoration of the people once the punishment is complete."[32] But what constitutes the LP for Daniel? To answer this question, we will explore the unit's (1) historical and (2) associative dimensions. First, the historical background of the LP is by no means straightforward and remains a prominent feature of the canon debate. Lang, for example, dates the construction "the Law and the Prophets" to around 561 BCE or "the date of the release of King Jehoiachin from his prison in Babylonia as recorded in 2 Kgs 25:27-30."[33] The literature of LP, according to Lang, is no more than the contents of "King Jehoiachin's Bible," containing "the First Bible" (Torah) and "the book of Jeremiah" (Prophets) and functioning as a "political programme for the restoration of a Hebrew

---

[31] Chapman, *Law and Prophets*, 109.

[32] Marvin Sweeney, "Foundations for a Jewish Theology of the Hebrew Bible: Prophets in Dialogue," in *Jewish Bible Theology: Perspectives and Case Studies* (ed. by Isaac Kalimi; Winona Lake, Ind.: Eisenbrauns, 2012), 165.

[33] Bernhard Lang, "The 'Writings': A Hellenistic Literary Canon in the Hebrew Bible," in *Canonization and Decanonization* (ed. A. van der Kooij and K. van der Toorn; Leiden: Brill, 1998), 62.

state in Palestine."³⁴ This argument fails to justify the proposed "editing" program behind the political ambitions of 561 BCE and does not possess the same textual evidence as the larger, second-century canonical model. More likely, the factors compelling the biblical authors to unite the books of the Pentateuch, for example, were equally authoritative in shaping the LP.

Henze sees Daniel using the LP as a literary device for making thinly veiled allusions to Antiochus IV:

> Both historical review and eschatological prediction are largely compilations of old prophetic oracles, pronouncements taken from different books in Scripture and reassembled here to tell the story of Antiochus and his imminent demise. Excerpts from the prophecies of Isaiah, Balaam, and Habakkuk in particular are reused to speak of Antiochus's military aggression, his humiliation, and the delay of his punishment.³⁵

A monochromatic understanding of the LP in Dan 9, such as this, is too static to explain why the author chooses *these* books or *this* content for the root system of his message. If Dan 9:3-19 is only a varnish used to make historical allusions to the Antiochene crises, why would Daniel be discerning or selective in his textual associations? Asserting a type of selectivity, that associates texts seemingly at random, contradicts the textual craft or logic in Dan 9.

Below, we will discuss the textual origins of the construction "the Law and the Prophets," but for now we can conclude that the LP is an authoritative centerpiece of the Hebrew Scriptures. Political programs and economic interests certainly claim some influence on its formation. In spite of such influences, however, the authority of the LP transcended religious, social and political circumstances, giving the dual-corpora the capability to make authoritative claims *over* these spheres. The wide and, at times, incongruous array of textual associations with which Daniel anchors his own writing (cf. Lev 26:34-35; Is 10:22-23) is evidence enough that the author did not pledge allegiance to a particular socio-political party.

Secondly, a unique associative function infuses the LP. Henze accurately describes types of association in Daniel: "While the concern for the eschaton is well pronounced and explicit, the connection with the past is, for the most part, *implicit and expressed* in the choice of literary genres, fictitious setting, and language, all at home in Israel's traditional writings."³⁶ There is a depth and intentionality to Daniel's associative activity that is able to *give voice* to older scriptures, rather than timidly borrow their authority. Depth, in this

---

³⁴ Ibid.
³⁵ Henze, "Use of Scripture," 294-295.
³⁶ Henze, "Use of Scripture," 279. It is difficult to know to which "setting" Henze is referring, but the other points are sound.

way, reveals "an extraordinary case in point of intertextuality" in 9:3-19, demonstrating textually how "history conforms to the divine template in new configurations."[37] Is it responsible, therefore, to restrict associations to a recoverable quotation or cross-reference? Does "interpretation" mean the effort of B to *explain* A, or does the *influence* of A on B also imply that B *interprets* A? As Henze states, any failure to look beyond a narrow system of cross-reference also "fails to capture the complex processes of adopting, reworking and recontextualizing the earlier materials."[38] Simply claiming something like "intertextuality" requires qualification and while tags like "allusions" or "partial quotations" are popular, these terms, even among the most generous definitions, will not fully apply to Dan 9:3-19. No clear citations occur beyond the level of a phrase or fragment and the only trace of an explicit association is in reference to Jeremiah's oracle (9:2). It seems *context*, not just quotation or influence, divulges enough to explain these relationships. The Law establishes the traditions unfolding in the Prophets, while the Prophets "provide the theological means within the Tanak by which Israel/Judaism constructively came to grips with fundamental challenges to their existence in a manner that enabled them to rebuild for the future."[39]

2.4. "Law of Moses" and the Pentateuch (Dan 9:11, 13)

At first glance, the occurrence of תורה seems too generic to be evidence for a five-book corpus. As it happens, all occurrences of תורה are in this chapter (9:10-11, 13). Dan 9:11, 13 are distinct in that the prophetic formula, "as it is written," precedes תורת משה, narrowing our search from the Torah and Former Prophets to the Pentateuch. However, the source (or sources) is still veiled: it may recount Moses' entreaty (ויחל משה את פני יהוה) on Mount Sinai during the Golden Calf incident (Exod 32:11-13) or the Song of Moses (Deut 32).[40] I suggest the expression transforms as it passes through the bodies of text preceding Dan 9.

The first, *formal* parallel to the phrase "law of Moses" (תורת משה) is in Josh 8:32, not, as logic would dictate, in Leviticus, Deuteronomy or Jeremiah. The meaning of the construction broadens as it proceeds through the Prophets (Josh 8:32, 23:6; 2 Kgs 14:6). Moving from the first inscriptions (Josh 8:32), to a "book" (Josh 23:6), to a more expansive work that includes Deuteronomy (2 Kgs 14:6; cf. Deut 24:16), we begin to notice a well-established stream of Torah

---

[37] Samuel Wells and George Sumner, *Esther and Daniel* (Grand Rapids: Brazos, 2013), 184; cf. Ephraim Radner, "Doctrine, Destiny and the Figure of History," in *Reclaiming Faith* (ed. Ephraim Radner and George Sumner; Grand Rapids: Eerdmans, 1993).

[38] Ibid., 280.

[39] Sweeney's conclusion, "Foundations," 186.

[40] Deuteronomy 32:28-29 describes a people who do not understand (שׂכל) and the nation is not able to discern their own end. This passage follows Deut 29:20—a strong contender for the "curse"/ "oath" language והשבעה האלה; cf. Num 5:21; Neh 10:29) in Dan 9:11.

in interpretatio. When we reach Dan 9:11, 13, the "law of Moses" means a full body of literature, including Lev 25, and certainly the capstone texts, Deut 29-34.[41] Daniel then merges the characteristics of Deut 29:20 and Jer 26:19:

> And the Lord will single him out from all the tribes of Israel for *calamity* (רעה), in accordance with all the *curses* (אלות) of the covenant written in this Book of the Law (Deut 29:20)

> Did Hezekiah king of Judah and all Judah put him to death? Did he not fear the Lord and *entreat the favor of the Lord* (ויחל את פני יהוה), and did not the Lord relent of the *calamity* (רעה) that he had pronounced against them? But we are about to bring great *calamity* (רעה) upon *ourselves* (על נפשנתינו) (Jer 26:19)

> As it is written in the Law of Moses, all this *calamity* (רעה) has come *upon us* (עלינו); yet we have not *entreated the favor of the Lord our God* (ולא חלינו פני את), turning from our iniquities and gaining insight by your truth (Dan 9:13)

Daniel performs two actions: first, he combines Deut 29:20 with Jer 26:19 and, second, shifts the referent in Deut 29:20 from the individual violator of the covenant (והבדילו יהוה לרעה מכל שבטי) to the first-person plural of 9:13. Daniel can merge these texts by virtue of working with two, intimately related bodies of literature, not single references.

2.5. Leviticus and the Pentateuch

Other portions of Torah bear a great deal of significance for Dan 9:3-19, and consequently how the author reckons the numerical images of 9:24-27. Prominent in the passage, the legal or *applied* Sabbath (derived from the roots of Sabbath [Gen 2:1-3]) revolves around a heptadic scheme or motif. These currents of tradition running through the tri-partite canon have their origins in the Pentateuch—the currents do not move in one linear direction, but radiate out from key texts. The texts of Leviticus commonly associated with Dan 9:2-19 are these:

> You will count *seven weeks of years* (שבתת שבע שנים; cf. Dan 9:2), *seven times seven years* (שבע השנים שבתת), so that the time of the seven weeks of years will give you forty-nine years (Lev 25:8)

> And in spite of this you will not *listen* (שמע; cf. Dan 9:6, 10-11, 17, 19) to me, then I will discipline you again *sevenfold* (שבע) for your sins (Lev 26:18; cf. 26:21, 24, 28)

---

[41] By the time of the promulgation of the Qumran texts, the "law of Moses" had become a conventional formula for citing Scripture (1QS V, 17; 1QS VIII, 14; 4QFlor, II, 3).

And I will lay *waste* (חרב; cf. Dan 9:2) to your *cities* (עירכם; cf. Dan 9:16, 18, 19) and *will make your sanctuaries desolate* (והשמותי את מקדשיכם; cf. Dan 9:17-19), and I will not smell your pleasing aromas (Lev 26:31)

Then the *land* (הארץ; cf. Dan 9:6-7) will enjoy its Sabbaths as long as it lies *desolate* (שמם), while you are in your enemies' land; then the land will rest, and enjoy its Sabbaths. As long as it lies *desolate* (שמם) it will have rest, the rest that it did not have on your Sabbaths when you were dwelling in it (Lev 26:34-35)

But if they *confess* (ידה; cf. Dan 9:4, 20) their *iniquity* (עון; cf. Dan 9:5, 13) and the *iniquity of their fathers* (עון אבתם; cf. Dan 9:16) *in their treachery that they committed against* me (במעלם אשר מעלו; cf. Dan 9:7) and also in walking contrary to me, so that I walked contrary to them and brought them into the land of their enemies—if then their uncircumcised heart is humbled and they make amends for their iniquity, then I will remember my *covenant* (ברית; cf. Dan 9:4) with Jacob, and I will remember my covenant with Isaac and my covenant with Abraham, and I will remember the land (Lev 26:40-42)

These five selections are by no means all of the associations between Lev 25-26 and Dan 9:3-19.[42] To my earlier point concerning Daniel's associative strategies, if we were to submit every association, we would have much of chs. 25-26. The prayer of 9:3-19 reflects a wider scope of reading and connecting. The passages above represent the core outline of Lev 25-26 as well as the highest volume of textual associations within Dan 9:3-19. Many of the associations we locate in 9:3-19 are also in 9:24-27, but we will treat that group of relationships in the next chapter; here, I want only to point out the first steps of interconnectivity taken by the author.

How do we find Lev 25-26 operating in 9:3-19? Four different types of association indicate Daniel's use of Leviticus texts: (1) a cluster of shared vocabulary; (2) evidence Daniel is reading a larger version of Torah, which includes Leviticus; (3) evidence Daniel is interpreting the text(s) of Jeremiah, who himself uses and interprets Levitical texts; (4) the contextual evidence that Daniel shapes his prayer to respond to the admonition of Lev 26:40. Meredith Kline sees Lev 26 in the glimpses of covenant lawsuit language scattered within the prayer (e.g. byr).[43] Collins, while noting the prevalence of Lev 25-26 in the

---

[42] Among the other options, we might include the conclusion of this two-chapter set—Lev 26:45-46—which coordinates with the conclusion to Daniel's prayer, 9:15-19. Both passages cite a fundamental Torah-reference, "the land of Egypt," however I do not include it among the above texts because of its common frequency in the Pentateuch.

[43] Kline, "The Covenant of the Seventieth Week," in *The Law and the Prophets: Old Testament Studies Prepared in Honor of Oswald Thompson Allis* (ed. John Skilton, et. al.; N.p.: Presbyterian and Reformed, 1974), 457-58.

prayer, also sees fragments of Deuteronomy, verifying how these texts associate with one another within their shaped corpus.[44] Goldingay entitles 9:11-13 "the 'Law of Moses' section" set in a context of "warning," with the prophets following and authoritatively echoing "Moses' own oral message" (cf. Deut 29:19-26).[45] Fishbane incorporates the prayer by focusing on the shared themes and traditions in Lev 26 and Jer 25, 29. For Fishbane, Daniel's motive is clear: he "avers the justice of divine wrath in recompense for the covenant disloyalty" spoken of in Lev 26.[46] Jeremiah's role is to give Daniel the implements (9:2) to respond to Lev 26:40.[47] Parallels, such as the consequence of "unfaithfulness" (מעל) and the need for "confession" (ידה; *hithpael*) bind Lev 26:40 to Dan 9:4-7.[48] This recurring cluster of elements, originating in Leviticus, plays out through Daniel's confessional response. Most likely, Lev 25:1-26:46 is the primary Torah text functioning intravenously throughout Dan 9.

Other scholars see a passing reference to Leviticus, usually grouping the association with other pieces of Torah.[49] Winfriend Vogel and Lacocque see the foundations of Jubilee in the text and a shaded exposition of Lev 25:9. After seven weeks of years (25:8), on the Day of Atonement, the Lord instructs the people to "sound the trumpet throughout all your land."[50] Before the legal form of Sabbath, however, we have a heptadic pattern set by God's completion of the created order. Leviticus 25:2-6 is the inevitable outcome of Gen 2:1-3. But Gen 1-3 must also be read in light of Lev 25-26: the same land (cf. Gen 1:11-12, 29-30; Lev 25:2, 26:4) which God appoints humanity to manage (cf. Gen 3:17-19; Lev 25:3-5) is under divine stewardship (cf. Gen 1:26-28).

Whereas Genesis holds a retrospective position, Deut 31:16-21 reshapes the threads of Lev 25-26 *prospectively*. New layers are added to the concept of land (31:21) and fruitfulness (31:20), sewing in "covenant" (31:16, 21) with older threads. Leviticus 26 is "the final parenetic discussion of the book" and parallels other receiving points in Torah, namely the summary texts of Ex 23:20-23 and Deut 28. This configuration of passages shows the thematic exchange occurring between Lev 25-26 and other texts in Torah. To explain how

---

[44] 9:4, Deut 7:9, 21 // 9:10; Deut 4:30 // 9:11; Deut 28:15-68, 29:20, 34:5 // 9:12; Deut 2:25 // 9:5 (Collins, *Daniel*, 350-51).

[45] Goldingay, *Daniel*, 245.

[46] Fishbane, *Biblical Interpretation*, 483.

[47] Ibid., 489.

[48] Labeling the section a "confession" justifies the textual associations in 9:3-19 *to a degree*. Conversely, a confession is difficult to defend when the framework of the chapter calls for further illumination (cf. Wilson, "The Prayer of Daniel 9," 92).

[49] Henze, for example, briefly notes the application of Lev 26:12-25 in Dan 9, but devotes more interest to the use of Num 24:24 in Dan 11:30, thereby setting up the downfall of Antiochus and the Seleucid Empire (cf. "and he also shall perish forever") ("Use of Scripture," 296).

[50] Vogel, 43-44. Cf. Lacocque, "The Liturgical Prayer in Daniel 9" *HUCA* 47 (1976): 119-142. We will discuss the details orbiting the "Jubilee" argument in a later section (Chapter 4—The Seventy Sevens).

Daniel includes Leviticus, one must look beyond the confines of a single book and consider its place within the five-book set.

Though these associations provide evidence of connectivity, it is the theme of sin and debt that binds these texts together on a theological level. Gary Anderson studies the notion of Israel's indebtedness throughout Lev 25 and 26, claiming it as "the common thread holding them together."[51] Sin is not normally treated with the nuance of "indebtedness," but Anderson convincingly argues for (1) a "new concept" tying Leviticus 25-26 together, as well as (2) projecting the tradition forward through the canon. He begins by acknowledging, "God is the true owner of the land, so that any sale of the land is really only a lease that allows the 'purchaser' to turn a profit from the crops he raises for whatever time remains until the next Jubilee" (Lev 25:23-24).[52] If the land belongs to God, no sale can ever be "final," which follows the logic of release and the Jubilee event.[53]

In Lev 26:18, we arrive at the rationale for setting the two chapters next to one another. The potential for a later actualization of Sabbath violation is revealed: the offense widens in 26:18-20 ("your *land* will not yield its produce") to an offense against God in 26:21-22 ("if you remain hostile toward *Me* and refuse to obey me ..."), resulting in a punishment, not of the land only, but of the people—"I too will remain hostile to *you* ... I will bring a sword against you to wreak vengeance for the covenant" (26:23-25a). The final verses of the chapter bundle these offenses together, into a single result: "For the land will be forsaken of them and will repay the debt (רצה) for its Sabbath years by being desolate of them, while they will repay their debt (רצה); for the abundant reason that they rejected My rules and spurned My laws" (26:43). The offenses take the form of a debt and it is a debt that Israel alone cannot repay. But the author does not end the warning there. A glimmer of hope remains and the topic abruptly turns from the land that repays debts to the "land of Egypt" from which Israel was herself redeemed: "Yet, even then, when they are in the land of their enemies, I will not despise them or abhor them so as to destroy them, breaking My covenant with them; for I am the Lord their God. I will remember in their favor the covenant with their forefathers, whom I freed from the land of Egypt in the sight of the nations to be their God: I, the Lord" (26:44-45). The writer assumes the reader knows this text—which concerns land ownership and debt repayment—is not only about the formal stipulations of the Sabbath. As Anderson continues, "It is not simply an ecological action that assures the ongoing fertility of the land. By leaving the land fallow every six years, one is keeping a divine command that instantiates the fact that land belongs not to human beings but to God.[54] To remind Israel that God owns the land is to require reparations from *both* the land and Israel. However, as we

---

[51] Gary Anderson, *Sin: A History* (New Haven: Yale University Press, 2009).
[52] Anderson, 56-57.
[53] Ibid., 57.
[54] Ibid., 65.

read in 26:44-45, this plan is not a "measure-for-measure punishment," Anderson notes, but "a process of restoration."[55]

Leviticus 26:40-45 not only completes the book's role in Dan 9, it also helps hold the chapter together. Aside from Lev 26:40 and Jeremiah "braided," as mentioned above, these verses contain the original impetus for Daniel's prayer and confession.[56] Israel is to "confess" (ידה) because of her "treachery" (מעל) and her resistance, or "walking away" (קרי), from Yahweh. The word קרי is unique to Leviticus, used only in ch. 26, and represents the contrary force pushing against Yahweh's own forceful reorientations (26:21-24, 27-28, 40-41). Moreover, Yahweh counters this opposition by striking Israel back "sevenfold" for her sins (שבע; 26:21, 24, 28). The full extent of Yahweh's sevenfold counter is not revealed in the final verses. Instead, it is left open. Consequently, the canonical shape of Dan 9 depends on more voices than just Lev 25-26. When these traditions and patterns, forged from these two chapters, are projected forward, images expand beyond land and feast days: the judgment will include exile, the dissolution of Israelite livelihood, and an apparent separation from the presence of God never before experienced.

These parting words of Lev 25-26, we will see below, are what the messengers the Prophets capture, and ultimately, Daniel. They are "ancient readers" who "were drawn to these chapters because of their detailed accounts of why Israel had been sent into exile and what had to transpire before redemption could occur."[57] As Anderson summarizes, "the time for warnings has passed" (cf. 26:27-38), Israel's cities and sanctuaries are marked for destruction, the land is in a state of desolation and Israel is to be scattered among the nations (vv. 31-33). Israel fails to visualize the progression of her sins; therefore, those linking Israel's sin, indebtedness and Sabbath violation to the transgression of God's Word in general are the "servants, the prophets."

2.6. "Servants the Prophets" and the Prophetic Corpus (Dan 9:6, 10)

Prophets are twice called "servants of the Lord" (9:6, 10) while Moses receives the title in the following verse: "the servant of God" (9:11; cf. Deut 34:5; Josh 1:13; 8:31-33; 11:12). This link is not a new development. Moses and the subsequent line of Prophets enjoy a well-established relationship (Deut 18:18;

---

[55] Ibid., 66.

[56] Apart from Daniel 9, the *Words of the Luminaries* (4Q504, frag. 1-2, col. 6:4-8), also contains a confession on behalf of Israel based on Leviticus 26, but shapes the passage (vv. 40-45) to achieve a different result. Rather than concluding with Lev 26:43 ("they will repay their debts..."), the author transforms the debt-claim to be filled ("[We have repaid the debt in that] we have not rejected the trials you have imposed ..."). Then, as Anderson concludes, "what had been a prediction of punishment in Leviticus now becomes a prescription for restoration in this prayer" (*Sin*, 92; cf. Esther Chazon, "Is Divrei ha-Meorot a Sectarian Prayer?," in *The Dead Sea Scrolls: Forty Years of Research* [ed. Devorah Dimant; Leiden: Brill, 1992], 3-17).

[57] Anderson, *Sin*, 75.

34:10). But by including the phrase עבדי הנביאים within the shape of this passage, Daniel calls attention to this relationship and augments it.

One might assume עבדי הנביאים originates with the prophet Jeremiah since the phrase implies a collective of prophets and contains Mosaic overtones (cf. Jer 7:25; 25:5; 29:19). Jeremiah is also cited by name (Dan 9:2). Unexpectedly, the construction, "servants, the prophets" (עבדי הנביאים), occurs in full form in the middle of the Former Prophets (2 Kgs 9:7). Daniel's field of reference ranges from the servant, Moses (Deut 18:18, 34:8-10), through the entirety of the Former Prophets (Josh 8:32; 2 Kgs 9:7), and to Jeremiah et al. Claiming 9:3-19 as a Deuteronomistic insertion is not out of the question, but it is insufficient. The use of עבדי הנביאים takes on new meaning when drawn through the *Latter* Prophets (Jer 7:25) as well. How then is Daniel using עבדי הנביאים? On one level, he is referring to the conjunctions between the Torah, the Former Prophets and the Latter Prophets. On another level, he is testifying to his sources and building upon the groundwork of the prophetic corpus.[58] To mention the "Law of Moses" and the "Prophets" is to refer to the authority, traditions and histories of these corpora in shorthand.

2.7. Jeremiah and the Major Prophets in Daniel 9:3-19

Daniel 9, as well as 7-12, proves the author is familiar with the Latter Prophets. Just as Lev 25-26 constitutes the center of Daniel's concentration on the Pentateuch, so also is Jeremiah at the center of the prophetic resource Daniel interprets.[59] For example, Habakkuk, though not a focal voice, is nevertheless present in Daniel's work. Daniel the author considers the "vision for the appointed time" in Hab 2:3 so as to draw attention to the "oppression by an invader" (cf. Dan 10-11).[60]

Before moving into Jeremiah, we must assess the place and impact of the other Major Prophets within the prayer. Ezekiel and Isaiah are two prophets to whom Dan 9:3-19 gives special attention.[61] With Ezekiel, Dan 9 share at least

---

[58] Consider Dan 9:16 // Ezek 28:14, 16; Dan 9:26-27 // Ezek 28:8, 17, 19. The "Teacher of Righteousness" also speaks of "the servants, the prophets" in terms of a collection (1 QpHab VII, 4-5).

[59] For these reasons, it is difficult to read the "shaped" Jeremiah as the first, lone voice of the prophetic corpus and even more difficult to consider this hypothesis based solely on the book's ability to placate concerns of a failed eschatology in the exilic community. See Wilson, "Persian Period," 110.

[60] Henze, "Use of Scripture," 297. In fact, the oracles of Habakkuk appear to be a source of "consolation and assurance" for Daniel (see originally Fishbane, *Biblical Interpretation*, 492).

[61] Sweeney proposes the notion that Daniel is "designed" to respond to the Prophets, ("End of Eschatology," 126); see also Koch, "Is Daniel Among the Prophets," 119-120. Conversely, Henze assumes Daniel's authors "continue to speak in the prophetic idiom, and, by doing so, make a powerful claim to prophetic, that is, revelatory authority" ("Use of Scripture," 303). Daniel's work, therefore, forms a "direct extension" to the

three critical themes: "ruin and desolation" (cf. 28:8, 17, 18), God's sacred mountain (cf. 28:14, 16), temple profanation (cf. 28:16, 18).[62] Ezekiel 39:23-26 also contains vocabulary found in Dan 9:16-18 (and Leviticus 26). In 39:23, the house of Israel went into captivity for their iniquity (עון), since they dealt treacherously (מעל) and the Lord proclaims twice, "I hid my face" (אסתר פני; cf. 39:23-24; Lev 26:40). Whether Yahweh's face is set against Israel or turned/hidden from her, the tragic message behind this imagery remains His absence and presence (מעל פני; cf. Jer 23:39). In truth, the passage in Ezekiel bears a stronger resemblance to Deuteronomy 32 than Lev 26:17-31. One example is Ezekiel's preference for the term "adversaries" (צרי)—the word is not in Leviticus, which prefers איבי in these contexts. Still, it is a dominant theme in Deut 32:27-43. Jeremiah also uses צרי, but with the distinct nuance of "devourers" who prey on God's people (30:16, 50:7; cf. 46:10). Other distinctives unique to Ezekiel's presentation includes the weight he places on "uncleanness" (טמא; v.24), "holiness" (קדש; v.25, 27) and "transgression" (פשע; v.24). Again, Daniel's associations justify a relationship more powerful than influence (evinced by the presence of a theological grammar), but not as rigid as quotation (usually reserved for unspooling a specific line of thought from one source).[63]

Isaiah is another voice in Dan 9. Beginning with the central prophecy of the book—Dan 2:20-23, 31-45—the reader finds familiar language. Besides reference to a growing mountain of massive proportions (Isa 2:2; Mic 4:1; cf. Dan 2:34), the closest associations appear between Dan 2, 9-12 and Isa 11, 41-45. Concluding that Daniel is integrating Isaianic material on a scale larger than one or two intertexts is not out of the question. In Childs' commentary on Isaiah, he expounds on this larger understanding:

> The point is not that editors simply adjusted the tradition to meet new historical realities, but rather that the coercion of the authoritative biblical text itself pressed the believing community to explore *the fuller meaning of the prophetic witness as an ongoing extension of divine revelation* that guided its faith and practice.[64]

It is not implausible to read Daniel performing this very action through his interpretation of the Isaiah. Neither is Isaiah the only prophetic text Daniel

---

prophetic tradition (303n59). Henze also refers to subsequent works pointing back to Daniel's prophetic roots (cf. 4QFlor ii, 3; Matt 24:15; *Ant.* 10.267-68).

[62] Goldingay, 232.

[63] Qumran also uses the Prophets to elaborate on an eschatological reality found in the Writings. The writer in 4QFlorilegium, for example, discusses turning aside "from walking in the way of [this people]"—a reference to Is 8:11—for the purpose of describing one who "walks not in the counsel of the wicked" in Ps 1:1 (Lines 14-18).

[64] Childs, *Isaiah* (OTL; Louisville: Westminster John Knox, 2001), 115.

reads from "a bird's eye view." Jeremiah, like Isaiah, accesses many of the same themes, oracular forms, imagery and traditions.

Based on this collection of witnesses, we are confronted with a question: Are these prophetic voices conclusive evidence for labeling Daniel a prophet? This question is an important strut in the supporting structure of a canonical approach to the book. The figure of Daniel appears to follow some of the conventions of a prophet, humbling himself and "lifting" his eyes to God's revelation (Dan 8:1-2, 15, 17-18; cf. Ezek 1:1-3; 2:1; 3:23-24; 8:3, 5).[65] This recuperation of prophet-like activity is yet another dimension of Daniel's incorporation of the LP. Henze tracks this activity in his account of Dan 10: "Daniel does not emerge from this episode as a prophet in his own right, but the reader is nonetheless struck by the extent to which the author reaches back and uses the language of the prophetic call narrative, specifically that of Ezekiel (Ezekiel 1-3) and Isaiah (Isaiah 6), to tell his own story."[66] Although Daniel uses language from prophetic call narratives, he still does not claim to be a prophet. He is presented as a wisdom figure, securely installed in the traditions of the Prophets. Clothing Daniel with too much prophetic garb diminishes his value as God's wise representative. Childs insightfully observes how Daniel's primary reason for not functioning prophetically is attested to by the contrasts within the text itself. These contrasts are not just differences in scribal practice or formula.[67] Whereas most prophets straddle the events of the present and the events of the future, in a "direct historical confrontation," Daniel speaks to the present by occupying or speaking *from* a teleological position "many days hence" (8:26).[68] Daniel fills the post of an interpreter of prophets, not a prophetic interpreter. This activity, entitled "prophecy by interpretation"

---

[65] Henze also considers "stars" cast down as permitting a loose link between Dan 8:10 and Is 14:2-3 (ibid., 291).

[66] Ibid., 292-3. Henze also compares Dan 10:5-6, the description of the angelic messenger, with the description in Ezekiel 1 (1:7, 13-14, 16, 26-27). Likewise, Fishbane observes similar comparisons in Dan 10, but as part of the scribal conventions of the day ("From Scribalism to Rabbinism: Perspectives on the Emergence of Classical Judaism," in *The Garments of Torah: Essays in Biblical Hermeneutics*, 64-80).

[67] Childs makes three distinct points: (1) Daniel does not use the traditional idiom of the prophet, "hear the word of the Lord" or "hear the word of Yahweh"; (2) Daniel is usually confused or unconscious (cf. 8:27), not as with the "direct historical confrontations" of Amos or Isaiah; (3) the Prophets usually had a message for the nations which surrounded Israel—Amos, Isaiah, Jeremiah—but Daniel did not view the nations from the perspective of within Israel" (*IOTS*, 614-15). Daniel has much more in common with Jeremiah's scribe, Baruch, who was "to write his words of prophecy (Jer. 36:4, 32; 45:1) and to provide the safekeeping of legal documents (Jer. 32:12-16), see Carr, *Writing on the Tablet*, 120. Koch also submits the existence of a thread connecting the prophetic line to Daniel's apocalyptic role without total equivalence ("Vom prophetischen zum apokalyptischen Visionbericht," in *Apocalypticism in the Mediteranean World and the Near East* [ed. David Hellholm; Tübingen: Mohr Siebeck, 1983]).

[68] Childs, *IOTS*, 614.

The Law and the Prophets

(*prophetische Prophetenauslegung*), is an appropriate tag for Daniel's position and the second-century writers composing texts in a Danielic vernacular.[69] This type of "prophecy" is more than a genre-type—it captures the gradual unveiling of God's mysterious work. In the end, Daniel's role as an interpreter of earlier prophetic texts is vital to the logic and message of Dan 7-12.

Daniel calls upon a multitude of prophets to shape a tradition, but it is Jeremiah on whom he relies the most. The reason for the prayer is, of course, Daniel's interpretation in 9:2, but, as Willis demonstrates, Daniel molds much of his material with Jeremiah in mind. The prophet is not a mere reference.[70] Both writers depend on a "word" (דבר) from God (Dan 9:2, 23; Jer 25:1, 13; 29:1, 19; cf. Deut 18:18) and both comment on the same trajectory of events by using a Sabbath-heptadic motif (Jer 25:11-12; 29:10-11; Dan 9:24-27). Jeremiah is present in the beginning (9:2), the end (9:24) and the *middle* of the chapter. We also find two examples illustrate Jeremianic influence within 9:3-19: Daniel calls Jerusalem a "holy hill" (הר קדש; 9:16, 20)—a designation used only once by Jeremiah (הר הקדש; 31:23) for the cities in Ephraim and Judah.[71] The second occurrence of this phrase in Daniel (9:20) lies outside the boundaries of the prayer and suggests an extensive reliance on the book of Jeremiah. The term רעה is key to Jeremiah's description of the trouble and calamity inflicting Israel (36:3, 7, 31) and, though common to the prophet, is only found in Dan 9:12-14, where a "great calamity" runs rampant. Furthermore, the Lord "keeps watch" (שקד) over this same "calamity" just as he "watches over" (שקד) the judgment upon Judah in Jer 31:28 and 44:27.

Still, reference to Jeremiah in Dan 9 concerns, primarily, the interpretation of "70 years." The pertinent texts are a matter of debate, but many studies cite the following two passages:

> This whole land shall become a ruin and a waste, and these nations shall serve the king of Babylon seventy years (שבעים שנה). Then after seventy years (שבעים שנה) are fulfilled (מלא), I will punish (פקד) the king of Babylon and that nation, the land of the Chaldeans, for their iniquity, declares the Lord, making the land an everlasting waste. I

---

[69] Marti Nissinen, "Pesharim as Divination, Qumran Exegesis, Omen Interpretation and Literary Prophecy," in *Prophecy after the Prophets*, 58. See also Odil Hannes Steck, *Die Prophetenbücher und ihr theologisches Zeugnis: Wege der Nachfrage und Fährten zur Antwort* (Tübingen: Mohr Siebeck, 1996).

[70] Willis, "The Plans of God in Jeremiah and Daniel" (paper presented at SBL Daniel section, San Francisco, November 2011), 1-20.

[71] Isaiah may also be responsible for Daniel's phrasing (10:32, 27:13). However, "Jerusalem" in Isaiah's context is almost always in conjunction with an intensified version of Mount Zion—the prophet's location of interest. The term הר is also more common in Isaiah since the dominant motifs are high mountain landscapes and low valley-floors (2:2; 30:25; 40:1-12; 54:10; 55:12). In Jer 31:23, there is one instance within a linguistic context similar to Daniel's own.

will bring upon that land all the words that I have uttered against it, everything written in this book, which Jeremiah prophesied against all the nations. For many nations and great kings shall make slaves even of them, and I will require recompense according to their deeds and the work of their hands (Jer 25:11-14)

For thus says the Lord: When seventy years (שבעים שנה) are completed (מלא) for Babylon, I will visit (פקד) you, and I will fulfill (קום) to you my promise and bring you back to this place. For I know the plans I have for you, declares the Lord, plans for welfare and not for evil, to give you a future and a hope (Jer 29:10-11)

Seventy years, much like its counterpart in 9:24, is not a clear-cut sum of time. An interpreter's first instinct may be to count the "seventy years" from the Babylonian Exile (586 BCE) to the dedication of the Second Temple under the edict of Cyrus (516 BCE). Likewise, one might push the date back to Nebuchadnezzar's initial sieges (c. 600-597 BCE) in order to settle, roughly, at the advent of Cyrus' edict (536 BCE). Sources such as the *Black Stone of Esarhaddon* also assign a semi-symbolic figure of "seventy years" until the destruction of Babylon.[72] Of course, the difficulties of such a tidy calculation are not lost on scholars. If we assign specific events to the *terminus ad quem* and *terminus ad quo* in Jer 25:11-12, then we must renegotiate our interpretation of שבעים. It is likely the "seventy years" in Jer 25:11 and 29:10 is a "round number," possibly "equivalent to a lifetime."[73] On the other hand, a purely symbolic value is not likely either. The figure truly encircles the descent of Babylon and the ascent of Persian rule, but also prompts the reader to recall the Sabbath-heptadic tradition of Leviticus—unrest is on the horizon and the cost of "over-fallowed land" (Lev 25:4-5) is Israel's unbearable exilic plight (Jer 25:34-38; *contra* Lev 25:5-6).[74]

2.8. The Bond Between Leviticus and Jeremiah

What possibilities arise when we recognize the bond between Leviticus and Jeremiah? As discussed above, the prophet Jeremiah moves the themes and language of Lev 25-26 forward and is, indeed, the most appropriate win-

---

[72] Cf. Daniel Luckenbill, "The Black Stone of Esarhaddon," *AJSL* 41 (1924-25), 167.

[73] Collins, *Daniel*, 348; also William Holladay, *Jeremiah 1* (Minneapolis: Fortress, 1986), 668-69.

[74] Some scholars attribute such complexities not to the canonical Jeremiah, but to multiple waves of editorial handiwork (Rainer Albertz, "Deuteronomistic History and the Heritage of the Prophets," in *Congress Volume Helsinki 2010* [ed. Marti Nissinen; VTSup 148; Leiden: Brill, 2012], 343-67, here 351). According to this model, the first editors speak to matters of the temple, the worldwide implications of the Lord's judgment, and expansive repentance (7:4, 13-15; 11:7-8) whereas the second wave of editors limits the scope to the Babylonian Empire and a newfound support of nationalistic policy (25:11-12; 27:7; 29:10; 36-38).

dow through which we can hear the message of Lev 25-26 (and the surrounding Torah). Jeremiah 25-29 has Lev 25-26 in view for multiple reasons, not least because, unlike Amos and Deut 28, "the words of restoration" in Lev 26 "have been incorporated into the very chapter that has spoken of the demise of Israel."[75] Both of these sections of Leviticus and Jeremiah are selections of "representative texts" from within the LP and, additionally, the prime vehicles from which Daniel understands their respective streams of tradition.

Barbara Schlenke comments on the "dialogue" between these two books and posits a theory.[76] The connections in Leviticus and Jeremiah are "als Anknüpfungspunkte für eine integrative Gesamtsicht auf den Textzusammenhang zu nennen, durch welche Gebet und Jahrwochenorakel zueinander in Bezug gesetzt sind."[77] Deuteronomic theology, the force of Lev 26:40 and the *Stichwort* ידע all work together as an *Ausgangspunkt* of the seventy year-weeks.[78] Schmid, implementing his notion of "continuation," comments on how Jer 25:11 and 29:10 "reciprocally augment one another and now, after the 'seventy-year' judgment on Jerusalem and Judah, expect salvation for Israel and an evil end for Babylon."

Childs adds that the seventy-year period and its consequences recall the "law of Moses" (Dan 9:10-11, 13) discussed earlier. Daniel associates his text closely to Jeremiah, utilizing the prophet's words in such a way that "the old prophetic text is adjusted to the new situation, but the new is still understood by means of the old text."[79] Specifically, Dan 9 "combines the prophecy of Jeremiah with the punishment of disobedience which the law of Moses (Dan 9:11) had threatened."[80] Childs' insight directs us back to the question of the prayer's intention: is 9:3-19 concerned with revelation or confession? The focal points of Jeremiah and Leviticus supply a partial answer: both. The conjunction of revelation and confession is concurrent with the revelatory content of "the prophecy of Jeremiah" and the confessional content of the "law of Moses." Childs rightly reconnects Leviticus and Jeremiah with a subtle appeal to the link between the LP. In step with Childs' conclusions, Sumner connects the place of each book in a continuum: "the intercessory prayer of Daniel has the

---

[75] Anderson, *Sin*, 64.

[76] See "Verantwortung angesichts des Endes Das Gebet des Daniel in Dan 9,4-20," in *Juda und Jerusalem in der Seleukidenzeit*. (ed. Ulrich Dahmen and Johannes Schnocks; Göttingen: Bonn University Press, 2010), 105-123.

[77] These connections are "examples of links to an overall, well-integrated context, in which the prayer and the seventy-year oracle are associated with one another" Ibid., 117 (trans. mine); cf. Christoph Berner, *Jahre, Jahrwochen und Jubiläen. Heptadische Geschichtskonzeptionen im Antiken Judentum* (BZAW 363; Berlin/ New York: De Gruyter, 2006).

[78] Schlenke, "Verantwortung," 118-119.

[79] Childs, "Midrash and the Old Testament," in *Understanding the Sacred Text: Essays in Honor of Morton S. Enslin on the Hebrew Bible and Christian Beginnings* (ed. John Reumann; Valley Forge: Judson, 1972), 47-59, esp. 55.

[80] Childs, *IOTS*, 617.

interpretation of Jer. 25 as its *text* and the call to contrition of Leviticus as its *mandate*, with the coming desolation of the present moment as its *occasion*."[81]

To conclude this section: associations certainly exist between Leviticus and Jeremiah, Daniel and Jeremiah, and Daniel and Leviticus. But the interpreter cannot stop here. Just as we cannot divorce these individual texts from Dan 9, neither can we divorce each of these sources from their corresponding corpora of which the author is keenly aware. To do so ignores the dynamics of the canon. The text follows the narrative from the Law through the Prophets: broadly speaking, Lev 25-26 narrates the importance of Sabbath rest and obedience; Jer 25 and 29 outlines the consequences of ignoring these two realities; Daniel recovers these claims and projects them forward.

2.9. Leviticus and Jeremiah as "Braided Texts"

Reading these bodies of literature as a unit also permits the author to make creative decisions about textual interplay within the early canon. It is misleading to think of these associations as having a monolithic connection to any one text (e.g. Daniel-Deuteronomy; Daniel-Leviticus), considering how the LP experience their own shaping process.[82] Daniel 9 requires readers to imagine wider vistas of textual association, or, according to Sumner, a "layered field or context" that must be heard within the "canon as a whole."[83]

Daniel 9:6-7 is a telling illustration and reveals multiple connections that are forged by unconventional means. Leviticus 26 and Jer 25 come together in a mixed unit. This "braiding" of texts suggests Daniel's view of the LP is a concerted effort to make theological sense of older traditions within a new context.[84] In 9:6, Daniel claims the words of the prophets were meant for "our kings (מלכינו), our princes (שרינו) and our fathers (ואבתינו)." It is an odd combination of figureheads. Both שרי and מלכי are a common pairing in Jeremiah (17:25; 25:18; 32:32). "Fathers," in this context, is also a group found in both Torah and Jer 34:14, 35:15. Jeremiah 44:21 refers to "your fathers (אבותיכם), your kings (מלכיכם) and your princes (ושריכם)," but unlike Dan 9:6, this verse fronts the term, אבות. Furthermore, the pairing is couched in Mosaic-like oracles (cf. 32:1-22, 26-43).

---

[81] Wells and Sumner, *Daniel*, 184.

[82] Goldingay also offers a parallel account of Daniel's reading of the Law and the Prophets. He argues Dan 2, in the development of the book, comes *after* chs. 3-6 so as to introduce the court tales; moreover, this move encourages readers to read the tales in light of Gen 41 and Isa 40-66 (*Daniel*, 38).

[83] Wells and Sumner, *Daniel*, 185.

[84] In Dan 11:36, Henze detects another instance of "braided texts," though he does not use the term. Isa 10:20-23 and Is 10:24-27a consist of two separate oracles which Daniel weaves into Dan 11:36, allowing Henze to conclude "the author of Daniel's final vision *combines the wording of both Isaianic passages*..." ("Use of Scripture," 295; italics mine).

In 9:7a, Daniel speaks of an "open shame" (בשת הפנים) reaching "to the men of Judah, to the inhabitants of Jerusalem, and to all Israel," echoing Jeremiah's address in 25:2 ("to all the people of Judah and all the inhabitants of Jerusalem"). Admittedly, this is typical vocabulary. But the convergence of terms is still significant since no other prophet uses such an address. The final line of Dan 9:7 gives the reason for the people's shame: it is "because of the treachery (מעל) that they committed (מעלו־בך) against you." Unlike in Jeremiah, the term מעל is not common. Some see a link to Ezek 39:23-26, which is also possible—but let us consider Lev 26:40. The "treachery (מעל) that they committed (מעל)" originates here in addition to the reuse of the *hithpael*-form of ידה Daniel uses in 9:4 (אתודה). It is likely Daniel is responding to the condition in Lev 26:40 by extrapolating the people-groups (cf. Jer 25:2; 44:21). Daniel offers a reading of Leviticus refracted *through* the prophet Jeremiah, not *in addition to* the prophet.[85] Readers of a non-traditional text such as Dan 9 should not be surprised, therefore, by a non-traditional method of interpretation.

The "braided" texts in Dan 9:6-7 are not the only examples of how these texts work in tandem. Daniel 9:16-17 exhibits features drawn from Leviticus, through Jeremiah, creating a fresh, theological statement. Nebuchadnezzar's conquest (Jer 25:9) is so severe and debilitating that the land and its inhabitants become "a destroyed place (שמה), a hissing (שרקה) and an everlasting waste (חרבה)," presumably in response to the forewarning of Lev 26:14-46. Leviticus 26:31 is indeed the original warning in response to Israel's iniquity: the Lord "will lay your cities to waste (חרב) and will make your sanctuaries desolate (שממ)." Daniel 9:16-17 follows alongside these texts, but limits the "destroyed place" to the "sanctuary" (מקדש) and replaces שרקה and חרבה with חרפה ("byword"). In addition, the text reaches back to Lev 26:17, leaving behind Jer 25, and responds to how the Lord set his "face" (פנה) against Israel by pleading with God, saying "make your face (פניך) to shine upon" the destroyed sanctuary (9:17c-d). Daniel pleads for the consummation of Israel's promises within the divine ecomomy, particularly a final restoration of people, sanctuary and city (9:16-19). These three elements rise and fall in frequency throughout the corresponding texts of Leviticus and Jeremiah. Each text emphasizes or "quiets" features within these streams of tradition (e.g. preservation of the sanctuary, abusing the Sabbath, representational confession). Such is the essence of, as Fishbane defines it, a "continuous tradition of oracular reinterpretation" and the result of two (or more) textual voices speaking at once.[86]

---

[85] In another example of this "reinterpretation," Fishbane notes that Is 58:14 makes use of Deut 32:9, 13 (477). It concerns the Sabbath and the land, emphasizing the land element as a natural reaction to the circumstances of exile. The interchange between Daniel and Jeremiah is the opposite: Daniel interprets Jeremiah in such a way as to redefine the land and relocate its position to the background.

[86] Fishbane, 479. He writes further: "Accordingly, the prophecy which had been formulated originally to forecast doom on the native land and the subjugation of its

Daniel's use of scripture is indeed "all-pervasive and operates on different levels simultaneously."[87] Realities already unfolding in the LP pour into 9:2, 3-19 and 24-27, in terms of both *textual reference* and *source material* laden with threads of tradition. Examples arise in 9:2-7, 16-17 and reinforce Daniel's general reliance on larger corpora. Scripture is not simply a deposit of potential references, but a hermeneutical framework anchoring and generating further theological reflection. This exegetical activity answers multiple questions: Is Daniel's use of Leviticus and Jeremiah, for example, confined to particles of confirmed textual associations? How do we read the prayer within the brackets (9:2; 24-27) of the chapter? How does this relate to the canonical re-shaping of Daniel's "rest"? Specifically, how does Daniel maintain the integrity of the previous narratives that speak to Sabbath rest while supplementing the metaphor of Sabbath unrest in 9:24? Continuing to answer these questions in 9:11-19 will clarify how the author slowly transitions from LP-traditions (Sabbath, heptads, rest and fulfilled promises) into a vision of complete rest (involves tyrants, exile, the role of the Temple and divine kingship).

3. Daniel the "Servant" and the Outpouring of a Tradition

A canonical feature long ignored by Daniel scholarship is the concept of servanthood in 9:3-19. Daniel labels himself a "servant" (9:17) and consistently injects the term "servant" into his prayer. As with many of Daniel's terms, a long-standing and recognizable tradition lies behind the inclusion. Alongside this tradition is an understanding that the LP speak to the tradition of "God's servant(s)" at length and in diverse contexts. Daniel presents himself as "a repository of the revelation of God's plans."[88]

Schmid, in a recently published work, asserts that servant-language throughout the LP is a product of strategic "continuations."[89] Servanthood, in this case, is inherited via scribal updates. These "continuations" are features of Persian literature and include the servant status of Cyrus in Is 42:1-4 (addition: 42:5-7) and Nebuchadnezzar in Jer 25:9-14; 30-31 (addition: 46:26-28; 50-51; cf. Ezek 37:24-25).[90] Reading these additions together might lead the interpreter

---

inhabitants in exile for a period of seventy years, was subsequently reinterpreted as a prophecy of hope for the diasporic community" (480).

[87] Henze, "Use of Scripture," 280; cf. Jacques Doukhan, *Daniel: The Vision of the End* (Berrien Springs, Mich.: Andrews University, 1987), 26-29.

[88] Lacocque, *Daniel*, 121.

[89] Schmid, *Old Testament*, 167-68.

[90] Apart from Isa 42:1-4, the section 52:13-53:12 has long been a recognized resource for parts of Daniel's material (cf. 12:2-13; 9:25-26; 1QIsa^a). The servant status of Cyrus is a subject of much debate (Is 45:1-6), compounded by a shift to the servant status of "Jacob"/Israel later in the same passage (45:4). Henze has no difficulty aligning the wise servant of Is 52:13-53:12, for example, with the wise servants of Dan 11-12 or

to identify Nebuchadnezzar as "the precursor of Cyrus."[91] While such redactional activity may explain how the various authors dealt with transitions in power as well as the process of divine appointment, this explanation falls short when we come to Daniel. The servant language of Dan 9 originates, in this case, with the paradigmatic servant, Moses. As we will discover, Daniel draws out the multiple traditions (or roles) that converge in the "servant," distinguishing himself as a "servant" within a line of servants.

Traditionally, the vocation of servant implies two additional roles: covenant mediator and suffering intercessor.[92] Daniel, like Moses and the Prophets, shares the responsibilities of *covenant mediation*. We know Moses, just as he is the paradigm of prophet, is also the paradigmatic mediator (Deut 34:10-12).[93] It follows that the prophets are each, to varying degrees, mediators of the covenant on Israel's behalf (cf. 1 Kgs 17:13; Jer 7:25-26, 25:4; Hos 4:1-6). When reading Dan 9:3-19, it is not difficult to detect the voice of Moses and his urgent pleas to God to lift Israel's curse. Jacob Milgrom presses even harder, arguing Daniel's representative confession, in conjunction with the Levitical notes of 9:3-19, grants the wise man a priestly function.[94]

Another facet of covenant mediation is the role of the *suffering intercessor*. Daniel concludes his confession with the striking claim "my people Israel" in 9:20, which is a claim usually reserved for Yahweh (cf. Ex 32:7; 34:10). Moses exemplifies the intercessor—he who embodies Israel, in all of her trials and flaws (Deut 1:37, 4:21, 9:6-29). Likewise, the Prophets following from Moses take on the burden of God's people, bowing humbly before God in the people's stead (cf. 1 Kgs 19:10; Amos 2:12; Jer 7:25-26, 29:19, 44:4; Ezek 3:22-27). How does Daniel enter into this stream of tradition? Two points solidify Daniel's position in this stream: (1) the centrality of Moses in biblical tradition and (2) how Daniel shares the role of "servant" with Moses.[95]

First, Daniel takes the mantle of "servant" (עבד) upon himself (9:17), a designation usually reserved for representatives (9:6, 10) or even Moses himself

---

"the oldest known interpretation in which the servant figure is identified with a group" ("Use of Scripture," 298).

[91] Schmid, *Old Testament*, 169.

[92] See Chapman, *Law and Prophets*, 121-22. Chapman sees evidence of covenant mediation and intercession in Dan 9:6, 10-12.

[93] The roots of Moses' servant-role go deeper than mediation and intercession. The Exodus expands Israel's function as "slave" to Israel's function as "servants" to the nations (cf. Lev 25:55).

[94] Milgrom, *Cult and Conscience: The Asham and the Priestly Doctrine of Repentance* (Leiden: Brill, 1976), 108.

[95] The nature of servanthood is a point that *distances* Daniel from the Maccabean literature, although many studies strive to connect the two. In 2 Macc 3-15, Jason of Cyrene cites the apostasy of the Jews as reason for the Hellenistic crisis, but instead of operating as a vicarious sufferer, Judas is portrayed as a mighty, conquering savior with Messianic overtones. A similar motif surrounds Judith, particularly in her "Hasmonean judge-like deliverer" persona (Carr, *Formation*, 157).

(9:11; cf. Exod 34:28; Deut 9:9).[96] Aligning with and representing this multitude allows Daniel to become a vicarious sufferer for "all Israel" (9:7, 11; cf. Deut 1:1; 5:1; 34:12). Daniel claims he is "confessing my sin and the sin of my people" (9:20). Briefly returning to the importance of the phrase "law of Moses" (9:11, 13), it is not a stretch to imagine the construction quietly vaulting Moses as both the lawgiver and the root of the prophetic line.[97] It follows that Daniel is the outgrowth of this root system and acts as a means of deliverance.[98] Leviticus 26 is a "collective confession without a representative petitioner," therefore Daniel must step in on behalf of a sinful nation.[99] Grammatical cues also confirm Daniel's intercessory role. Goldingay, referring to the shift in person from 9:2 "I"/9:3-19 "we"/9:20 "I," writes "[w]hile the 'we' is appropriate to a prayer that concerns Israel's sin, the 'I' puts Daniel in the position of intercessors such as Moses and Jeremiah."[100]

Second, tradents have long placed Moses at the center of many biblical traditions, not least as the gravity pulling together textual units and giving coherence to the theological grammar of LP. Chapman writes, following Childs's own position, "the biblical text itself depicts Moses as its ultimate source, indicating the continued importance of the figure of Moses for understandings of the canon's received shape."[101] Moses' role as the paradigm of the prophet goes beyond prediction and fulfillment. Chapman and Childs rightly associate Moses' role with ongoing patterns and hopes (e.g. the Former Prophets), role *modeling* (e.g. Jeremiah) and critical points of canonical transition (e.g. the "seams" of the Hebrew canon). "The point to be made," Chapman concludes, "is that while Moses is depicted in deuteronomistic traditions as mediator and intercessor par excellence, neither of these roles belongs exclusively to him—only the extent to which he initiated and unified these roles remains unsurpassed."[102]

---

[96] Chapman writes, "the variation between the second and third person singular pronoun in Dan 9:11d may have resulted partly because the identification between Moses, the Prophets and the revealed will of God had become so close" (*Law and the Prophets*, 239-40).

[97] John Watts evaluates Moses' place in the text according to the popular, socio-religious attitudes of the day. The Hasmonean monarchy did not revitalize the Davidic hope; therefore, sentiments changed regarding the Davidic kingdom between the span of the fourth century BCE and first century CE. As Watts notes, "the literature produced thus far, the Torah and the Prophets, suggests that Moses had been the authoritative figure most acceptable to Judaism in the period" (*How We Got Our Bible: Files from an Alttestamentler's Hard Drive* [Eugene, Ore.: Wipf & Stock, 2011], 168).

[98] Goldingay, 233.

[99] Lacocque, *Daniel*, 126.

[100] Goldingay, 233; cf. Gilbert, "La priere de Daniel," 303-4; see also Claus Westermann, "Struktur und Geschichte der Klage im Alten Testament," ZAW 66 (1954) 48-49.

[101] Chapman, *Law and Prophets*, 151; see Childs, IOTS, 62-63.

[102] Chapman, *Law and the Prophets*, 121.

Jeremiah's status as a Mosaic prophet is another point of contact in our analysis of Dan 9:3-19. Jeremiah situates himself on a continuum of biblical prophets beginning with Moses (cf. Deut 18:18; Jer 1:9b, 7:25).[103] Childs reminds us, "Jeremiah was understood as the prime example of the messenger of God—a picture shared and decisively formed by the scriptural tradition of Deuteronomy—who forecast the divine judgment."[104] What begins with Moses continues through to the Major Prophets, creating a thread of prophetic activity. The reader encounters glimpses of this thread in the prayer (cf. 9:25 and Ezek 28:2, 14; 9:26-27 and Is 10:22-23). This holistic perspective is also in sources from Qumran, for example, which merge Jeremiah, Isaiah, Ezekiel and Daniel into a single voice (4QapocrJer^c; 4QPs-Ezek.).[105] Even though Daniel is not a prophet in a formal sense, as Jeremiah or Ezekiel, these voices share a broad sense of "prophecy," embodying the role of servant and announcing God's kingly design.

Asking how Daniel's role reconnects to earlier versions of servant-hood also requires we ask how his role *differs* from prior tradition—to be sure, "servant(s)" in 9:3-19 is not a replica of its older iterations. Daniel uses the tradition for his own purposes and, as it follows, a new context will render a new meaning.[106] Evidence for this new appropriation is present in the servant paradigm, as it expands throughout the book. No longer confined to a prophet in the line of Moses, this "servanthood" becomes characteristic of the beloved, wise man Daniel and the discerning community to which he is speaking (12:2-3, 10-13). The servant also takes further action: exercising wisdom (יַשְׂכִּיל).[107] The root

---

[103] It is no secret that Jeremiah is a "Mosaic" prophet in form and content. One well-known example is Deut 30:15, 19 (cf. 30:20, 32:47), which summarizes an essential two-fold belief concerning the blessing of "life" and the curse of "death." Jeremiah 21:8 recovers these very words—"I set before you the way of life and the way of death"—to illustrate Zedekiah's detainment under Nebuchadnezzar, "King of Babylon."

[104] Childs, *IOTS*, 346.

[105] Henze, "4QApocryphon of Jeremiah C and 4QPseudo-Ezekiel: Two 'Historical' Apocalypses," in *Prophecy After the Prophets? The Contribution of the Dead Sea Scrolls to the Understanding of Biblical and Extra-Biblical Prophecy* (ed. K.D. Troyer and Armin Lange; CBET 52; Leuven: Peeters, 2009), 25-42.

[106] Here, we discover an example of "transposition": the idea of a word taking on new meaning by being placed in a different context. The transposition of "servant" is complicated further with the shared features between Daniel and Joseph. As with Joseph, Daniel is "an exemplar of wisdom" and possibly an "exilic Joseph" who "knows its origin and ... its end in the purposes of the God of Israel" (Wells and Sumner, *Daniel*, 105).

[107] Driver, "Isaiah 52:13-53:12: The Servant of the Lord" in *In Memoriam Paul Kahle* (eds. M. Black and G. Fohler; BZAW 103; Berlin: Töpelmann, 1968), 90. Driver emends ישכל to ישקל "to be hanging, suspended" based on the Akk. *sakkîlu* and Arabic derivatives; Jim Adams reads a combination of nuances: the action may describe someone who understands (Is 44:18; Jer 9:23), wise (Prov 15:24) and ultimately leading to success or prosperity (Josh 1:8; Jer 10.21) (*The Performative Nature and Function of Isaiah 40-55*

שׂכל can function a number of ways in the context. On its own, שׂכל speaks of wisdom and success in general terms.[108] But given the short distance to a variety of other sapiential images and motifs (righteousness, instruction, the wicked as antonym, etc.) within the passage, the reader recognizes a "complex of wisdom" directly related to the mantle of servant.

Much can be added to Daniel's adoption of the servant-mantle, but space forces us to conclude that "servant," in this case, is but one description for a role within a rich heritage of inspired messengers and mediators.[109] Daniel is an intercessor and mediator of Yahweh's covenant promises (as Moses *et al.*) by his self-identification as servant, his place within an expanding stream of tradition, and his representative confession (9:3-20). Daniel is able to speak to the unfolding and reshaping of Sabbath-heptadic tradition in 9:24-27 due to his authoritative placement alongside (but also subsequent to) Moses and the Prophets.[110]

4. The Seams Between the Torah-Prophets and Daniel 9:3-19

Daniel studies the theological contours of the LP by reading these corpora as a grammar. In Chapter 2, we acknowledged the importance of the grammar for understanding the compilation of the Hebrew canon. We now turn to the *textual* roots of this grammar and their place in Dan 9. Daniel depends on certain "hermeneutical guides" to aid in the right construal of the tradents who came before him.[111] Therefore, it should come as no surprise that the language at the seams of the tri-partite arrangement resembles the LP language of Dan

---

[JSOTSup 448; New York: T&T Clark, 2006]. Given the paradigmatic and syntagmatic relationships between wisdom and other wisdom-lexemes (e.g. בין, ישׁר), Adams' appeal is appropriate; cf. Magne Sæbø, "שׂכל" TLOT 3:1269-72.

[108] First, the word could mean "to prosper, succeed" (*hipʿal*), usually accompanied by חכם, בין or צלח (cf. Deut 32:29; Josh 1:8). For translations along these lines, see Blenkinsopp who renders the verbal construction, "will achieve success" (*Isaiah 40-55* [AB 19A; New York: Doubleday, 2000], 347). The *Targum of Isaiah*, for example, replaces שׂכל with צלח (formally translated "to be successful, prosperous"). Second, we can render the term "to be wise" (in the *hipʿal*, "to supply wisdom"). This possibility has support in the LXX συνίημι (cf. Is 52:15d LXX) and the book of Daniel itself (1:4, 17; 7:8; 8:25; 9:13, 22, 25; 11:33, 35; 12:3, 10). Both of these options are somewhat interchangeable. But we must not forget that no matter which avenue of translation we take, the semantic location of שׂכל is within the sphere of wisdom.

[109] Lacocque labels Daniel the "acting representative of Israel," confessing "in order to remove the last obstacle on God's road to vindication" (*Daniel*, 123).

[110] Goldingay notes, "to speak of Israel, then, is to make a significant theological claim for the little community of Judeans who survived the Exile, by seeing them as the successors of that whole people with whom Yahweh entered into covenant (vv. 11, 20)" (*Daniel*, 246).

[111] Chapman, *Law and Prophets*, 103-104.

9:3-19.[112] In the conclusions to both the Law (Deut 34:10-12) and the Prophets (Mal 4:4-6 [3:22-24]), we find the same language:

> And there has not arisen *a prophet since in Israel like Moses* (כמשה נביא עוד בישראל) whom the Lord knew face to face, none like him for all the signs and wonders that the Lord *sent him* (שלחו) to do in the land of Egypt, to Pharaoh and to all his servants and to all his land, and for all the mighty power and all the *great deeds of terror* (הגדול המורא) that Moses did in the sight of *all Isra* (כל ישראל) (Deut 34:10-12)
>
> *Remember the law of my servant Moses* (זכרו תורת משה עבדי], the statues and rules that I commanded him at Horeb for *all Israel* (כל ישראל). Behold, I will *send to you* (שלח לכם) Elijah *the pro-phet* (הנביא) before *the great and awesome* (הגדול והנורא) day of the Lord comes (Mal 4:4-5 [3:22-23]).

What we see are "two self-conscious 'endings'" that reflect "the mature theological reflection of Israel's ancient traditions, summarizing those traditions in terms that illuminate their significance ... and convey their significance to future readers."[113]

Daniel 9:3-19 also contains this language in a condensed form. These phrases, "law of Moses," "my servant," "servants, the prophets" are not tied to a single cross-reference as many commentaries note (and remain confounded), but connect to key locations *within* the LP—as in the example of servanthood—and the *seams* of this dual-unit. The conclusion to Deuteronomy is the first seam (34:10-12). Not only do we read about the establishment of the prophetic line beginning with the agent of Torah (Moses) but we also see a juxtaposition of Moses with the typified, prophetic figure, Elijah (Mal 4:4-5 [3:22-23]). Chapman argues that these endings are "concerned to coordinate 'the Law' and 'the Prophets' as related scriptural traditions; both pursue their task of coordination primarily with deuteronomistic language and ideas."[114]

---

[112] Outside the flagship studies by Childs, Seitz and Chapman, numerous appeals are made to a network of "seams" binding the Law and Prophets together: Ronald Clements, *Old Testament Prophecy: From Oracles to Canon* (Louisville: Westminster John Knox, 1996); Julio Trebolle Barrera, "Origins of a Tripartite Old Testament Canon," in *The Canon Debate* (Peabody, Mass.: Hendrickson, 1995), 129-145; for a more detailed study on how Daniel and the Writings join with the previous corpora, see Stone, "The Compilational History," 20-25. Stone refers to "framing devices" as a type of intertextual criterion (20); similarly, see Bernd Janowski, "Die 'Kleine Biblia': Zur Bedeutung der Psalmen für eine Theologie des Alten Testaments," in *Der Psalter in Judentum und Christentum* (ed. Erich Zenger; Freiburg: Herder, 1998), 381-420.

[113] Chapman, 112. Erich Zenger also acknowledges the editorial significance of these two texts, calling them "programmatische Schulsstexte" (Deut 34:10-12//Mal 3:22-24) and concluding with 2 Chr 36:22 ff. in the Writings (*Einleitung*, 23).

[114] Chapman, 146.

Can we infer that Daniel consulted fully "closed and fixed" materials? No, we need not insist on Dan 9:3-19 drawing from a fixed body of LP since the inherited authority of these books did not rely on their "closed" status.[115] However, this "seam" language occurs in Daniel's prayer and in association with the earmarks of the passage: we must take seriously the *location* of these texts in the LP.[116] Daniel 9:4-15 reacquires these terms and fits them accordingly. He prays to the Lord, "great and awesome" (הגדול והנורא; 9:4) on behalf of Israel's broken "rules and commandments" (משפטים; 9:5), namely the "law of Moses" (משה תורת; 9:11, 13). And, as discussed above, Moses is both a "servant" (עבד) and member of the prophetic line (9:10-11). These condensed forms make their theological sense in the textual webs and constructions of Dan 9:3-19.

Seam-language occurs at the conclusions of the corpora, but this language can also *initiate* a corpus. Moses' servanthood is a prime example (Dan 9:11, 13) of these transitions. The death of Moses (Josh 1:1-2) attaches the book to Deuteronomy with the added layer, "Moses, my servant" (משה עבדי; 1:2, 7). As Dempster claims, the only other instance of this phrase is "at the end of this section of the canon," namely, the Prophets (cf. Mal 4:4 [3:22]).[117] The close proximity of Joshua to Jeremiah in Dan 9:3-19 is not a coincidence. Dempster argues the books of Joshua-2 Kings "sketch a historical context for most of the Latter Prophets."[118] Repetition of themes and vocabulary is paramount to the operation of these seams. Mark Boda, for example, explains the "scriptural impulse" of the Old Testament is to relay "various reflective summaries and rehearsals of what lay at the core of Israelite theology."[119] Taking form in these seam-texts, it is not difficult to see "a pattern of presentations and 're-presentations.'"[120] Boda is alluding to a rolling, textual instinct meant to mark out the pathways of Israel's unfolding narrative. If we continue with this "nar-

---

[115] Separating an "original" from a "canonical" meaning creates an artificial distinction, rather "the original meaning took on a certain extension and development once it was allied to other prophecies in a written collection *which held a proto-canonical status*" (Clements, 194; italics mine).

[116] Limiting such textual relationships to quotation alone risks oversimplification. Reference to associations based on location can be fruitful. In the case of Dan 9:3-19, at least two areas of association are evident: (1) connections between texts within vv. 3-19 and (2) the association of books and corpora Lange refers to a specific brand of intertextuality that may be effective: those associations "which are created by tradition without a link to a specific text (convention, configuration, genre)" (cf. Armin Lange and Matthias Weigold, *Biblical Quotations and Allusions in Second Temple Jewish Literature* [JAJS 5; Göttingen: Vandenhoeck and Ruprecht, 2011], 22).

[117] Dempster, "An 'Extraordinary Fact': Torah and Temple and the Contours of the Hebrew Canon, Part 2," *TynBul* 48.1 (1997) 191; cf. Blenkinsopp, *Prophecy and Canon*; Sheppard, "Theology of the Book of Psalms," *Interpretation* 46 [1992] 153).

[118] Ibid., 194; see also J.W. Miller, *The Origins of the Bible: Rethinking Canon History* (New York: Paulist, 1994), 115.

[119] Mark Boda, "Biblical Theology," 126.

[120] Ibid.

rative" metaphor, we may view these seams as "bookends" to the various corpora. Seams running between the corpora bind the theological grammar together, providing a theological construct.[121]

In the case of Dan 9:3-19, we can now add at least one more mode of association: the association of books and corpora.[122] We established the layered depths of Daniel's lexical and grammatical associations and, again, we encounter a type of association that is not confined to one-to-one citations, or an ephemeral sphere of influence. Intimately tied to Daniel's strategy of association is this, that "from the larger perspective of canon, a deliberate editorial strategy is clearly discernable—one that links up a new section of the canon with the old while maintaining the priority of the old."[123]

5. The Deuteronomistic Editor as Main Interlocutor?

Having examined the textual relationships in and canonical locations familiar to Dan 9:3-19, we are better equipped to weigh one of the most prevalent readings of the chapter's context: Deuteronomism.[124] Not to be confused with "Deuteronomic passages" or the "deuteronomistic history," such a literary presence greatly influences the goal one assigns to the confession (9:3-19) and, subsequently, the interpretation (24-27). Beginning with the seminal work of Martin Noth, scholars have long invoked a deuteronomistic redactor (Dtr.) to support the editing/writing of particular texts.[125] Gradually, the Dtr. gained a full-fledged persona in contemporary scholarship, possessing theological convictions, intentions, influences, and political leanings. Texts, such as Dan 9, are now judged according to its anti- or pro-establishment rhetoric while little remains of a Deuteronomic voice. Interpretations in this vein radically redefine notions of "determinism" (e.g. anti-establishmentarianism), "restoration" (e.g. pro-Hasmonean) and "free will" (e.g. pro-Judean, but anti-Hasmonean). Is 9:24-27 nothing more than a quick memorandum (c. 165 BCE) or an instance of mantic historiography penned to *counter* (or foil?)

---

[121] Seitz, *Goodly Fellowship*, 4.

[122] To be sure, Childs limited the majority of his work to the shape of individual books; however, he adds, "the canonical process involved the shaping of tradition not only into independent books, but also into larger canonical units, such as the Law, Prophets, and Writings" (*OT Theology in a Canonical Context*, 13).

[123] Dempster, "An Extraordinary Fact, Part 2," 192.

[124] Martin Noth, *The Deuteronomistic History* (trans. J.A. Clines; JSOTSup 15; Sheffield: JSOT Press, 1981). With the work of Martin Noth, however, the status of "Prophets" was quickly replaced with a division of history that was itself the product of "a few large compilations" (the Deuteronomist and Chronicler).

[125] The theories of Noth have long since been augmented since some scholars, such as Rainer Albertz, consider his approach "too basic," opting for a Deuteronomism that "shows traits of a longer growing process, some internal disputes and a number of Deuteronomistic additons" ("Deuteronomistic History," 350).

deuteronomistic thinking?[126] A large contingent of Daniel scholars appeal to the power of this deuteronomistic influence and how it shapes the entirety of the chapter's message.[127] Jeremiah, for example, is a text upon which Daniel 9 hinges and is also arguably shaped with a Dtr. edition or "JerD" (550-520 BCE).[128] However, few interpreters negotiate the level of this influence and, consequently, do not anticipate how such a theologically charged framework might disengage from the canonical shaping. Rather than asking how such a voice contributes to the final form of the text—a distinct voice among other distinct voices—the question shrinks into myopia: "Is this Deuteronomistic material from a former day inserted later?" or "Is this the hand of a contemporary, Deuteronomistic editor?"

Two recent studies are informative for our purposes here. First, Konrad Schmid: he believes the deuteronomistic history creates a critical theological bridge within the *corpus propheticum*—the bridge moves from "the older history of salvation (from the patriarchs to the occupation of the land) through the history of perdition (monarchial period) to a new salvation history promised by the prophets."[129] The result of Schmid's summary unfolds in his comments on Dan 9, where Deuteronomism is alleged to fit. He believes including notes of Deuteronomy and Deuteronomism "discredits" dream-interpretation, but such interpretation is "rehabilitated" as the tradition takes a new turn: the introduction of an *angeles interpres* in Dan 8-9.[130] It follows that the determinism wrought by the angelic message sufficiently replaces the determinism typical of Daniel's dream-interpretation.

Christoph Berner confirms the work of the Deuteronomist within the nexus of several key themes: "Die Zusammenschau von Exil und eigener Gegenwart untër dem Aspekt der fortdauernden Sündenschuld Israels und des ihr korrespondierenden göttlichen Zornes bildet eine Vorstellung."[131] Familiar motifs revolve around שׁוב, היום, תורה, חסד, and אהב and are elements attached to "Moses, kings and prophets as scribes, hearers, and preachers of Yahweh's

---

[126] Willis, *Dissonance*. Willis argues that Daniel "uses mantic historiography and its strategy as a way of adjudicating the conflicts and tensions emergent in divine sovereignty" (29).

[127] See O.H. Steck, *Israel und das gewaltsame Geschick der Propheten: Untersuchungen zur Überlieferung des deuteronomistischen Geschichtsbildes im Alten Testament, Spätjudentum und Urchristentum* (WMANT 23; Neukirchen-Vluyn: Neukirchener Verlag, 1967). Others building on the work of Noth: Hans van Deventer, "The End of the End Or, What is the Deuteronomist (Still) Doing in Daniel?" in *Past, Present, Future: The Deuteronomistic History and the Prophets* [ed. Johannes C. De Moor and Harry van Rooy; Leiden: Brill, 2000], 62-75); Schlenke, "Verantwortung," 119.

[128] Rainer Albertz, "Deuteronomistic History," 343.

[129] Schmid, *Old Testament*, 159-60.

[130] Ibid., 165.

[131] "A summary of Exile and its present expression is best conveyed in these dual concepts: the persistent sin-guilt of Israel and the wrath from god that corresponds with it." Berner, *Jahre*, 29; cf. Steck, *Israel*, 186.

instruction" (cf. Dan 9:6).[132] Unlike Schmid, Berner makes a small distinction between the remarks of Dtr. and an author-editor drawing from the Pentateuch. Both of these studies demonstrate how the language of the passage takes on wholly different shades of meaning with the application of Deuteronomism. It is evident champions of Deuteronomism sometimes leap to matters of human freedom, determinism, apocalypticism, counter-deuteronomistic narratives and conditionality—some or all of which are smuggled in at the cost of other contexts.[133] This model sets two opposing forces against one another—deuteronomistic covenant-faith and apocalyptic—and manages to overshadow the express, canonical intent behind the passage's coherence.[134]

I am not suggesting there were no editorial practices surrounding Joshua-2 Kings, or an "overarching narrative" within the Former Prophets or even the possibility of a late author registering his prophetic message in deuteronomic imagery.[135] At issue is how the unique theological contours of Dan 9:3-19 and 24-27 may be hostage to a rigid distinction: on one side apocalyptic determinism, on the other, a nascent deuteronomistic philosophy of human freedom. The canonical shape of Dan 9 is more complex and multivalent. As argued above, neglecting the centrality of passages *outside* of this prophetic history (cf. Lev 26:40; Jer 25:11, 29:10) dismisses the interests of the chapter (Dan 9:2-3, 24).[136] There is no doubt that texts subsequent to the Pentateuch make use of and celebrate both Deuteronomy and Mosaic theology. The immediate example of the Former Prophets (or "Deuteronomic History") begins to build upon

---

[132] Goldingay, 234; Sweeney correctly highlights "deuteronomic principles" in the passage ("Foundations," 175). Also, Van Deventer leans heavily on potential allusions to Deuteronomy in Daniel to legitimate a Deuteronomistic editor ("End of the End," 67-68).

[133] Cf. Koch, "Das Profetenschweigen des deuteronomistischen Geschichtswerks," in *Die Botschaft und die Boten: Festschrift für H.W. Wolff* (ed. Jorg Jeremias; Neukirchen-Vluyn: Neukirchen-Verlag, 1981), 118; Albertz, "Deuteronomistic," 347.

[134] See also William Adler, who summarizes the apparent tension between the prayer and 9:24-27: "It is as if to say that the plan of redemption has been decreed independently of Daniel's supplications for forgiveness." ("The Apocalyptic Survey of History Adapted by Christians: Daniel's Prophecy of 70 Weeks," in *The Jewish Apocalyptic Heritage in Early Christianity* [ed. James VanderKam and William Adler; Assen: Van Gorcum, 1996], 203).

[135] Deuteronomy, 1 Kgs 8, Jeremiah, Leviticus, Chronicles and the Psalter all have a place in the prayer. In truth, a reader may see hymnic or poetic elements in 9:3-19, adding yet another component to the debate over deuteronomistic influence. The prayer has repeated expressions, hendiadys, parallel clauses and a distinct "liturgical style" (Goldingay, 233).

[136] Deuteronomic theology in Dan 9, Henze states, is "the exception rather than the rule" and "can hardly serve as a model for Daniel's use of Scripture in general" ("Use of Scripture," 280)

the language of Torah and feeds into the collection of the Latter Prophets.[137]

To conclude this section, editors were at work in Dan 9; however, I submit arguments for a program of Deuteronomism that archs over Dan 9 are too heavy handed. In commenting on the final form of the text, Childs rightly insists on restraint when attempting to pin down editorial personalities:

> The clearest evidence for this position is found in a consistent manner in which the identity of the canonical editors has been consciously obscured, and the only signs of an ongoing history are found in the multi-layered text of scripture itself. The shape of the canon directs the reader's attention to the sacred writings rather than to their editors[138]

The canonical shape of Dan 9, particularly the interpretive work of Dan 9:24-27 functions, not with inserted clippings of post-exilic theology, but on a "continuum of textual shaping."[139] The scene in 9:3-19 is an accompaniment of prophetic messengers with Deuteronomic lineage, speaking to a greater eschatological reality: "If those in exile acknowledge their wrongdoing and the justice of Yahweh's punishment of them, he will remember his covenant with them (Lev 26:39-45); if they return to Yahweh, he will restore them (Deut 30:1-10; cf. 1 Kgs 8:46-53; Jer 29:10-14)."[140] Daniel, while preserving the relevant traditions, incorporates a *telescopic* view of where these traditions have come and will proceed. While these traditions do not fundamentally change, Daniel reveals they are expandable; therefore, themes, motifs and vocabulary buttressing such traditions shift (e.g. Deuteronomic covenant-traditions) but remain familiar.[141]

---

[137] The Former Prophets are a canonical "accomplishment" in conjunction with the prior division of Law and the subsequent collection of Latter Prophets (Seitz, *Goodly Fellowship*, 26-28). The deuteronomistic history is part of a larger corpus of Prophets, which "were construed together in antiquity as a scriptural 'intertext'" (Chapman, *Law and Prophets*, 112). By this reasoning, a Deuteronomistic history is "not a continuous historical narrative but in a grammar of Law and Prophets" (26).

[138] Childs, *IOTS*, 59.

[139] Ibid., 111.

[140] Ibid.

[141] Goldingay argues on a thematic basis, "the prayer is not an acknowledgement of wrongdoing and acceptance of responsibility for it, like Josh 7:20-21 ... and the Deuteronomistic History as a whole" (*Daniel*, 233). Instead the reader witnesses a display of "Deuteronomistic covenant tradition" (234).

6. Conclusion to 9:3-19 and Transition in 9:20-23

6.1. Conclusion 9:3-19

A canonical approach to Dan 9:24-27 requires we pay ample attention to the layers of context preceding the section. Framed by two numerical images (9:2, 24), the chapter "grafts" a confession into the text and growing organically—especially with the matching pairs of words occurring between 9:3-19 and 9:24-27—arrives at an informed conclusion. The coherence of the chapter is a result of canonical shaping, or, as Sumner puts it, "interpretation in a canonical mode."[142] Corresponding fragments, texts, themes, source-references, images and style choices all coordinate purposefully, leading many to believe that the "coherence in substance and style of the book appears to indicate a unitary origin" or at the very least, "a very thorough final redaction."[143] On many levels, the book of Daniel is "self-referential."[144]

These layers are not only the sum total of various textual associations, but also thick streams of tradition tracing back to Leviticus.[145] The LP, by now a well-recognized scriptural resource, sustains the narrative. Entering Daniel's interpretation (9:24-27), this same set of familiar traditions transforms into a *renewed* (not different) theological claim: the "rest" promised by Yahweh is thwarted by sin. Seitz details this dynamic well:

> Certain obvious arrangements of the literature of the canon pointed not to a driving forward of restless traditions but to an opposite tendency: the establishment of the past (especially Sinai) as founda-

---

[142] Wells and Sumner, *Daniel*, 101.

[143] Jan-Wim Wesselius, "The Writing of Daniel," in *The Book of Daniel: Composition and Reception, Vol. 2*, 291; cf. H.H. Rowley, "The Unity of the Book of Daniel," in *The Servant of the Lord and Other Essays on the Old Testament* (London: Athlone, 1952), 235-68. Also note J.E. Miller, "The Redaction of Daniel," in *JSOT* 52 (1991): 115-24.

[144] It is worth reading Henze's full quote: "The book of Daniel is self-referential, in the sense that its final authors/redactors were also its earliest interpreters" (287). His assertion that the divisions of the book (chs. 1-6; 7-12) are held together "through inner-Danielic reference" *only* is too simplistic. Henze uses the example of Dan 7 and its recasting of Dan 2 or its "historical recontextualization, or actualization, of the historical schema introduced in Daniel 2" (288). Daniel 7, in this way, is implementing the "four-kingdom schema" from Dan 2 in order to "contemporize" or update the older material. This reconstruction is unlikely—rather than adding bits of material to "contemporize" the book, it seems the author/editor sought to base *much* of the theological shape of the work (even chs. 8-12) upon Dan 2 (cf. Childs, *IOTS*, 618).

[145] However, Carr and others treat biblical traditions as though they only move in one direction, namely, *reaching back* to cultivate some semblance of authority. The validity of an association, so the axiom goes, is determined by the text's ability to cross-reference with a quotation. But Dan 9:24-27 *moves forward* and accounts for the organic growth of these traditions—a true outworking of realities originating in and dependent upon the Law and Prophets.

tional and stable and constitutive. One thinks above all the relationship between Law and Prophets as the major theological categories of the present Tanak. The Torah is not seeking some fulfillment beyond itself. If anything, it contains its own seconding and dynamic voice...and this witness looks backward and forward at once, with no restlessness or eschatological pressure for completion by later traditions.[146]

The voice of Leviticus is not lost: the land is still forfeit and God, seemingly absent. Will Israel always pay for the land's unrest? In Dan 9:24-27 something greater is necessary; namely that which moves beyond building projects and civil cooperation with oppressive regimes. Such is the tenor and setup of Dan 9.

6.1. Daniel 9:20-23: Transition to Interpretation (9:24-27)

Daniel 9:20-23 concludes the prayer (9:20; mirror-effect with 9:3-4) and introduces the interpretation in 9:24-27. In short, the section revolves around "understanding" (בין)—a term repeated four times in the span of two verses. The term "understanding" buttresses the theme of these verses as well as the hinge upon which the prayer and the interpretation swings: the wisdom of Daniel, the "greatly desired" (חמודות; 9:23). This designation cuts between the form-critical dichotomy of "prophet" or "court sage." Daniel is "more than a prophet."[147] To be sure, Daniel is a wisdom figure reinforced by the sapiential connotations surrounding חמודות. He is also an interpreter, a suffering servant, a mediator, a visionary and a sacrificial representative.

Context such as this sets the stage for 9:24-27. Moreover, the reader is gradually aware of a complex horizon upon which to interpret the numerical images. It will require more than chronology and reference. Undoubtedly, our conclusion, that Daniel is shifting the stream of tradition from the Sabbath-heptadic "rest" of the LP to a "completion" based on this same heptadic pattern, is only tenable if 9:2, 3-19, 20-23 sanctions such an argument. What makes this position defensible? A canonical approach demonstrating the shape of the chapter, the resources consulted and the intuitions (partially) of those charged with the task. Proposals for 9:24-27 that acquire evidence outside of the immediate context, as I suggest above, are isolated from Israel's inscripturated history and confined to a scant number of historical reconstructions.

---

[146] Seitz, "Two Testaments," 36.
[147] Koch, "Is Daniel Among the Prophets?" 125.

CHAPTER 4
Daniel 9:24-27

Turning to 9:24-27, the chapter transitions—no longer do we read a penitential framework or an exchange between Daniel and the angelic messenger, but an interpretation of Yahweh's long-standing decree. This chapter approaches the interpretation (vv. 24-27) in three parts, with two verses making up each section: (1) an analysis of the phrase "seventy sevens," through lexical, semantic and comparative study; (2) the promise and trajectory of Dan 9:24-25; (3) Dan 9:26-27 and the downfall of oppressive rule.

1. The "Seventy Sevens"

Reexamining the contexts from which the phrase "originates" (the Law, Prophets, immediate context of Dan 9), our task is to find a reliable location from where to interpret the construction, "seventy sevens." The task, as we have seen, is not as simple as tying the seventy sevens to a direct or partial quotation. We also know Daniel is no stranger to ambiguity—the bulk of his message lies in shadowy images. It is the imagery of *time*—not incomplete historical record—that complicates our reading of Dan 9 more than any other device. The way we construe the seventy sevens will also determine how we interpret the whole of 9:24-27. Our task also includes asking questions: how are these time-images operating? Do they function in conventional terms, portraying one event after another in a sequence? To answer these questions, we will (a) give a brief history of the research on the seventy sevens, (b) consider the lexical and semantic features of the phrase, (c) compare (and distinguish) similar constructions in select interim-period texts (3rd cen. BCE-3rd cen. CE), (d) and evaluate the phrase's overall role as time-image in 9:24-27.

1.1. Past Research on the Seventy Sevens

Descriptions of the seventy sevens are understandably broad and compel interpreters to quickly move from the prayer to the divisions (vv. 25-27). Still, we must be aware of the landscape on which many scholars view the puzzling number. Sweeney locates the sum of the whole book in the seventy sevens, based on the connection between Dan 2 and chs. 7-12: the kingdom of "the holy ones of the Most High" will arise "at the time of the end" (Dan 9:17; 10:40; 12:4) through the actions of hands which are not human (Dan 2:34; 8:25).[1]

Lacocque comments on the conclusion of the chapter: the resultant seventy sevens are actually the "true meaning of the *Jeremian* text being in fact 'seventy weeks of years.'"[2] He asks if the construction is one point in a "chiastic relationship of the same expression" between 9:2 and 9:24?[3] Other analyses of the seventy sevens are content with arguing for an "exact mathematical fulfillment," with the adjective "exact" taking on various nuances.[4] Alternatively, those who do not hold to a chronological line to Jesus Christ tend to consider the seventy sevens a 490-year expansion hastily formed in some inaccurate attempt to represent the "span of ancient Israelite history"—from the destruction of the First Temple (587/86 BCE) to the alleged entrance of the "abomination of desolation" as/by Antiochus IV Epiphanes (175-64 BCE).[5] In this case, the author/editor is at fault. Using the seventy sevens as a baseline, Daniel, according to one commentator, may be working with poor, historical calculations.[6] Others see the number as both literal *and* figurative. He finds that while the number itself is not "jeglichen Bezug zur absoluten Chronologie," the overall chronology is still "einen konkreten Anknüpfungspunkt in dessen Observanz zur Zeit des Verfassers" and not just "einen imaginäern Kalender von Sabbatjahrzyklen."[7]

It is true asking what lies behind the seventy sevens is not a misguided question as long as the interpreter is aware of the complexities of the text. On the other hand, treating the numerical imagery as a series of historical points, and then assigning theological values to those points, can be problematic.[8] Koch is correct in casting Daniel's interpretation of the seventy sevens in the

---

[1] Sweeney, "The End of Eschatology," 123.

[2] Lacocque, *Daniel*, 125 (italics mine). It is the ambiguous character of the seventy-year figure set by Jeremiah that, as Lacocque states, emphasizes "the full responsibility of the wicked whose arrogant lack of repentance prolonged the time of chastisement... although in so doing they fulfilled the secret purpose of God" (125).

[3] Vogel, 148.

[4] David Lurie, "A New Interpretation of Daniel's 'Sevens' and the Chronology of the Seventy 'Sevens,'" *JETS* 33.3 (1990) 303-9.

[5] Fishbane, *Biblical Interpretation*, 479. Regardless of where these sequences lead (either to Christ's ministry or another "anointed" figure), both attempt to distill the images into historical solutions that lie behind the text.

[6] Norman Porteous, *Das Buch Daniel* (DATD 23; Göttingen: Vandenhoeck & Ruprecht, 1985), 58.

[7] Is not "strictly a reference to an absolute chronology," the overall chronology is still "a concrete link in its observance at the time of the author," and not just "an imaginary calendar of the Sabbath-year cycle" Berner, *Jahre*, 95.

[8] Such approaches were common in the Early church; see, e.g., Julius Africanus, a third century church father who saw the seventy weeks spanning from the 20th year of Artaxerxes to the 22nd year of Tiberius Caesar; see Martin Wallraff, ed. *Julius Africanus Chronographie: The Extant Fragments* (Berlin: Walter de Gruyter, 2007), 237.

light of careful, coordinated theological "research and exegesis."[9] Of course, noting this type of "exegesis" is not an immediate contemporary to current exegesis, we can assert the level of craft and intentionality is part of the DNA of the text. The construction "seventy sevens" is also *itself* an exercise in Danielic exegesis, both in its lexical, semantic and cultural expression.

1.2. Lexical and Semantic Characteristics of the Seventy Sevens

The seventy sevens are a heptadic scheme functioning as an umbrella over the remaining verses.[10] Beginning with a syntactical observation, the "seventy sevens" (שבעים שבעים) is a construction fronting 9:24, thereby supplying the reader with a topic (9:24-27).[11] Analysis of the phrase indicates this construction is not as easily translatable as some interpreters let on. If one assumes some influence from the seventy years of Jeremiah in 9:2 (and Lev 25.1-55), then the rendering, "seventy *weeks*," is misleading.[12] Goldingay rightly asks "why we should accept the basis of this computation, that of a 360-day year?"[13] The notion of "weeks" (in multiples of seven) already has a designation, שבתות שבע (cf. Lev 23:15, 25:8). Automatically translating the word "weeks" often compels interpreters to understand the entire passage in terms of 365-day "years." The rendering "seventy *sevens*" is preferable since it retains the figure of speech Daniel is implying—a semi-referential time-image.[14] Examples of this

---

[9] Koch, *Das Buch Daniel*, 154. To Koch, the "seventy sevens" are an "apokalyptische Einteilung der Weltchronologie" (152).

[10] Or, as Fishbane describes the image, we are acknowledging a *"schematic span of time* based on multiples of 7 and 70" (483; italics mine). Daniel locates himself in the symbolic scheme, considering it the "final Sabbatical 'week.'" See also Poythress, "Hermeneutical Factors," 143.

[11] Cf. Rigger, *Siebzig*, 110; Schlenke, "Verantwortung," 119. Though I disagree with Schelnke's emphasis on the rift between apocalyptic and non-apocalyptic revelation, the fact the seventy sevens appears at the converging point of the prayer (vv. 3-19; 20-23) and the interpreted revelation (vv 24-27) is noteworthy.

[12] Like the seventy sevens, the seventy-year period of Jeremiah is not a simple matter of historical association if we restrict our reading to exact numerical calculations. Does the seventy-year period begin in 586 BCE and end with the decree of Cyrus (2 Chr 36:20-22; cf. Ezra 1:1), possibly to line up with "Sabbath" observance (36:21)? Do we begin with Judah's submission to Babylon in 605 BCE? Does the period end in the second year of Darius, 519 BCE (Zech 1:12)? What if the *terminus ad quo* depends upon the *capture* of the city by Nebuchadnezzar (597 BCE) and not its occupation? For the *terminus ad quem*, do we seal the timespan at the fall of Babylon (539 BCE) or the completion of the rebuilt Temple (517 BCE)? Clearly, any combination of these historical waypoints would change the sum of years.

[13] Goldingay, *Daniel*, 258.

[14] If one takes the phrase as 490 years, whether exact or inexact, the number might be a "collective" of years, emphasizing the *composition* of the collected item(s) (Bruce Waltke and M. O'Connor, *An Introduction to Biblical Hebrew Syntax* [Winona Lake, Ind.: Eisenbrauns, 1990], 119.) The descriptor שָׁבֻעִים may also have a "distributive sense" (cf.

language are common in the book: Dan 3:19 tells of Nebuchadnezzar's fiery temper rising with the rising temperature of the furnace, heated "*seven times*" (שבעה) the normal amount. Similarly, Nebuchadnezzar incurs judgment for his high-minded monologue on his high rooftop (4.26-27[29-30]). As a result, his judgment spans "*seven periods*" (שבעה) without any further specification.[15] One of the texts under discussion, Lev 26:18, states, "And if in spite of this you will not listen to me, then I will rebuke you *sevenfold* (שבע) for your sins" (cf. 26:21, 24, 28). In these instances, it is important to differentiate between reporting "seven" objects and adding a heptadic value to an object or objects, not unlike changing "seven" into a verbal descriptor.

Those who think of the שבעים שבעים in terms of technical "weeks" tend to interpret the phrase as either factors (e.g. 7 x 70) or products (e.g. 490 years). If the message intended to convey a technical nuance, one would expect something like a numeric *waw* (e.g. שבעים ושבעה for the number "seventy seven," as in Judg 8:14), upon which the author could add however many sevens or tens were necessary to fix a point in time. Also, there is the use of מלא in 9:2, which is often translated as time "passing" (ESV) when, in fact, the number is *filling*— the "fullness" of time. Completing or filling is a common part of heptadic structures in earlier passages (cf. Gen 29:27; 41:7, 22; 50:3; Exod 7:25; 23:26; 29:35; Lev 8:33). The phrase bears all of the characteristics of a figure of speech or convention.[16]

Grammatically, the phrase itself is unique: "שָׁבֻעִים" ('weeks', 'besevened') is only found in Dan 9:24 and 10:2-3. The word's scarcity lends to its ambiguous spelling. What does it mean to "beseven" a measurement of time, so to speak? In light of the other theological tactics Daniel employs, the ambiguity in spelling (שָׁבֻעִים שָׁבְעִים) may be another example of Daniel's exegetical construction of large patterns.[17] Though the plural שָׁבֻעִים is common, it is only here that

---

Deut 14:22) of the object שָׁבֻעִים, akin to "one seven after another" for an indeterminate amount of time.

[15] As a comparison, see the "seven periods of time" (שבעה עדנין) will end for Nebuchadnezzar once he knows that "the Most High rules the kingdom of men and gives it to whom he will" (4:22, 32 [25, 35])

[16] We can liken the figure of speech to the exchange in Matt 18:21-22: "Then Peter came up and said to him, 'Lord, how often will my brother sin against me, and I forgive him? As many as seven times?' Jesus said to him, 'I do not say to you seven times, but seventy times seven.'" Clearly, Jesus does not mean for Peter to enact 490 instances of forgiveness, but an unlimited amount of forgiveness befitting one who follows Christ.

[17] The "seventy years" (שבעים שנה) of Jer 25:10-11 can be repointed from שָׁבֻעִים to שָׁבֻעִים thereby rendering a fresh interpretation of an old prophecy. Sweeney, for example, takes a traditional Jewish interpretation to the phrase by considering the wordplay inherent in the allocation of vowel points (*Tanak: A Theological and Critical Introduction to the Jewish Bible* [Minneapolis: Fortress, 2012], 454-55); also Lawrence Willis, "Daniel" in *Jewish Study Bible* (ed. Adele Berlin and Marc Brettler; Oxford: Oxford University Press, 2003), 352-56. Problems arise, however, when Sweeney adds "years" (שנה) to the final

the plural שָׁבֻעִים is tied to the plural absolute שָׁבוּעַ in these forms and in this sequence.[18] Such adjustments to the wording do not illuminate points in time, but *veil* points in time so that the reader is compelled to step back and take in a panorama of images and events. The phrase also omits the addition of שׁנה ("years") which is found in Leviticus and Jeremiah; we do not read "seventy sevens *of years*," but simply "seventy sevens." Here, we witness Daniel's "economy of style" and use of "generalization" in full effect.[19] Figures of speech that are shaped by ambiguity allow for more interpretive possibilities. By leaving the interpretive field open, the imagery can freely attach itself to the textual associations in vv.2-19 and vv.20-23. The seventy sevens also remain rooted in Leviticus (e.g. the heptadic scheme) and Jeremiah (e.g. the interpreted number, seventy)—this multivalent view of Daniel's numerical image is, according to Childs, "the layering of tradition."[20]

After layering these traditions, we find Daniel is likely elaborating upon a stream of tradition rooted primarily in the "solemn rest" (שׁבתון) of Exod 16:23, 31:15; Lev 23:3. Like Daniel's construction, this image in Lev 23:3 is unique: it is a "sabbath of sabbaths" or "an unclear specific sense of שׁבת."[21] Another similarity between the two constructions is the likeness evoked by the full, implied construct of שׁבתון. The implied construct is שׁבת שׁבתון, wording not far from the "heightening" sense of שׁבעים שׁבעים.

The repeated combination of *shin-bet* (שׁ-ב) is another stylistic feature binding the Sabbath-heptadic pattern together. Daniel does not use "rest" (שׁבת) in its lexical form, but the associations with the Sabbath-heptadic tradition in Leviticus and Jeremiah make an alliterative connection for the reader. As far back as Exod 31:15 (cf. 16:23; Lev 23:3), we find this configuration of Sabbath-heptadic terms and their *shin-bet* combinations: "But the seventh day (השׁביעי) is a Sabbath (שׁבת) of solemn rest (שׁבתון)." Apart from the *Ruhetag* in Gen 2, this configuration stands as the baseline for much of the Sabbath-heptadic tradition moving forward. Is this simply clever artistry behind the wordplay, keeping the imagination of the reader loosely within the confines of a well-known pentateuchal motif? The play on letters appears to produce im-

---

interpreted construct, rendering the phrase in Dan 9:24a as שָׁבֻעִים שִׁבְעִים שָׁנָה instead of simply שָׁבֻעִים שִׁבְעִים (455).

[18] Given the language of Sabbath, one may expect שׁבתת ("Sabbaths") as Lev 23:15, 25:8 instead of שׁבעים ("weeks"). There is also a variation on the sequence of descriptor and object: here the descriptor is first (tobv hobv or "seven weeks"), as in Deut 16:9, but Dan 9:24 makes the object first.

[19] G. B. Caird, *The Language and Imagery of the Bible* (Grand Rapids: Eerdmans, 1980), 26-33. Imagery and ambiguity cross paths, giving way to what Caird calls "associative thinking" (107-8).

[20] Childs, "Response," 54.

[21] *HALOT*, "שׁבת," 1407. This heightened Sabbath is also rendered in the NT, holding special significance for the crucifixion narrative: "Since it was the day of Preparation, and so that the bodies would not remain on the cross on the Sabbath (for the Sabbath was a high day [ην γαρ μεγαλη η ημερα εκεινου του σαββατου]) ..." (John 19:31).

ages of the first interchange between the ש-ב in שבע ("seven") and the ש-ב in שבת ("completeness"). Vogel notes, that "from the beginning, the seven-day week cycle became the quintessence of the completeness of time."[22] However, the *absence* of שבת is equally important. Apart from reference to heptadic structures, Daniel's only reuse of the ש-ב alliteration is the brief mention of Jerusalem's restoration (שוב). In his vision, the notion of "rest" (שבת) is oblique, running in the margins, as the tradition expands to include Israel *and the nations* in the completion of the "end" in 9:24-27 (קץ, כלה).

The lexical and semantic nuances of the phrase pose another question: does the semantic range of the construction justify an emphasis on a Jubilee year or "super-Jubilee," as many scholars argue?[23] At least three problems plague this association. First, Daniel does not use any of the key words (יובל, שמטה, דרור) that link the Jubilee-year context of Leviticus and Deuteronomy to Dan 9. No reference is made to the "fiftieth year" of Lev 25:11 or the following "eighth day" of Lev 23:39.[24] Second, the calendration of Daniel's timetable would have no problems with *precision* if it were based on the Feasts. In the Pentateuch, the Feast times were nothing if not precise (cf. Exod 13:6; 23:14-18; Lev 23:34-40). For example, the Feast of Booths goes hand in hand with the "year of release" (cf. Deut 31:10), yet we have no hint of such observance in Dan 9:24. One would expect the same level of precision when speaking to the Jubilee year or "fiftieth year." Third, proponents of a jubilee theology in Dan 9:24 seem to unintentionally fixate on the interpretations of Qumran apocalyptic. Texts, such as 11QMelchizedek, freely associate Lev 25:8-17 (the primer on jubilee-years) with a grand jubilee or, in this case, a scheme consisting of

---

[22] Vogel, 147; cf. Johannes Hehn, *Siebenzahl und Sabbat bei den Babyloniern und im Alten Testament* (LSS II/5; Leipzig: Zentralantiquariat der DDR, 1968), 130.

[23] According to Lacocque, Daniel means to "symbolically place the end of the tribulation of exile and the inauguration of the restoration after a symbolic time-span of ten sabbatical cycles (cf. Lev. 25:2-7; Deut. 15:1-11)" (*Daniel*, 121). Vogel offers one of the most recent and extended cases for a strong connection between Dan 9, Lev 25-26 and the Jubilee year. Following Koch's argument ("Die mysteriösen Zahlen der judäischen Könige und die apokalyptischen Jahrwochen" [*VT* 28 [1978], 433-41] here 439), Vogel relates the seventy weeks of years to a "prophetic" or "powered" jubilee wherein the readers of Daniel are meant to associate the number with "the concept of 'release' (שְׁמָטָה) from slavery and the hope of a new beginning inherent in the sabbatical year injunction" (Vogel, 180). Goldingay, on the other hand, takes issue with the notion of Jubilee-traditions hiding behind the seventy sevens by pointing towards the remainder of the passage: "the seven-sevens of Dan 9:25 are insufficient to indicate that Dan 9 reflects Jubilee thinking, given that it does not describe the 490 years in these terms" (*Daniel*, 232).

[24] Cf. Bergsma, *The Jubilee from Leviticus to Qumran: A History of Interpretation* [VTSup 115; Leiden: Brill], 2007).

"ten jubilees."[25] With Qumran texts that depend on chronology, such as Jubilees, a theology of Sabbath and calendration are inextricably linked.[26]

This relationship results in a transfer or back-reading onto Daniel's Sabbath-heptadic strategy. Daniel never comes to a firm conclusion about what full restoration looks like. He does not endorse a "happy ending," even at the end of the book (cf. 12:12-13). The vision of final rest is difficult for Daniel to sharpen, even as he implements his exegetical skills on the LP. A reenactment of the Jubilee year in an intensified form does not account for the dark days *in parallel* with Jerusalem's restoration. The expanse of the seventy sevens includes events and figures that, though veiled in obscurity, imply a powerful clash where chaos (v. 25-26) and restfulness (v. 24, 27d) entangle one another. We, therefore, cannot reduce the construction seventy sevens to one theological concept, but we can gather potential nuances to show the complexity of this phrase.

1.3. "Seventy Sevens" and Sabbath-Heptadic Themes in Interim Period Literature

Texts from the interim period (3rd cen. BCE-3rd cen. CE) play a large part in determining how the Sabbath-heptadic scheme was understood on and around the time of Daniel's earliest reception; for many scholars, the Qumran scrolls specifically offer the definitive key to understanding why Daniel uses a Sabbath-heptadic scheme.[27] In either case, references to the Sabbath-heptadic tradition in a select group of interim period texts are useful for ascertaining the many sides of this convention. In what follows, we will examine where and how the combination of Sabbath and heptadic language occurs in certain post-Danielic texts.

1.4. Jubilees and Dan 9:24-27

Qumran studies frequently draw parallels between *Jubilees* (c. 150 BCE) and Daniel in order to compare time-imagery, eschatology, philosophy and socio-political attitudes. The book retraces the events running from Creation to the circumstances involving the children of Israel at Mount Sinai. A major impetus for the book is a revelation received by Moses on the mountain (cf. Exod 24:12, 15-18) by means of an *angeles interpres* (*Jub* 50:2).[28] Of interest, however, is the

---

[25] For full discussion, see Joseph Fitzmeyer, "Further Light on Melchizedek from Qumran Cave 11," in *JBL* 86 (1976) 25-41.

[26] See Martin Abegg, "The Calendar at Qumran," in *Judaism in Late Antiquity, Vol. 1* (ed. Alan Avery-Peck and Jacob Neusner; Leiden: Brill, 2001).

[27] Zakovitch interprets the omission of written Qumran traditions in the Hebrew Scriptures to be a matter of maintaining the theological *status quo*. The "popular, but *problematic*" traditions of Qumran "whether in oral or written form ... were *rejected* by the biblical writers and not *admitted* into the Sacred Scriptures" ("Inner-biblical," 37; emphasis mine).

[28] The intention of the book, according to Jacques van Ruiten, "is to confirm the authenticity and authority of its version of the revelation of Moses" ("Biblical Interpre-

shared Sabbath-heptadic language permeating the book of *Jubilees*.²⁹ The book uses a "continuing chronological system" of 2450 years that spans from creation to the entrance into the land. This total is delineated by a heptadic structure—the periodic celebration of Jubilees (every 49 [7x7] years). In this way, the author can determine 49 sets of 50-year units or 2450 years total. *Jubilees* bases its telic perspective on the phrase, "in the year of jubilee" (בשנת היובל), from Leviticus (cf. 25:10-54; 27:17-24; cf. Num 36:4), and is eschatologically charged through contact with Deut 15:2—"for the *final days* (לאחרית הימים) concerning the captives."³⁰ The text is, therefore, equally concerned with matters of Sabbath.³¹ The last year in the system is "toward *the year of grace* (לשנת הרצון) of Melchizedek" (Lines 8-9).

Leviticus, however, marks the jubilee (יובל) at periods of *50 years*, not 49 years (25:10-11). The significance is not that a late book such as *Jubilees* takes up the themes of Leviticus, but that the author transforms the time images in order to make a statement about the whole of time or even issues not entirely chronological. While not strictly an "apocalyptic" text, the final unit of time or culmination of the time imagery is the last Jubilee, or as Vanderkam calls it, "the climax of chronology."³² By implication, *Jubilees* is preoccupied with communicating an "enduring exile" or the capacity for the Exile not just to speak as a fixed, historical event, but as a manner of living (1:15-18).³³ Exile, according to *Jubilees*, is a recurring pattern of existence.

---

tation in the Book of Jubilees: The Case of the Early Abram [Jub. 11:14-12:15]" in *A Companion to Biblical Interpretation in Early Judaism* [ed. Matthias Henze; Grand Rapids: Eerdmans, 2012], 123); cf. Hindy Naiman, "Interpretation as Primordial Writing: Jubilees and Its Authority Conferring Strategies," *JSJ* 30 (1999) 379-410.

²⁹ Cf. James VanderKam, "Enoch Traditions in Jubilees and Other Second-Century Sources," *SBLSP* 1 (1978) 229-51.

³⁰ The clear jubilee-teleology of *11QMelchizedek* is also a valuable resource for comparing Sabbath-heptadic structures and Isaianic prophecy. At a textual level, the author combines the words of Dan 9:24-27 and Isa 52:7 in order to proclaim "the year of favor" or "to proclaim liberty to the captives" (Henze, *Biblical Interpretation*, 151). As Puech terms it, the focal point of the text is "the tenth jubilee as the age of redemption" (E. Puech, "Notes sur le manuscript de X1QMelkisedeq," *RevQ* 12 [1987] 483-513, here 483). It is also a recognizable divergence that the final years and days of text's heptadic sequence consist of the administration of justice and military force, referring to Pss 82:1-2 (cf. *Jub* 7:8-9).

³¹ Sabbath theology, for example, is regarded so highly in *Jubilees* that it affects the Qumranic calendration: events transpired almost exclusively on a Sunday, Wednesday or Friday—not a Sabbath day (Abegg, "Calendar," 148).

³² VanderKam, "Questions," 125.

³³ Martien Halvorson-Taylor, *Enduring Exile: The Metaphorization of Exile in the Hebrew Bible* (Leiden: Brill, 2010), 9-10.

1.5. Enochic Texts and Daniel 9:24-27

Many Enochic texts make little effort to hide their reintegration of Danielic material, especially Daniel's use of Sabbath-heptadic structures.[34] The text of *1 Enoch* (late 3rd BCE-2nd BCE) sketches a loose timeline of seven weeks over the course of which the "chosen righteous" will endure and receive from God "sevenfold teaching concerning his whole creation" (93:10; cf. Dan 12:10-13).[35] In the latter section of the book, we find the following heptadic structuring of time: "Then after that there shall be many weeks (בעון [שׁ]) without number forever; it shall be (a time) of goodness and righteousness, and sin shall no more be heard of forever" (91:17).[36] Apart from the theological parallels to Dan 9:24-27 (cf. "end of sin"), the "weeks" are escalated to a degree of atempor-ality. The figurative nature of the expression is more pronounced since neither text includes the specification, "years" (שׁנים). The author also adds that, like Daniel, the interpretation of "weeks" comes out of a "recounting from the books" (ד[ו...ח].נון מתלה; 93:1, 3). Clearly the author of *Enoch* sees himself in a post-Danielic role. However, unlike *Jubilees* or Daniel, the heptads in *Enoch* convey a figurative, theological and a-temporal sense.[37] Heptadic descriptors in *Enoch* can even express their theological sense without any reference to time, as with the "*seventy* shepherds" (*1 En* 89:59-77). Again, these literary conventions tell us such expressions were at least possible, if not likely, at the inception of Daniel's own heptadic structuring.

1.6. Other Scrolls and Daniel 9:24-27

In the *Rule of the Congregation*, the term שׁבוע designates "a week of years" or a point in every seven years (1QS 10, 7-8; also CD 16, 4; [שׁ]בועותיהם). 1QS 10, 7-8 also includes the designation, "seasons" (מועדי) into its heptadic structure, possibly to unite the Levitical institution more closely to a unit of time, as with

---

[34] The *Enochic Astronomical Book* (4QEnast ar*a*) is a version of *1 En.* 72-82 reportedly precedes the final form of Daniel—setting the scroll around the late third century BCE or early second century BCE. (Dimant, "Seventy Weeks Chronology," 59); see also A. Mertens, *Das Buch Daniel im Lichte der Texte vom Toten Meer* (SBM 12; Stuttgart: Katholisches Bibelwerk, 1971). The *Damascus Rule* (CD), according to Mertens, is also the first of a long line of commentaries on Dan 9:24-27.

[35] Cf. Beckwith, "The Significance of the Calendar for Interpreting Essene Chronology and Eschatology," *RevQ* 38 (1980) 167-202.

[36] James H. Charlesworth, ed. *The Old Testament Pseudapigrapha: Volume 1, Apocalyptic Literature and Testaments* (Peabody: Hendrickson, 2009), footnote t2, gives the optional translation of "sabbaths." In an Aramaic translation from one *Enoch* scroll (4QEn*g* ar), we find the word שׁבוע shares the same lettering as the Hebrew singular from Dan 9:24 (שָׁבֻעִים).

[37] Texts such as *Enoch* and *Jubilees* use a particular "solar" calendar (364-day year) whereas most ANE texts use a 29.5 day/month "lunar" calendar (354-day year) (Abegg, "Calendar," 146). We cannot dismiss how these calendrical values in *Enoch* and *Jubilees* are interlaced throughout their theological expressions while keeping a considerable, semantic distance from the images of time portrayed in these texts.

"seasons of the years up to their seven-year periods" (מועדי שנים לשבועיהם); The construction may point to an active/passive relationship ("sevened sevens") similar to the effect of a singular verb and a plural subject (e.g. "unleavened bread" [מצות יאכל] in Exod 13:7). While not the exact same construction in the Hebrew construction in Dan 9:24, the nuances are familiar. The compounded heptads relay a theological message *in the first instance* and then a chronological message in the second. Though these configurations do not permit us to equate a hybrid of temporal and theological nuances to the seventy sevens of Dan 9:24, they do expand our options for classification.

This heptadic structure in a section of *Nedarim* (b. Ned. 60a-61a), a Talmudic source, sets the "weeks" to a seven-year cycle (השבת ושבת שעברה חדש). Also, the *Damascus Document* refers to "the book (ספר) of the divisions of the periods according to their *jubilees* and their *weeks* (שבועותיהם)" (CD 16, 3-4). "Weeks," here, convey *divisions* of time rather than a timespan in itself. A noticeable pattern emerges: with the exception of CD 16, these sources maintain a broad stance on Sabbath and eschatological fulfillment, *without* recourse to the details of Lev 25:1-55 (esp. vv. 8-10).[38]

Additional clues from *pseudo-Daniel* (4Q243), dated to the early first century CE also help refine the picture of Sabbath-heptadic structures we have in the canonical Daniel.[39] Within these scrolls (4Q196-4Q363), texts shed light on Danielic theology, its reception and, in some cases, units of "seventy years."

---

[38] Roger Beckwith, "Early Traces of the Book of Daniel," *TynBul* 53.1 (2002): 74-82, argues that these various inter-testamental works (Tobit, *1 Enoch* and Ecclesiasticus) received Daniel in such a way as to front the book's prophetic message and expand its eschatological claims. This is certainly true of Qumran. See Dimant, "Seventy Weeks." These are intertestamental communities with their own "chronological purposes" (David Miano, *Shadow on the Steps: Time Measurement in Ancient Israel* [Atlanta: Society of Biblical Literature, 2010], 73).

[39] Dimant, "Seventy Weeks," 60. In close proximity to the Danielic psedapigrapha, 1-2 Maccabees (2nd cen. BCE) also "theologizes" heptads by tailoring specific dates to possess Sabbath-heptadic features. In 1 Maccabees 6, the author describes Judas Maccabee offering surrender to Antiochus V and relinquishing the city of Beth-zur, due to starvation. Occurring in 163-162 BCE, the writer shifted the calendar (not Elul [164-163], but Tishri [163-162]) in order to align the starvation with the observance of *shemittah*, because "it was the seventh year" (6:53). To see this same historical accommodation working in Josephus and other Maccabean texts, see Ben Zion Wacholder, "The Calendar of Sabbath Years During the Second Temple Era: A Response," in *Origins of Judaism, Religion, History, and Literature in Late Antiquity, Vol. 5, Part 2* (ed. Jacob Neusner and William Scott Green; New York: Garland, 1990), 193-203. Much Aramaic literature post-dating the rededication of the Temple (164 BCE) depends on Daniel, not unlike the historical "appropriation" of events by 1-2 Maccabees (cf. 4:36-59; 2 Macc 10:1-8; Dan 11). We can compare, for example, the events of "the abomination of desolation" in 1 Macc 1:54 to Dan 11:31, 12:11; cf. 9:27. When a sequence of historical events appear in the apocalyptic interim literature, it is possible—and, in some cases, likely—that the account relies on the shaped historical events of Daniel itself (e.g. 8:13-14, Dan 11).

Peter Flint, in analyzing one of these texts (4Q243), strikes a balanced approach to the mention of "[seven]ty years" (שבעין שנין) in 16.1. The fragment may denote a restoration or renewal on the one hand, but it does not necessarily "denote the 'seventy years' of the Babylonian Exile."[40] As Koch also observes, this text moves beyond the Maccabean epoch into its *own eschatological timetable*.[41] This apocalyptic narrative covers the sweep of Israelite history as opposed to a single, series of events. What is more, the author is clearly in touch with the Daniel tradition: "The literature proves in spite of their *Naherewartung* the Qumranites (and related Essene circles) were eager to connect the destiny and future of their movement not only with the history of Israel, but also with universal history and its end along the lines prevalent in proto-Masoretic Daniel."[42] Even units of "seventy years" carry theological import in post-Danielic literature, by virtue of their ability to build upon a heptadic structure.[43]

The "Seventh Vision of Daniel" or *7Dan* (5th cen. CE) also capitalizes on the figurative understanding of seven and heptadic formations. Originally in Greek, this Armenian text attaches a "seventh vision" to the six visions present in the book of Daniel. It also merges vocabulary and themes from Matt 23-24 and Revelation. This extra vision outlines the eradication of the Roman Empire, the coming of the Antichrist and the end of days. Throughout Daniel's vision, reference is made to a "seven-hilled Babylon"—so named "because all the nations of the Persians entered into you, O Rome; they shall not reign until the *completion of eternity*" (25.2; cf. 3.1).[44] Explicit is the connection between the heptadic description, "seven-hilled," and the temporal nature of Rome's rule, "the completion of eternity." The factor of "seven" is a common interpretive tool in these texts used as far back as the mid-second century BCE exegetical texts.[45]

LXX Daniel 9:24 (OG) also interprets the seventy sevens as a time-image by dividing the content of 9:24-27 according to two different schemes of chronology: first, the "seventy weeks for ... Zion" and, second, "seven and seventy and sixty-two weeks" (v. 26). Though two different schemes are conveyed, the

---

[40] Flint, "The Daniel Tradition," 340.

[41] Koch, "Stages," 428.

[42] Ibid.

[43] The *Epistle of Jeremiah* also reshapes the seventy years of Jer 29, using the familiar chapter as a "jumping off point" (Goldingay, 232). In this case, the seventy years become "seven generations" or 280 years. Dividing timespans in terms of generations is also a common practice in biblical chronology (cf. 1 Kgs 6:1; "480 years" or "12 generations").

[44] An amalgamation of terms is likely occurring, as the value of "seven" in Daniel is combined with the "seven mountains" (επτα ορη) in Rev 17:9.

[45] The exegetical text 4Q177 (frg. 10-11; lines 1-2) describes a "furnace on the ground, purified *seven times* (שבעתים)" from Ps 12:7, and "a single stone with *seven facets* (שבעת עינים), its inscription is engraved" from Zech 3:9.

timeframes refer to the same events. Within the "seventy weeks" the vision is to be "consummated" (συντελέω), while "the consummation of times" (συντελέω καιρῶν) in v. 27 is "after seven years and seventy times and sixty-two times, until the time of the consummation of the war." Notably, the "seventy weeks" of LXX 9:24 is an image *representing* the augmented timeframe—"seven and seventy and sixty-two weeks"—unfolding in LXX 9:26-27.

What are some conclusions we can draw from this survey of Sabbath-heptadic structures in the post-Danielic sources? Three summary points reconnect these comparative analyses to our understanding of the seventy sevens. First, most of these texts, as Goldingay states, "represent a way of thinking that Daniel takes up rather than one it initiates."[46] Accounting for this reality, it follows that while the logic behind the seventy sevens originates in the LP, the notion of a heptadic time-image describing the course of Israel's history and/or life is a culturally accessible idea. Many of these scrolls and fragments that are of an apocalyptic milieu and nearly contemporaneous to the final form of Daniel see Sabbath-heptadic structures as an opportune literary device for broadening, deepening, associating divisions of and "theologizing" time (both in its human and divine sense). Dividing heptadic structures into their chronological parts—constructing a timeline—appears to be a secondary function of this literature.[47] It is *this* world and textual culture of which Daniel is a part. We cannot ignore Daniel's imperial education either—it is worth remembering he is versed "in every branch of wisdom" (1:4), a trait that plays a significant role throughout the book. In the case of 9:24-27, chronography was likely a component of such education and should be considered in light of Dan-

---

[46] *Daniel*, 232. On the discussion of Danielic dependence or influence in calendrical entries in Qumran, see C.H. Cornhill, "Die siebzig Jahrwochen Daniels," in *Theologische Studien und Skizzen aus Ostpreussen* 2 (1889) 1-32; Barbara Thiering, "The Three and Half Years of Elijah," in *NovT* 23 (1981): 41-55. Many of the apocalyptic texts were amenable to intertexts, allusions and formulaic crossovers (cf. Henze, "4 Ezra and 2 Baruch: Literary Composition and Oral Performance in First-Century Apocalyptic Literature," *JBL* 131.1 [2012] 181-200); see also Michael E. Stone, *Features of the Eschatology of IV Ezra* (HSS 35; Atlanta: Scholars Press, 1989), 143-45. It is safe to affirm that Daniel is not the single source and architect of second to first century apocalyptic nor is Daniel a *pastiche* of borrowed apocalyptic thought, devoid of any generative claims.

[47] Considering the background of this time-imagery, we can conclude with Goldingay that, "none of this background suggest that either the total period of 490 years or its subdivisions are to *be expected necessarily to correspond numerically to chronological periods*. Our attempt to link them with such periods is to be made on the basis of exegetical considerations as these arise from the passage, not of actual chronology" (*Daniel*, 258). Assembling large blocks of time into a meaningful, theological order is an "interest...typical of Jewish apocalyptic texts" (Adele Collins, *Cosmology and Eschatology in Jewish and Christian Apocalyptic* [JSOTSup 50; ed. John Collins; Leiden: Brill, 1996], 56). Apocalyptic texts demonstrate "minimal interest" in hard chronology as such, but nevertheless show a "familiarity with chronological data" (57).

iel's grooming as a court seer.[48] Likewise, practicing numerical symbolism in the ANE was an activity of "discovering order in environment and experience."[49]

Second, the foundational themes and mental furniture around which these texts arrange their heptadic structures are also active in Dan 9:24-27. Qumran interpretation, in particular, utilizes thematic coherence to pull one text to another (as opposed to only intertexts or fragmented quotation).[50] George Brooke calls the biblical interpretation active in Qumran, the work of "thematic commentaries on prophetic scriptures."[51] Commentary on Dan 9 was from "a special vantage-point" and written in light of concurrent revelation–revelation that "was not confined to the distant past but continued in their time and fellowship."[52]

The third point is crucial: there are significant differences between the interim literature and Dan 9. These differences, in the end, are stark enough to conclude Daniel is forging his own path by means of his Sabbath-heptadic structure, despite the features shared with interim texts. Interpretive methods, for example, differentiate between the two presentations of time-imagery. Both Daniel and the interim period texts tie their heptadic expressions to their interpretive approaches. Qumran authors associate "a combination of prophetic settings" to suit specific purposes. For example, certain historical apocalypses link Daniel, Jeremiah and Ezekiel, not for their prophetic content necessarily, but because they offer glimpses of the early phase of the Exile (cf. 4QApocryphon of Jeremiah C and 4QPseudo-Ezekiel).[53] Daniel 9 distinguishes itself by directing the reader to a *network* of interlocking texts and applying the ever-growing traditions that sprout from Israel's scriptures. This feature of an interlocking network would remain incomprehensible if not for evidence that Daniel is drawing from the collective, textual message of the LP. All too frequently contemporary Daniel studies will equate the textual associations in

---

[48] Adler, "Apocalyptic Survey," 204.

[49] A. Collins, *Cosmology*, 56.

[50] Certain interim-period texts correlate the theme of the "fulfilled" age with various time references, but these are either in terms of "epochs fulfilled" (מלאי קצים y; 4QFlor, line 19-20) or ages. An unspecified "number" (מספר); line 20) is even a rubric for interpreting the times. Still, interpretations within these interim texts are fragmentary and always in conjunction with *an assortment of passages*; moreover, a set teleological motif or theme is in play as one might encounter in a synagogue reading or sermon (e.g. Davidic messiah, the path of the wise and the like).

[51] Henze, *Biblical Interpretation*, 134.

[52] Koch, "Stages," 432; also VanderKam, "Questions of Canon," 270. Here, VanderKam is commenting on the Teacher of Righteousness and his relationship to *concurrent* revelation (cf. 1QpHab 7:4-5).

[53] Henze, "4QApocryphon of Jeremiah C and 4QPseudo-Ezekiel: Two 'Historical' Apocalypses," in *Prophecy after the Prophets? The Contribution of the Dead Sea Scrolls to the Understanding of Biblical and Extra-Biblical Prophecy* (ed. Kristin De Troyer and Armin Lange; Leuven: Peeters, 2009), 35.

Daniel with the type of association we interpret in Qumran or other pseudapigrapha, risking either a limitation on types of textual association or an *artificial addition* that only befits specific sectarian theologies.[54] We must stress how both literatures possess their own canonical "loyalties" which, consequently, leads to a different appropriation of texts and cultural norms.[55]

Doubtless, many characteristics of Dan 9 are comparable to the interim apocalyptic literature. Broadly speaking, we can classify these texts as a *type* of literature. But such a claim is different from concluding that, in the second century BCE, there was no distinction between "scripture," "pseudapigrapha," and "apocrypha," just different "types of text" in one homogenous group of

---

[54] These additions and limitations are commonly within the range of "eschatologizing" (events exclusively in the eschaton) to "modernizing" (updated material for contemporary application). Fitzmyer outlines four classes of OT *quotation* in this example: (1) literal/historical—quoted and used in the same way it was before; (2) modernization—originally a reference to the contemporary scene, but was vague enough to apply to a new event; (3) accommodation—the OT text was "wrested" from the original context and modified/changed to adapt to the writer's new situation; (4) eschatological—"the Old Testament quotation expressed a promise or threat about something to be accomplished in the *eschaton* and which the Qumran writer cited as something still to be accomplished in the new *eschaton* of which he wrote" ("The Use of Explicit Old Testa-ment Quotations in Qumran Literature and the New Testament" in *The Semitic Background of the New Testament* [Grand Rapids: Eerdmans, 1997], 3-58). VanderKam cautions, rightly in my view, against such language as "wrested from the intention of the original author" ("To What End?" 309). Geza Vermes moves beyond simple quotation in his taxonomy. Like Fitzmyer, he provides a limited selection of possible intentions, but adds "sub-classes" to his own list: (1) eschatological actualization (e.g. 1QM 10.1-2); (2) direct proof—a "self-explanatory" selection; (3) reinforced proof—explanation is needed in such cases; (4) proof of historical fulfillment—the way a passage is fulfilled in the author's own time. The sub-classes of usage range from (a) a doctrinal statement, (b) an introductory formula, (c) a citation, to (d) an interpretation ("Biblical Proof-Texts in Qumran Literature," in *JSS* 34 [1989]: 493-508). With such strict categories in place, a large-scale appeal to the roots and traditions of the LP, as we find in Daniel, seems less than plausible.

[55] To illustrate these interpretive differences, many cite Dan 9 as an example of canonical texts interpreted with a Qumranic method (i.e. *pesher*). Schmid, for example, argues for this method in concert with the seventy years of Jeremiah: "Dan 9 steht mit seiner Auslegung der *siebzig Jahre* aus Jer bereits sehr nahe bei der Hermeneutik der Qumran-Pescharim (vgl. v.a. 1QpHab)," translated "Dan 9, with its interpretation of Jeremiah's *seventy years*, remains closely associated with the Qumran-Pesharim hermeneutic" (Schmid, "Innerbiblische Schriftauslegung," 21; Goldingay, 231). Dimant also sees hints of a "characteristic *pesher* method" in Daniel's study of the "books" (9:2) since the mutual application of multiple biblical statements is a feature common in Qumran interpretation (Dimant, "Seventy Weeks," 59). The intent behind *pesher* interpretation and the like within these extra-biblical materials, was to create an apologetic that "did not depend on canonicity, but on verisimilitude" (Beckwith, "A Modern Theory of Old Testament Canon," *VT* 41.4 [1991], 385-95, here 388).

literature.⁵⁶ VanderKam, for example, reminds us that no full *canon* (meaning a "supremely authoritative list") existed as of yet in early Second Temple Judaism, but such a claim should not invite the conclusion that all biblical and interim period literature is equivalent in method and authority.⁵⁷ The text of Daniel, rather, was woven into a canonical context that allows the book to speak with a chorus of voices. Canonical texts deliver their message on many levels and with many unique layers.⁵⁸ The canonical posture of Dan 9:24-27 demonstrates "a new way of reading the literature has emerged from the larger canonical context."⁵⁹

Attention to parallel passages in the Hebrew Scriptures takes us even further. Zechariah 1:12 and 2 Chr 36:21 include heptadic schemes as running literary conventions, each author communicating his own unique extrapolation of Jeremiah's seventy years. Within the context of Zechariah's time (522-486 BCE), the seventy years held a particular post: to "encourage people to take as a precise calculation a figure that did not have this significance for Jeremiah."⁶⁰ For 2 Chr 36:20-22, the movement of heptadic time is from the destruction of the Temple (586 BCE) to the "fulfillment" of Cyrus (cf. Ezra 1:1).⁶¹

---

⁵⁶ Carr, *Formation*, 184.

⁵⁷ VanderKam, "Questions of Canon," 269. His conception of the canon is revealing: "All we have are hints over a considerable historical span suggesting that some books were regarded by certain writers as sufficiently authoritative that they could be cited to settle a dispute, explain a situation, provide an example, or predict what would happen" (270). Obviously, the primary scaffolding erected alongside this definition of "canon" is a utilitarian one—but does this option convey the on-the-ground meaning of "authority" that we find in the canonical process? For VanderKam and others, the sequence of "authority" runs in reverse: an author authorizes an authoritative text. Conversely, a confessional stance submits that authority runs in the other direction: authoritative texts convey authority to readers and subsequent editors. This reversal may explain how some scholars see maximum compatibility between the book of Daniel and the traditions popular in Qumran.

⁵⁸ Here, we find a characteristic of Qumran generally considered to be reserved for only these scrolls: a gradient "from authoritative texts to writings intimately related to them, to works that cite authoritative books, to ones that only allude to scripture or employ scriptural language" (VanderKam, "To What End?" 302). However, such a "spectrum" of association-types is equally true of Dan 7-12.

⁵⁹ Childs, *BTONT*, 71. Childs' statement has a two-fold meaning. First, the immediate shaping of the text and its inclusion into theological setting (i.e. Dan 9 within Dan 7-12) is a dimension of "the larger canonical context." Second, Childs' is referring to the development of an OT text within a two-testament arch is also "the larger canonical context." Acknowledging the magnitude of this claim for the early Church, Seitz speaks to the latter meaning in his own words: "But as a total witness, an eventual New Testament canon will serve to describe the apostolic limits and public character of Christian claims as a comprehensive matter" (*Character*, 195).

⁶⁰ Goldingay, 231.

⁶¹ Many Daniel scholars link these texts so closely they merge the two messages and conventions and unconsciously allow for a "totality transfer" of the Sabbath-

The interaction between Zech 1:12, 2 Chr 36:21 and Dan 9:24 is an example of "the interaction of the various parts of Scripture," and how it "often serves to balance, check, and subordinate individual elements."[62] These instances demonstrate how the canonical witness makes sense of these Sabbath-heptadic traditions and helps show Daniel's work with streams of biblical tradition. The seventy sevens do not stem from a pure, abstract concept unique to Daniel nor is it solely an inheritance from extra-canonical sources.

1.7. The Seventy Sevens as a Time Image

Daniel crafted a way of looking at time episodically and never at the expense of his theological proclamation. This is one reason it is difficult to determine a precise *terminus ad quo* and a *terminus ad quem* for either the seventy-year period (cf. Jer 25:11-12; 29:10; Dan 9:2) or for the span of seventy sevens. The seventy sevens are not a strict time-reference, but a time-*image* meant to encapsulate a period moving from exile to restoration.[63] Generally, when a scholar speaks of a symbolic number in prophetic or apocalyptic discourse, it is simply the opposite of "literal." But "image" or "symbol," in this case, is more than that.[64] Images do more than refer.[65] The heptadic image, in particu-

---

heptadic scheme. According to Collins, the reason for the disparity between Dan 9:24-27 and these two texts is that Daniel "rejected their interpretation of the prophecy" (*Daniel*, 349.). Schmid suspects multiple sources lying behind the Sabbath-heptadic scheme: "Die Aufweitung der 70 auf 490 Jahre (Dan 9, 24) ist keineswegs willkürlich eingeführt," ("The widening of 70 years to 490 years...is by no means introduced arbitrarily...") (Schmid, "Innerbiblische Schriftauslegung: Aspekte der Forschungsgeschichte," in *Schriftauslegung in der Schrift: Festschrift für Odil Hannes Steck zu seinem 65. Geburtstag* (ed. Reinhard G. Kratz and Thomas Krüger; BZAW 300; Berlin: DeGruyter, 2000), 21, n. 115). Schmid's argument, though insightful, floats over any evidence of a hermeneutic, save for an appeal to the *pesher*-method. Goldingay, on the other hand, sees 2 Chr 36:20-23 nuancing Zech 1:12 by interpreting the seventy years in light of Lev 25:1-7; 26:31-35, 43. For the Chronicler, the timespan represents "the approximately 490 sabbathless years of the monarchic period" (231).

[62] Childs, "Response," 55.

[63] Ancient texts, such as Ugaritic poems, already use heptadic conventions and images to not only refer to events: "The seven-year convention—or rather, the end of a seven year period—is a more fixed literary formulation, well known, for example, from the Ugaritic poems, and is meant to point out a change, the end of a cycle, the beginning of the final arrangement: 'for seven years there was such a state of affairs, but in the seventh year finally the situation changed,' or 'for seven years I had to wait, but in the seventh year I decided to act,' and so on" (Mario Liverani, "The Chronology of the Biblical Fairy-Tale," in *The Historian and the Bible: Essays in Honor of Lester Grabbe* [ed. Philip Davies; JSOTSup 530; New York: T&T Clark, 2010], 77).

[64] Metaphor is another descriptor one could attach to the seventy sevens, but with qualifications. Different *gradations* of metaphor are at work (David Aaron, *Biblical Ambiguities: Metaphor, Semantics and Divine Imagery* [BRLAJ 4; Leiden: Brill, 2001], 20-29). On the first metaphorical level, the "seventy sevens" depict a complete unit of time. Further along the continuum of metaphor, the image takes on the nuance of completion by

lar, communicates numerous layers of significance. Literary conventions such as the seven-year period have ancient roots and anticipate Daniel's own use by centuries,[66] and, as we discussed above, are attested in the centuries following the book's reception.

But what are the theological implications of the seventy sevens as a time-image? The seventy sevens are (a) a clarification of earlier scriptures, (b) a connection to Sabbath and rest and, lastly, (c) a starting point for the patterns in "regime history" (vv. 25-27). The seventy sevens are, first, the result of earlier biblical texts, a normal convention of the surrounding culture, and, as Childs defines it, an inspired word of clarification: "The point of this reinterpretation is not that Jeremiah was mistaken in his prophecy, but that which he correctly envisioned was further *clarified* by a fresh illumination of scripture through the Spirit."[67] The image of the seventy sevens is significant, in that, it is the "clarification" of a stream of traditions flowing through the Hebrew canon.[68] The shift to the seventy sevens from seventy years "presupposes read-

---

depicting a pattern of Sabbath "weeks." On a deeper level, the metaphor extends beyond itself into an eschatological vision of Sabbath rest and unrest (9:24b-27). Subscribing to this definition of metaphor does not constrain the interpreter to choose between "real" and "imaginary" persons, places or events.

[65] The language is not merely referential, but performative, expressive and cohesive.[65] Daniel supplies imagery that is able to capture and communicate or to respond to an experience (cf. Caird, *Language and Imagery*). These dynamics surrounding the phrase "seventy sevens" are even more distinct when we compare the time images of 9:24-27 to the other numbers in the book: the "2300 evenings and mornings" (8:14) and the "1290-1335 days" (12:11-12) are clearly operating with some precision (Lacocque, *Daniel*, 250).

[66] In Hittite chronology, the reign of a king, Urhi-Teshub, lasted "for six-years" and "on the *seventh* year," the usurper Hattusshia III took the throne. Again, in the autobiographical inscription on a statue of King Idrimi of Alakah, we read, "seven years I resided among the Habian, but in the *seventh* year the god Adad turned toward me." One last example, in the Mari archives (ARM I. 131), an officer writes about a siege and reports that "on the seventh day I took the town"—less precise in chronology, but appropriate in terms of motif. Heptads can, therefore, take on a nuance of finishing and not just a point in a sequence.

[67] Childs, *IOTS*, 617 (italics mine).

[68] Proponents of a strict chronology in 9:24-27 usually claim the text is an anti-Seleucid gloss, ruling the seventy sevens a defensive maneuver used to fuel or contest the war effort. But to propose 9:24-27 is a final gloss or insertion imposed upon Jeremiah's word—consequently, drowning out the theological notes of the text—is to misunderstand the function of a canonical shape and erect a later section to rule the message of the first. As Childs states in a word to his detractors, "[T]o suggest that the final canonical form reflects only the theology of the last editor's hand is a misunderstanding of my position. My concern in showing the process of canonization is to demonstrate that the *entire history of Israel's interaction with its traditions* is reflected in the canonical text" (Childs, "Response," 54). This canonical point is a way of rephrasing the idea surrounding Daniel's elucidation of earlier scriptures.

ing Jer 25:11/29:10 in the light of other passages as well as Lev 25-26."[69] This wider significance constitutes the message of Dan 9:24-27. Concluding that the seventy sevens is no more than an update meant to guard against shattered hopes does not consider the deeper levels of meaning the image carries.

Another example of clarification is found in how the seventy sevens functions structurally in the passage: as one end of a framework. The placement of the seventy sevens suggests the construction carries a theological value that incorporates the material in the preceding prayer.[70] To cast the seventy sevens another way, Daniel is explaining how the seventy years are to be "filled" (9:2; cf. Jer 25:12). The time is "prolonged" and, thereby, constructs the frame connecting the two time-images. If the seventy years of Jeremiah are congruent with Daniel's narrative (cf. 1:21), then Dan 9:24 is commenting on, as one author puts it, *"den chronologischen Rahmen der Wirksámkeit Daniels."*[71] The seventy years in 9:2 and the seventy sevens in 9:24 are *bridged* by 9:3-19; this roots the time image in Leviticus (e.g. the heptadic scheme) and Jeremiah (e.g. the interpreted number, seventy). Such a multivalent view of Daniel's numerical image is, according to Childs, "the layering of tradition."[72]

Second, we learn this clarification contains a Sabbath element. Sabbath is a "blessed and holy" span of time (Exod 20:11) that is defined in terms of *rest*.[73] As Childs traces the theme in a section devoted to the Sabbath, he observes how it is "the creative act of God who ... rested on the seventh day" (Exodus), that which is "grounded in God's redemption of Israel" (Deuteronomy) and, in addition, a "sign of the covenant" (Exod 31:13, 16-17).[74] Implicit to "Sabbath

---

[69] Goldingay, 232.

[70] To call this a "chiasm," however, may obligate the reader to claim more than what 9:3-19 conveys. Traditionally, a chiastic structure brings certain statements within the core of the passage into sharp relief, denoting emphasis. Daniel 9:3-19 does not appear to present its centralized texts in this way (vv. 8-10).

[71] Berner, *Jahre*, 24. How should the reader organize the "number of years" (9:2), the "decreed end" (9:26-27) and the "appointed time" (11:27, 29, 35; cf. 10:14)? Are these varying descriptions of the same time-period? If each idiom is distinct, what differences can we detect? It is easy to mix these expressions together, but such is the harm interpreters inflict when not reading with care. One example, in Dan 11:27, is "an *end* at the appointed time." Already, we uncover nuances and slight shifts in meaning—the "appointed time" is not simply equivalent to the "decreed end" (9:26-27). Alternatively, Dan 11:35 describes an "interval of the end" (Xq to) running up until the "time appointed."

[72] Childs, "Response," 54.

[73] We can differentiate between the Jubilee year and aspects of the Sabbath through positive and negative outcomes. Unlike the Jubilee year, which stands as a positive, rewarding command, the Sabbath is both "boon and bane." Childs expands this two-fold outcome, saying "although the Sabbath was originally intended to be a positive sign of Israel's special relation to God, it also proved to be a negative sign of Israel's failure to regard God's command (Ezek 20:12)" (Childs, *OT Theology*, 71).

[74] Ibid., 70.

time," according to Childs, are the vague "limits of observance" (cf. Lev 23:2, 32; Exod 31:16).[75] Unlike the Jubilee—which is a divine command toward certain social actions—the grand Sabbath or "Sabbath of Sabbaths" is first to the Lord (Exod 31:15; 35:2) then to the people (cf. Lev 16:31; 23:32) and finally to the land (cf. Lev 25:4). This time image captures a deep, Edenic sense of Sabbath rest (cf. Gen 2:2, 3) where land *and people* undergo restoration, and goes even further.[76] Connections to Genesis are indirect, but Daniel does use שׁבעים and not the formal שׁבתת from Lev 23:15 (cf. 25:8). We may ask: why not use the original word? The text intentionally refers to the skeleton or the boldest outline of the sabbatical institution to make room for new images (desolation of the temple, full restoration of land and people, etc.). Daniel, in his redirection of the Sabbath tradition, departs from any focus on a Jubilee year or the land promises of Leviticus, and emphasizes the fullness of God's intended Sabbath rest. These emphases, though related, cannot be *conflated*.

Third, the time image of seventy sevens presents the interpreter with a starting point or "a platform from which exegesis is launched rather than a barrier by which creative activity is restrained."[77] Time, space and promise are spacious enough in this image to allow for oppressed communities to see themselves (and their plight) reflected in the words of Daniel. For our own understanding of the images in 9:25-27, *we also* require some understanding of our starting point: the seventy sevens. The Sabbath-heptadic understanding of ruling powers—from human to divine kingship—is neither completely new nor completely old. Like many Qumran sources, the heptadic convention represents a theological interpretation of "regime history" or *theo-chronology* that results in the completion of a (usually toilsome) span of time (cf. Dan 9:25-27). The goal is not another, more lenient human government, but the end of exile, oppression and, ultimately sin itself.[78] To achieve this expression theologically (and exegetically), the interpreter Daniel does not resort to chronology with exact calendrical values, but *theo*-chronology, or even a subset of historiographical inspiration.

---

[75] Ibid. The concept of Sabbath itself was construed as a *metaphor* parallel to its chronological aspect (cf. Robert Johnston, "The Sabbath as Metaphor in the Second Century C.E.," *AUSS* 49.2 [2011] 321-335).

[76] Vogel, 169. See also Michael Burer, *Divine Sabbath Work* (Winona Lake, Ind.: Eisenbrauns, 2012). In his study, Burer considers Gen 2:1-3 to be the "central passage" around which divine Sabbath work revolves (29).

[77] Childs, *IOTS*, 83.

[78] The end of sin, as Goldingay reminds us, comes at the end of "the seventy Sabbath years that were due" and "have been exacted sevenfold" (*Daniel*, 232).

2. Daniel 9:24-25—Introduction to the Kingdom Pattern

2.1. Daniel 9:24

Oddly enough, this final section of the chapter begins with the *ending* (9:24). Daniel 9:24 opens with a vision of a *completed* people and city—the summary and core of the section—and ends with a curious unit of time (seven weeks and sixty weeks) in a "troubled time" (9:25). What follows is the entire "decree" (חתך) to people and city (9:24a)—a notion of "decree" (חרץ) to which we will return at the close of the passage (cf. 9:26-27). The main idea of the section is fronted by 9:24 and, if we cut off v. 1 and vv. 25-27, we have a short answer to the events following "the desolations of Jerusalem" in 9:2.

In structure, Dan 9:24 is a triad of theological elements (9:24b-d) with three mirror images reflecting back on the first (9:24e-g).[79] "Seventy sevens," therefore, are *decreed* in order to:

> "finish the transgression" (24b) // "to bring in everlasting righteousness" (24e; cf. Is 45:17)
> "to end sin" (24c; cf. 8:23) // "to seal both vision and pro-phet" (24f)
> "to atone for iniquity" (24d) // "to anoint the most Holy" (24g)

Completing or finishing "the transgression" (הפשע), a reference to the sinful trajectory of Israel in 9:3-19, introduces the three-part sets. But the goal of the following phrases allows for a much larger reality to come ("everlasting righteousness," "to seal both vision and prophet"). Phrases initiating each of the lines mark the completion of *all* sin by collecting common terms for wrongdoing (פשע, חטא, עון) and stacking them on one another. The ambiguity of the triadic construction as a whole, however, supports a number of interpretive possibilities and references.[80]

Though the triad is a clear stair-step model, the relationships are quite vague: Are they appositional ("in other words ...") or instrumental ("by means of ...")? One could argue for a sequence of loosely related events: "to finish the transgression *then* to end sin *then* to atone for iniquity." But there is still no way of determining if such a sequence is in a consecutive order. A cautious, albeit helpful, strategy is to read the list as a non-sequential summary or as three different renderings of the same event. But this move still leaves the question of scope—are these triadic elements the expectation of a one or two faith-communities in the second century BCE? Is this a timeless epigram or

---

[79] Cf. James Montgomery, *A Critical and Exegetical Commentary on the Book of Daniel* (3d ed.; Edingburgh: T&T Clark, 1959). Collins notes how we have "six infinitives, with God as the implied subject (*Daniel*, 353).

[80] Dimant, for example, observes how the term is matched with eternal justice and "may allude to activity of dispensing justice by the Davidic messiah" (cf. Isa 11:5) ("Seventy Weeks," 59).

creed that functions regardless of time or circumstance? Or, are these actual expectations best understood in the context before (vv. 3-19) and the material after (vv. 25-27)?

It is with good reason the descriptions for sin in 9:24b-d are interchangeable (פשע, חטא, עון). Although the first three phrases in the construction (24b, c, d) refer to one reality, the three responses (24 e, f, g) refer to three different panels. These panels are windows into the finality of Yahweh's decree. Indeed, the whole of the triad, according to Dimant, is meant to foil the unfolding "contemporary evil situation" in vv. 25-27.[81] Interpreted this way, Daniel is likely revisiting a similar construction found in Jeremiah: "I will *cleanse* (טהר) them from *all the guilt* (כל־עונם) of their sin (חטא) against me, and I will forgive all the guilt of their sin and *rebellion* (פשע) against me" (Jer 33:8).

Though the structure lacks a second triadic panel to balance the negative sin-language, Jeremiah still imagines a time when sin in *all its descriptions* will be purified (טהר), using priestly vocabulary for the city and her people (vv. 6-7, 9, 16). Daniel widens the "end of sin" by including an array of names for God's final action (כלה, תמם, חתם, כפר). But the hardships leading up to these final panels have been, are being and will be costly—in this manner Daniel emphasizes the larger dimension of "completion" and not the more positive condensed notion of "rest."

2.2. The Most Holy? (קדש קדשים)

The construction קדש קדשים is also a matter of debate. To comment on this phrase, we will begin with (a) an analysis of the construction itself and then (b) discuss scholars' emphasis on the temple-sanctuary context. First, the construction: "the Most Holy" (קדש קדשים) is obscure. Is it the sanctuary (cf. 8:14), or altar (cf. Exod 29:36, 30:26ff), a priestly service (cf. 1 Chr 23:13) or a holy people (cf. Exod 12:16; Dan 12:7)? Apart from holy structures, the term קדש tends to be an abstract notion of "holiness."[82] Those who read a strong cultic line through the chapter might immediately see the "Holy of Holies" (Ex 29:36-37). Collins interprets the construction as "a rededication of the Jerusalem

---

[81] Dimant, "Seventy Weeks," 59. Collins sees a possible parallel in *1 Enoch* 10:20-22, which mentions a command from Michael to cleanse the earth from "all wrong and from all iniquity, and from all sin, and from all impiety, and from all the uncleanness, which is brought about from the earth ... [A]nd the earth will be cleansed from all corruption and from all sin, and from all wrath, and from all torment; and I will not again send a flood upon it for all generations forever." It is difficult to tell if the author has Daniel in mind, especially with the absence of the priestly language we find in the triadic construction of 9:24.

[82] Cf. H. Müller, "קדש *qds helig*" in *Theologisches Handwörterbuch zum Alten Testament* (ed. Ernst Jenni and Claus Westermann; Munich: Chr. Kalser, 1984); Baruch Levine, "The Language of Holiness: Perceptions of the Sacred in the Hebrew Bible," in *Backgrounds for the Bible* (ed. Michael P. O'Connor and David Noel Freedman; Winona Lake, Ind.: Eisenbrauns, 1987), 241-55.

Temple" by the hand of Judas Maccabeus after the passage was supposedly penned.[83] Another tack is to interpret the phrase as a messianic figure—a "Holiest One"—which is an alternative long held by early interpreters.[84] Vogel argues קדש קדשים can be "an inclusive term for the location as well as the atoning services of the sanctuary" (cf. 1 Kgs 18:36; 1 Chr 23:13), not just a reference to the inner sanctum described in Torah.[85]

A case can also be made for an *attributive* sense—reference to that which is "Most Holy." According to Lev 8:11, this motif of sprinkling (נזה), anointing (משח) and consecrating (קדש) seven times—as Aaron did for the altar—is first an attributive idea before taking on a locative nuance (cf. Exod 26:33; 29:37; 30:10, 29). Under Yahweh's direction, an object or person is conferred holiness. But the sanctuary and the people (9:3-19) are both unclean and require the very presence of Yahweh to attain what is "Most Holy." The altar and temple location are defiled and though these can be physically restored, the full, spiritual implications tied to both the actions of the "desolator" and the behavior of Israel will only be repristinated when the kingdom, city and sanctuary "built-without-hands" exist. We also know the pattern of the destroyed sanctuary likely continues in recompense for Israel's sin-debt (cf. 9:26), until the decreed end. The referent remains vague, leaving the interpreter to account for what is "Most Holy" (sanctuary, priest, altar, defiled vessels, etc.)?

Moving to the second point, if one's interpretation of קדש קדשים overemphasizes the temple sanctuary, this can potentially sway the context of 9:24-27. Joining the rendering "Holy of Holies" (קדשים קדש), references to the "evening sacrifice" (9:21) and the priestly imagery of 9:24, incline many scholars to make the temple sanctuary the unequivocal center of 9:24-27. Though this point seems to be a secondary, exegetical disagreement, favoring a single theme or context can be abrasive to the grain of the canonical context of Dan 9:24-27, even run contrary to it.

There is, of course, no doubt about the confluence of priestly themes in Dan 9: Daniel's "priestly" role (vv. 3-20), reference to the "sanctuary" (v. 17), and the act of "anointing" (v. 24) are only a handful. Sweeney sees the *Tanak* revolving around the temple in many respects—the central topic of the tripartite canon.[86] Temple, in Sweeney's terms, is the "holy or ideal center of canon and creation, insofar as the temple, represented in the Pentateuch as

---

[83] Collins, *Daniel*, 354.

[84] Most LXX mss. have the indeterminate construction agion agiwn with one manuscript adding a new verb (και ευφραναι [not χριω] αγιον αγιων). Latin renderings, of both Tertullian and Jerome's Vulgate, have the masculine *sanctus sanctorum*. The Peshitta substitutes the noun ajyvm instead of the verb jvm. Collins concludes, rather haughtily, the "messianic interpretation was for long the central issue in the interpretation of Dan 9:24-27 but is now abandoned by all but the most conservative interpreters" (*Daniel*, 354).

[85] Vogel, 65.

[86] Sweeney, "Foundations," 173.

the wilderness Tabernacle, serves as the context for the revelation of divine Torah both to Israel/Judaism and the world at large throughout the Jewish Bible."[87] Sweeney continues by describing the "fundamental concerns" of the Writings and how they "centered around its restored Temple in Jerusalem."[88] But while this affirmation of the centrality of the temple is true of the corpus, superimposing the theme textually diminishes the text's ability to speak with different voices.[89]

Supplanting multiple contexts and images with a single theme—especially one based on alignment with the historical record of the second century—calls into question the way one associates texts. Vogel's treatment of the temple in his work *The Cultic Motif in the Book of Daniel* illustrates this point. As a consequence of this centralization, textual associations that might otherwise have their own voice on a matter get caught within the gravitational pull of this theme. Vogel makes this position clear: "[W]hen the holy mountain is in view the sanctuary is *clearly* in mind as well, and when the sanctuary is mentioned its location on the holy mountain is *always* implied."[90] Vogel argues for an extreme level of association in order to establish Daniel's alleged emphasis on the temple-sanctuary.

A major problem in Vogel's mode of association is the transfer of meaning between terms and contexts. He first connects the phrase "holy hill" (9:16, 20)

---

[87] Ibid., 166. In another article, Sweeney finds Jewish interpreters approaching the Temple in Dan 9 "are also influenced by the perspectives of Christian theology, which views the destruction of the Jewish state and the Jerusalem Temple as a confirmation of Jesus' messiahship are a justification for the spread of Christianity throughout the world" ("End of Eschatology," 125). The statement does not do justice to the strength of Jesus' claims or the role of the Temple in Christian eschatology. Jesus, the Son of God, is the embodiment of God's presence and is, therefore, the Temple realized. In Christian eschatology, the return of the Son of God reintroduces this "Temple presence," but in a state of glory.

[88] Sweeney, "Foundations," 185. Although Sweeney argues for Temple as the ideological center of the canon, he also detects a reorientation of temple-language within Dan 9. The mythological/symbolic descriptions surrounding the Temple are a convention of the priesthood, in Sweeney's estimation, which seeks to wrest the holy sanctuary of Jerusalem from foreign control *through literary ingenuity*. For Sweeney, the inability to guard holy places by force makes it necessary to guard the sanctuary with words (or redefinition and redescription).

[89] Centering the temple and cultic elements will also affect how one interprets the message of the book. Goswell presses Daniel's temple language to the point of saying that any profanation of the sanctuary is "a direct challenge to God's rule," touching on the theological arch of the *entire* book ("The Temple Theme in the Book of Daniel," *JETS* 55.3 [2012], 518). This may be true—however, Daniel's primary concerns divert attention from the temple, whether through the terminology he chooses or simple omission.

[90] Vogel, 35 (italics mine).

directly to the sanctuary in the prayer (used once in 9:17).[91] He ignores descriptions that force the reader to consider these locations with nuance: "your city Jerusalem" in apposition (9:16), "the city that is called by your name" (9:18-19), "Jerusalem" (9:25) and the delineation between "the city and the sanctuary" (9:24, 26). Vogel's transfer circles back to Dan 2:45, based largely on the cultic atmosphere he dictates.[92] Under the assumption that 9:16, 20 refers to temple imagery, Vogel takes this nuance of "holy hill" and places it on the "mountain" (הר) in 2:35, 45.[93] But the stone/mountain image is not contained within a temple structure.[94] Rather, the stone/mountain represents a larger

---

[91] Greg Goswell sees this focal point as the climax of the events in 9:24, even a "reversal" of the temple's fate portrayed in 8:13-14 (Goswell, "Temple Theme," 519). William Shea also reads Dan 8:9-14 reinforcing the cultic setting of 9:24-27 ("The Prophecy of Daniel 9:24-27," in *70 Weeks, Leviticus, Nature of Prophecy* [ed. Frank Holbrook; Washington, D.C.: Biblical Research Institute, 1986], 75-118).

[92] Some track the "mountain imagery" originating in Dan 2:34-35, 44-45 through the entire book (9:16, 20, 11:45; cf. Is 2:2-4, 28:16; Zech 12:3) while connecting the imagery to the temple theme. However, those espousing this connection fail to see the unique nature of the mountain imagery in Dan 1-6 and the new vocabulary it takes on in Dan 7-12 (cf. Goswell, "Temple Theme," 509-20). Goswell goes further by saying 9:24-27 has a focus on "sanctuary." He makes a subtle transfer from temple to "the city" since it is conjoined with the sanctuary (9:26)—the city becomes imbued with temple-significance (515-16). Vogel also bestows special significance on שמם, deeming it a "state of the sanctuary" (35n75). He cites Dan 8:13, 9:17-18, 9:26, 11:31 and 12:11 and even Lev 26:31 and Ezek 6:4 for their various ties to the temple-sanctuary. Unfortunately, he fails to mention Jer 19:8, 33:10, 50:13 which reports the desolation of the *city*, an image Daniel constantly uses, certainly more often than any reference to the sanctuary (9:16, 18-19, 24, 26; cf. 9:25, ולבנות ירושלם).

[93] The word for "mountain" (טור) is not common. Outside of Daniel's two occurrences the word, to Vogel's point, can only be found in the context of temple preparation (Exod 28:17-20, 39:10-13; 1 Kgs 6:36, 7:2-4, 12, 18, 20; Ezek 46:23; 2 Chr 4:3, 13). However, Daniel is also the only work use טור as "mountain" whereas all other occurrences use rwf to refer to "rows" or measured lines of objects (precious gems, gourds, pomegranates, etc.).

[94] The stone cut "without human hands" (2:34-35, 44-45) refers to the ultimate reign overtaking all human powers, whereas the depiction of reigns in Dan 7-12 takes on animal imagery. Muddling the images in Dan 1-6 with temple imagery from Isaiah and Ezekiel improperly shades the imagery in Dan 9:16, 24-27. It is not possible to lay out all the research here, but there are links between Daniel's portrayal of the sanctuary and Ezek 40-48. On closer inspection, however, Dan 9:24-27 remains vague about the appearance and ministry of the "sanctuary," while Ezekiel offers a detailed account, albeit of an unseen temple that is difficult to imagine. If we are not careful, we may see the temple everywhere and ignore the possibility that the author wants to think about Yahweh's presence and rule in a different light. Goswell's statement proves this notion: "[E]ven in chapters *where the temple itself is not mentioned*, it is present by means of related motifs: the "great mountain" (Daniel 2), the "palace" of Nebuchadnezzar (Daniel 4), the confiscated temple vessels (Daniel 5), and the throne scene of Daniel 7" ("Temple Theme," 520; italics mine).

edifice—a mysterious *reign or kingship* in contradistinction to the other kingdoms or "metals/minerals." The point of Dan 2 remains the inbreaking of God's supreme reign. We also cannot marginalize the "stone," which seems to sketch the humble beginnings of God's kingship in broad strokes, becoming the "mountain" embedded in every faithful Israelite's theological vocabulary. It is where God, the nations and His people reside.

Denying these emphases or story-arcs does not mean we must also deny the historical realities of a future for Israel's sanctuary. By the end of the first century, it is true that there is precedent for a sanctuary in a broader sense. But at no point, is the real temple structure relegated to a memory, or the absence of a temple a foregone conclusion. We can compare this expectation to the hope in a physical, messianic figure—though these actualizations are in flux[95] and the emphases have shifted, the canonical shape, nevertheless, tethers them historically. To argue that Israel's testimony must be either "necessarily historical" or that history is "irrelevant to Israel's faith" is to bypass, what Childs call, "the subtle complexity of the Old Testament."[96] It is a natural activity of the canonical reader "to follow the biblical text in its theological use of historical referentiality."[97] Therefore, whereas many authors see Daniel's preservation of the temple center, we find Daniel *extrapolating* the purpose of the temple structure beyond its physicality. At this point (9:24), the temple is no longer envisioned to be the place where one deals with sin, but is a place within a "city" (v. 24a) where sin no longer reigns.

The temple is indeed paramount and underpins many areas of Jewish theology—the scarcity of details, images or visions by no means lowers its level of importance for Daniel. However, it is precisely in this paucity of description that Daniel directs the reader to the new, grim reality of "non-temple" life. What does worship and holiness look like after the Babylonians or after the "abomination"? How does Daniel's people live under the cloud of temple defilement, especially in light of Israel being the responsible party? We encounter a "holy hill" and "a city called by your name," but Daniel does not utter the words: "Zion" or "holy mountain" (cf. Is 65:11; 66:8). We read of a sanctuary, but without God's presence, without description and without Yahweh's "name"—rather, it is a "byword" (9:16-18; cf. Jer 23:40, 24:9, 29:18, 51:51; Ezek 5:14-15, 22:4). Daniel diverts his energy and emphasis onto the "people" (9:15,

---

[95] Within Qumran and Maccabean circles, the question as to whether the Messiah would resemble an anointed priestly figure (cf. CD 19.10-11) or a latter-day warrior and liberator in the mid-first century was asked with increasing fervor. Gerbern Oegema calls this fluctuation the "two messiah theory" (*Apocalyptic Interpretation of the Bible: Apocalypticism and Biblical Interpretation in Early Judaism, the Apostle Paul, the Historical Jesus, and their Reception History* [London: T&T Clark, 2012], 26; cf. F.M. Strickert, "Damascus Document VII, 10-20 and Qumran Messianic Expectation," in *Revue de Qumran* 47 [1986] 327-50).

[96] Childs, "Response," 57.

[97] Ibid., *OT Theology*, 16.

19-20, 24) who are the true object of his prayer *and* revelation.[98] Taking into account the Persian context in which Dan 9 is to be read (9:1), we know the Temple restoration to be a sensitive subject following Cyrus' decree in 538 BCE. Anderson summarizes the attitude of the day:

> Cyrus the Persian announced that the Judean captives were free to return to their homeland and to begin restoring Jerusalem and its temple (see II Chron 36:22-23 and Ezra 1-3), it was felt that God had bigger plans for the restoration of his people throughout the Second Temple period. Surprisingly, Jewish writers often ignored the rebuilding of the temple in retelling Israel's sacred history. The reason for this was the widespread acknowledgment that the building erected in the late sixth century did not meet the grand expectations that had evolved during the exile.[99]

Discussion of the Sabbath, according to Lev 26:2, is also (commonly) a reason to reflect upon the sanctuary: "You will keep my Sabbaths (שבתת) and revere my sanctuary (מקדש)." The "holy hill," like the theological heightening of the Sabbath, is a vision far off, but is nevertheless a supreme image, as Koch describes: "Der Zionstempel bleibt *Hauptheiligtum*, doch sein Kult wird umgestaltet."[100] Although the land is central to the conditions of Sabbath, it is holy *time* rather than holy space that preoccupies Dan 9:24-27. Like the veiling of the temple in Dan 9, explicit reference to Sabbath is missing despite the presence or "footprint" of the language that commonly encircles the term. With the fronting of the seventy sevens and the Sabbath-heptadic language connected with references to holy space, it is difficult to miss the hallowed position of the Sabbath tradition, partiularly how this holy time is sanctified

---

[98] After interpreting this triad of momentous occasions (9:24b-c), appeal to an anti-Seleucidian program seems less likely. How can we reconcile these assurances of hope, peace and finality (overtly *passive* circumstances) with a propagandist's agenda to incite rebellion (overtly *active* circumstances)? To illustrate the problem, consider how Sweeney bases the production of the book (167-164 BCE) on support for the Judean revolt against Ephiphanes (175-164 BCE). Those interpreters who emphasize the book's intent to mobilize Jewish revolutionaries overlook, I suggest, scenes in which Daniel exhibits some counter-revolutionary behavior ("End of Eschatology," 123). At the end of Dan 10, an angelic messenger "strengthens" (חזק) Daniel, an action repeating three times over the course of two verses (10:18, 19b-c). This same action immediately occurs in the first verse of Dan 11, where Daniel not only "strengthens" (חזק) Darius the Mede, but also "stands" by him (עמד) and "fortifies" him (עוז). It is apparent that Daniel's function is not to promote the dissolution of government or even to use scriptural language as a type of subterfuge. One must, at the very least, concede a tension in Daniel's "political affiliations."

[99] Anderson, *Sin*, 75.

[100] "The Zion-temple remains *Hauptheiligtum*, therefore, the cult follows suit" (Koch, *Das Buch Daniel*, 129, translation mine).

above the temple practices and furniture (Exod 31:13-14). Central to the arch of the passage is the original *Ruhetag* in which the whole of Yahweh's creation is located within the space of his kingdom and rest.[101]

In concluding our analysis of 9:24, we find the writer leaves the answer to Daniel's major question (v. 2; vv. 3-19) open-ended: how long until our sin-debt is paid? Rather than supply a date, the final "decree" envisions a people and place without sin. As for time, all things are to be complete, followed by the long-awaited *Ruhetag* (cf. Gen 2:2-3; Ex 31:13-17). At most, the verse is a "quasi-prophecy" (in predictive terms).[102] "Prophecy," here, is augmented by the promises and language of the LP. The text is elevated above a single prediction because the prospective vision is massive in scope. Not even the alleged "determinism" of 9:24 can give an answer due to its ambiguity. Both vv. 3-19 and v. 24 contain promises unrealized ("to finish [כלה] sin," v.24a) as well as an awe-inspiring account of forgiveness (not just salvation, but "insight and understanding" for Yahweh's people [9:22; 12:3, 10]). A fullness of time is to come. If the seventy sevens are set *first* in the summary, then the finality of sin is in the *center*—a hope that reaches back to Leviticus 25-26, Jeremiah 25-29 and is echoed by communities who look forward to a similar end (cf. 2 Macc 6:14-15).[103]

2.3. Daniel 9:25

Daniel 9:25 follows the constructions in 9:24 with a logical course of action: with the time and promise both revealed, you must *now* "know and understand" (v.25a). From this point onward, the course of the seventy sevens unfolds. It is also from this point that we encounter a large deposit of chronologies, readings, historical allusions and submissions by interpreters. These submissions offer nearly every conceivable configuration of these three

---

[101] Although Daniel is shifting the language of "rest" to include a more holistic resolution to God's creation—one which includes Israel's judgments—he is, nevertheless, tapping into a well-known sequence of Jewish thought: dissolution and restoration. Sweeney considers this sequence a "basic pattern" that "calls for the building and rebuilding of the ideal Jewish people and its relationship to the world at large..." ("Foundations," 186).

[102] Goldingay compares the quasi-prophetic status of 9:24 to the status of "actual prophecy" demonstrated by 9:27 (231). I suggest recalibrating this tag to prophetic interpretation, since this section of Dan 9 is a substitution for the vision sections in chs. 7-8 (231).

[103] "With the other nations the Lord waits patiently, staying their punishment until they reach the full measure of their sins. Quite otherwise is His decree for us, in order that He should not have to punish us after we have come to the complete measure of our sins" (2 Macc 6:14-15). When a reader joins in this call for the "end of sin," he or she begins to recognize the "process of restoration" referred to in Lev 25-26. But, lest we reduce Daniel's interpretation to an exegesis of Leviticus alone, we must consider the vision of the prophet (likely Jeremiah's contribution) and the future of the holy "city" (cf. Jer 33:9) in what follows.

heptadic figures (7 wks-62 wks-1 wk). Just as 9:24 begins with a "decree" (חתך) "against your people and your city" (על־עמך ועל־עיר),[104] so do we read of "a word going forth" (מן־מצא דבר; 9:25b) to restore Jerusalem, a decree ending at an indeterminate time.[105] From there, a shadowy figure arises: "an anointed one (משׁח; 9:24g "למשׁח"), a prince."[106] Over the course of these 69 weeks (9:25-26), this (same?) leader is "cut off" (כרת)[107] and is subject to some type of upheaval or overpowering force (ואין לו).[108] Is it the figure Onias III (171 B.C.; cf. 2 Macc 4.23-28), Joshua, Zerubbabel or Jesus of Nazareth? Daniel 9.26c leaves the referent open-ended: who or what experiences an "end" (קצו)?[109] What do interpreters make of these questions? Fortuitously, the list of rulers from both the

---

[104] "Against" (על) as opposed to "about" (ESV) since the decree appears to be an indictment or "legal debit" (Montgomery, 371). This rendering is also consistent with the indictments regarding Sabbath violation in Lev 25.

[105] Daniel 9:25 marks another obstacle for interpreters: how do we separate the verse breaks? The lack of punctuation allows for a vast number of translations: "from the going out of the word to restore and build Jerusalem to the coming of an anointed one, a prince, there shall be seven weeks. Then for sixty-two weeks ..." (ESV); "from the issuing of the command to restore and rebuild Jerusalem until an anointed one, a prince arrives, there will be a period of seven weeks and sixty-two weeks" (NET); OG omits any reference to seven or sixty-two weeks whereas θ' resembles the NET. Yet again, Daniel's style of ambiguity and imagery jostles any attempts at a referential timeline.

[106] The figure behind the text could be Cyrus (cf. Zech 1:12), known to be an "anointed" ruler (cf. Is 45:1). But this title does not explain the restoration of "Jerusalem," the title "prince" (נגיד), and the strange comments in 9:26 stretches this association too far. Joshua, the high priest (cf. Zech 6:11-12) and Zerubbabel (cf. Ezra 5:2; Hag 1:1; Zech 4:6-10) are also candidates. Of course, in order to avoid the odd remark in v.26 (יכרת משׁיח), scholars separate the משׁיח into two figures; for example, Redditt, "Daniel 9," 246.

[107] כרת may refer to a separation from a community (cf. Gen 9:11) or the death penalty (cf. Lev 7:20); it is noteworthy that those who do not "afflict themselves" on the tenth day of the seventh month (Lev 23:28-29) will be "cut off" (כרת) from his or her people.

[108] The construction ואין לו is highly generalized, an "unexplained crux" to the verse (Montgomery, 381).

[109] The referent for the 3ms possessive could be the immediate ms noun, נגיד, or the prior ms noun, הקדשׁ, which makes more contextual sense if the עם (26b) causes the subsequent "flood" of destruction (26c). Note the text-critical possibilities: MT ואין לו; Collins sees a mistaken emendation (originally ואין עוזר לו) "and there will be no help for him/from him" from 11.45; q'= "he will have no judgment" (ואין און לו); Collins could be right since the construction אין + a prepositional pronoun tends to carry a participle (cf. Gen 40:8, 41:24). On the other hand, some instances render the construction as a normal copula + object ("there is no ..." or "he has no..."; Exod 22:2, Lev 11:10, 1 Sam 27:1, Is 55:1); these have a sense of possession, always with an object, substantival participle or preceded by a relative clause marker (אשׁר).

Persian/Hellenistic sphere and the Hasmonean sphere provide many potentialities for historical reference.

2.4. Various Breakdowns of the Heptadic Units

By highlighting several constructions, we can demonstrate the sharp divergences that occur when we parse out the "weeks" of the seventy sevens. For those committed to deciphering the historical allusions, these verses tend to describe the tyranny of Antiochus IV and the dissolution of the high priesthood.[110] For example, if we begin at Jeremiah's prophecy (605 BCE) and continue to Cyrus's accession (556 BCE), which is a span of 49 years or seven "weeks," and to the death of the high priest Onias III (171 BCE). After this span of 434 years or 62 "weeks," an insignificant passage of time leads to the rededication of the temple in 164 BCE. The alleged 434 years (62 weeks) assigned to the accession of Cyrus spanning to the death of Onias III is exceeded by some 70 years. As Adler observes, this is not a miscalculation or "an idiomatic attempt by the author to update Jeremiah's prophecy."[111]

A *Christian* messianic model, on the other hand, frequently outlines the chronology as follows: beginning with the period of Nehemiah (445-444 BCE) to the crucifixion of Jesus or Passover (32-33 CE), a sum of roughly (?) 483 years, proponents of this model "suspend" the final seven years to a future week.[112] The *Testament of Levi* 16-17 is an example of constantly reworked heptadic chronologies that move toward the high priest, Jesus Christ (*T. Levi* 18). In response to the failed Jewish priesthood, the author uses theological chronology to move from the seventy weeks of Daniel to the "eschatological

---

[110] For a source that highlights these comparisons, see Hanan Eshel, "The Roots of the Hasmonean Revolt: The Reign of Antiochus IV," in *The Dead Sea Scrolls and the Hasmonean State* (Grand Rapids: Eerdmans and Jerusalem: Yad Ben-Zvi, 2008), 13-27.

[111] Adler, "Apocalyptic Survey," 203. Adler sees a precedent for idiomatic updating in 2 Chr 36:21.

[112] One of the original submissions of this model that gained a great deal of traction in conservative Christian circles is by H.W. Hoehner ("Daniel's Seventy Weeks and New Testament Chronology," BibSac 132 [1975] 47-65); see also R. Anderson, *The Coming Prince* (London: Hodder, 1881). Koch divides these two models (historicist/Christian) into "inclusive" and "exclusive" approaches (*Das Buch Daniel*, 152). Gerhard Hasel critiques these "systemic" approaches and identifies the "basic problem" to be the assumptions underpinning calendrical statements (e.g. Artaxerxes' decree on Nisan 1 [March 5] in 444 BCE) and doctrinal differences (e.g. the "gap theory," demarcating the Church Age from the other "weeks") ("Interpretations of the Chronology of the Seventy Weeks," in *70 Weeks, Leviticus, Nature of Prophecy: Daniel and Revelation Committee Series 3* [ed. Frank Holbrook; Washington D.C.: Review and Herald, 1986], 4-5). He concludes his assessment stating, "there is ... no agreement as to whether this period is to be understood as completely literal, or partially literal and partially symbolic or totally symbolic" (7).

high priest."[113] Most chronologies are a variation of these two constructions, but both timelines exhibit the same hermeneutical inconsistency and, as Goldingay puts it, "arbitrariness."[114]

Some configure the weeks to accord in a *non-linear* fashion. Sweeney appoints each section an "appropriate" set of historical events regardless of whether or not the years run in a consecutive order. At some points, he divides the epochs by entire decades. According to Sweeney, these events most likely coordinate with the vague activities outlined by 9:25-27: the seven weeks of 9:25 span the Exile (586 BCE) to the decree of Cyrus (536 BCE); the sixty-two weeks of 9:25-26 span Cyrus' decree (536 BCE) to the "enthronement" of the high priest Aristobulus I, who was also the first self-appointed Hasmonean monarch (104 BCE); the final week of 9:27 begins with Aristobulus' appointment and ends with the succession of his brother, Alexander Jannaeus (103 BCE), who married Alexandra Salome and claiming the title "high priest and king" of Judah.[115] A similar approach is outlined in Berner's interpretation: the first seven yearweeks initiates an "effektiven Dauer des Exils" with a pointed, heptadic significance while the final yearweek functions as an "unbestreitbarem Bezug zur Verfasserzeit" (170/169-164/163) into the midpoint of the "Kultreform Antiochus IV."[116] Again, the interpreter is forced to manipulate the sequence of events, even stagger them, in order to accommodate the vagueness of these numerical images.[117]

---

[113] Cf. Berner, "The Heptadic Chronologies of Testament of Levi 16-17 and Their Sources," *JSOP* 22.1 (2012) 40-52.

[114] Goldingay comments on the two primary timelines and the assumptions that underlie each chronological instance: "In the case of the first, it is not obvious why two partly concurrent figures should be added together. In the case of the second, it is not obvious why the word about building a restored Jerusalem should be connected with Artaxerxes' commission of Nehemiah to rebuild the walls of Jerusalem; nor why we should accept the basis of the computation, that of a 360-day year; nor why we should date Nehemiah's commission in 444 B.C. or Jesus' crucifixion in A.D. 32—the computation requires one or the other, but the usually preferred dates are 445 and A.D. 30 or 33" (*Daniel*, 257).

[115] See details of Sweeney's timeline, *Tanak*, 455-57. Setting aside the problem with inconsistent numerical values (i.e. the final "week"), the language must stretch to the point of breaking if we accommodate Sweeney's historical overlay. One major example, in 9:25, is the secondary reference to the anointed one as "prince" (נגיד) which we must assume is Aristobulus I. However, in as much as the Hasmonean monarchy functioned beneath the Greek political complex, Aristobulus I was a "king," not a prince. Moreover, Daniel uses the term "king" (מלך) often and appears to reserve it for particular figures (1:1; 5:1; 6:6; 7:17; 11:2-3). We must also agree with Sweeney's application of the punctuation in 9:25 before we make any further judgments.

[116] Berner, *Jahre*, 95.

[117] The false assumption that one must recalibrate the times and events of the text (for the text's sake), is not lost on Childs. It is often "assumed," he notes, "that the

Others believe it possible to *replace* one figure with another in order to achieve the desired alignment of time and event. Bergsma does just that in his rendering of the seventy sevens:

> It would be better to recognize that Dan. 9.24 announces a 70-week penitential period that does not start with Jeremiah's prophecy of '70 years', but rather is subsequent to the Jeremianic period. Cyrus' decree—the 'word to restore and build Jerusalem' of Dan. 9.25—terminates the '70 years' of Jeremiah and inaugurates the '70 weeks' of years of Daniel. Jeremiah's 70 years were unsuccessful in producing repentance, so a seven-fold longer penitential period is to begin at their termination.[118]

Constructions that favor the Seleucid interpretation are not without fault either, though these interpreters are the majority. It is the reality of these theological texts, as Childs observes that, "at times, the witness to events is so thoroughly impregnated by Israel's faith that the depiction bears little resemblance to our ordinary understanding of history."[119] Here, we encounter the problems that afflict those who fully commit to the referential system operating in a Maccabean reading of 9:24-27. Therein, also, is the root of Childs' dissatisfaction with such an approach (although he himself dated the material to the second century BCE). Speaking to the scene of contemporary Daniel scholarship, Childs concludes that, "the emphasis has fallen on sketching the profiles of the diverse and conflicting ideologies of post-exilic Judaism, and in determining the relation between religious beliefs and the political struggles of the period."[120] In an intense pursuit of the historical references behind the Antiochene crisis, it is not just possible, but likely that a reader will forego any theological explanation for the "chronology" of 9:24-27.

Two reminders are necessary before interpreters "unpack" 9:25-27 (or the seventy sevens): (1) the breakdown of heptadic sections, the 7-62-1 week constructions, are part of the theological message emitted by the seventy sevens of 9:24; (2) the parallel commentary provided in Dan 8, 11 that speaks to the events of 9:24-27. First, we consider the sequence of heptadic constructions. Most contributions isolate only a few events (and allusions) at the expense of a holistic chronology. Disconnecting text and history encourages a reading that does not reflect the goals of the 7-62-7 heptadic sequence. Why do the weeks divide into this tri-partite, rounded formation? In a chronographical context, how do these divisions communicate theologically? That significant events

---

time-conditionality of the canonical witness can be theologically 'corrected' by means of historical critical reconstructions ("Response," 55).

[118] Bergsma, "Penitential Prayer," 60.
[119] Childs, "Response," 57.
[120] Ibid., *IOTS*, 613.

occurred *exactly* at the beginning and end of each of these three divisions (7 wks–62 wks–1 wk) is unlikely and, as we observed through the inexactness of date-event specificity, should be read within the Sabbath-heptadic context. Many studies on 9:25-27 seem to neglect the context: the necessary "completion" of sins and the enduring character of God's people in exile. Omitting this context invites an approach governed by nothing more than the hopes of securing a historical figure or event on a disjointed constellation of historical points. These groupings, rather, indicate a pattern of kingdom ascendancy for a period of "seven weeks," the turmoil, violence and ultimate downfall of the kingdom for the majority of time ("sixty-two weeks"), and the final period in which the circuit of oppressive kingdoms is cut and the pattern *itself* comes to an end ("one week"). We are indeed tracking a *motif* or set of concrete images as well as actions and/or objects that recur through a particular narrative.[121] In this case, images that are concurrent with the Sabbath-heptadic stream of tradition.

Second, the inner-Danielic references between ch. 9 and chs. 8-11 give a more resolute picture of vv. 25-27. The unity of the book itself invites the reader to consider inner-Danielic references. Childs notes that, "the last vision in chs. 10-11 with an epilogue in ch. 12 ... explicitly develops the themes of ch. 2 along with the interpretation of chs. 7-9."[122] Seitz continues this train of thought, commenting on Childs' observation:

> Though Daniel appeared as a figure in these later chapters, as he had in the first chapters, what was at issue was God's prior word pressing for fulfillment, beyond the moment of its original utterance or seeming reception, and this high view of God's word did not require anything more than obedience to it–even when it seemed, for it could only seem, to remain unfulfilled.[123]

The words of 9:24-27 press forward in fulfillment and are not sealed in with a single community.

References from Dan 8 indeed come into play and enhance the reading of 9:24-27. A handful of scholars associate Dan 8-9 so closely, that the latter becomes a *variation* on the former.[124] Associations between the two chapters are plentiful and certainly strengthen this position. Both chapters begin with ruler

---

[121] David Beldman, "Literary Approaches and Old Testament Interpretation," in *Hearing the Old Testament: Listening for God's Address* (Grand Rapids: Eerdmans, 2012), 72; see also Robert Alter, *The Art of Biblical Narrative* (New York: Basic, 1981), 95. Few would identify Dan 9 with narrative, but some scholars have detected narrative qualities to the passage (De Long, "Daniel and the Narrative Integrity.")

[122] Childs, *IOTS*, 617.

[123] Seitz, *Figured Out*, 31.

[124] The only marker that differentiates Daniel 9, according to Berner, is its relationship to Dan 8:27 and Daniel's return to his court service (Berner, *Jahre*, 21).

and reign: "the third year of Belshazzar" (8:1) and "the first year of Darius" (9:1). A "little horn" (8:9) opposes the "prince of the host" to whom belongs the "sanctuary" and "offering" (8:11-13). In 9:25-26, an "anointed prince" precedes the 62 weeks (9:25) and an "anointed one" who is "cut off" prior to the "prince who is to come" maintains a force that "destroys" the city and "sanctuary" (9:24-26). Both chapters also include a span of time: "2300 evenings and mornings" (8:14) and "seventy sevens" (9:24).[125] Chapter 8, I suggest, is an actualization of the pattern outlined in Dan 9, hence the links between the two without perfect parallelism. The positioning, therefore, is not accidental.[126] With Dan 8 and 11 as actualized versions of the patterns in 9:24-27, these depictions, in turn, make sense of the 7-62-1 dividers (or figural waypoints) throughout the passage.

These verses (9:25-27), therefore, are not part of a repetition—recycling a task that could have been performed by Daniel 8 and/or 11—but are a paradigm for interpretation. Daniel 9 does create a *break* in an otherwise unbroken line of visions.[127] It is true that Dan 9 connects and orders our understanding of chs. 8-11, but such description also works *in reverse*. In offering detailed accounts of kingdom upheaval, we see the theological function of Dan 9:24-27 "in action" within the text of Daniel itself.

2.5. To 'Know and Understand' the Word Going Forth (v. 25a)

With these two reminders in place, we can move to the opening phrases of 9:25: to "know and understand." Compared to studies on 9:3-19 and 9:24-27, the call for Daniel to "know and understand" (ותדע ותשכל) receives little attention. It is a critical retrospective, however, on the interpretation language in 9:2—"to understand (בין)...the number of years." The combination of interpretation-language illumines another point that is significant in any reading of Dan 9:24-26: the context of *wisdom*. Along with the language in the first frame ("understand" [בין]; 9:2), one can make a convincing argument for the influence and exercise of wisdom throughout the chapter.[128] Outside of Proverbs,

---

[125] As with Daniel's seventy sevens, if we assign a value of "years" to 2300 days, the reader would require a 330-day calendar which aligns with neither the solar or lunar arrangements popular at the time.

[126] It may not be coincidental that Daniel's interpretation of "desolations" (9:17-18, 26-27) is linked to the last verse of ch. 8, where Daniel is "appalled" (שמם) by his vision.

[127] Reinhard Kratz, "Die Visionen des Daniel," in *Schriftauslegung in der Schrift*, 219-36, here 236. For a longer treatment, see *Das Judentum im Zeitalter des Zweiten Tempels, Kleine Schriften I* (Tübingen: Mohr Siebeck, 2013), 240-44.

[128] Moving beyond the limits of Dan 9, we detect a broad network of wisdom-terms spread throughout the book—perhaps even at key points (introduction—1:4, 17, 20; conclusion—12:3-4, 8, 10). The network of wisdom language shifts attention from an over-focalization on "scribal" wisdom many assign to the book. B. Lang reads the whole book as an expanded "novella" (cf. Esther, Ruth): "In the 160's BCE, the older Daniel story (Dan 1-6), a court novel about a Jewish boy who made a career at the Baby-

Daniel uses the term שׂכל the most.[129] Here, the reader is called to participate in Daniel's puzzling over the unfolding of the seventy sevens. Along with the theological markers, 7-62-1 weeks, we notice a space for Daniel (and the reader) to articulate how Yahweh's decree will appear.

As it happens, wisdom is what the exilic community sorely needs; they refuse to "listen" (9:6, 10-11). This need is reflected in the structure of the book, as Childs comments, noting how "the stories about Daniel in the first part of the book describe him as one granted 'understanding in all visions and dreams' (1:17), which are then recounted in the second part of the book."[130] Daniel is the embodiment of wisdom and understanding, the representative exilee and an example of how Israel is supposed to relate to Yahweh's revelatory character. Childs continues the thought, saying, "the challenge of the visions of the last chapters which call for endurance to hardship as faithful servants of God is illustrated, above all, in the example of Daniel and his companions." Converse to this embodiment, readers are called to "know and understand" by receiving/hearing the material and, thereby, locating themselves on the book's theological map (see Chapter 6). These concepts appear contradictory, but actually function side-by-side, ebbing and flowing from the foreground to the background, depending on the shape of the received text. The canonical shape of the text, therefore, affords a place for subsequent generations of interpreters and communities who are to "know and understand" the following texts.

The first timeframe to consider spans from "the going out of the word to restore and build Jerusalem until the time of the anointed one, seven weeks." For some interpreters, the "word" (דבר) is obvious—it is a reference to Daniel's "word" which the angelic messenger answered, offering an understanding of the vision (9:23).[131] Or does this "word" simply play on Jeremiah's role—it is a "word...to the prophet Jeremiah" (9:2) that is now a word proceeding *out* or going forth from Daniel (9:23, 25; 10:1, 11-12)?[132] Scholars also read a human decree in v. 25, ranging from one of the decrees in the book of Ezra to Cyrus'

---

lonian court, was enlarged to include visions that echo the Syrian persecution of the 160's and the rise of the Maccabean liberation movement" ("The 'Writings,'" 59).

[129] One might make the case Daniel is the wise response to the negative portrayal of Jehoiachin at the end of the book of Jeremiah: Jehoiachin was freed (Jer 52:31; cf. Dan 1:18), took a seat alongside Nebuchadnezzar (v. 32; cf. Dan 2:48), put off prison garments (v. 33; cf. Dan 5:29), ate at the kings table (cf. Dan 1:5) and, finally, was supplied with all his daily needs (v. 34; cf. Dan 2:49, 5:29, 6:28). This account immediately follows the recounting of how many exiles were captured in Judah and Jerusalem, and transported by the king of Babylon and the captain of the guard (52:28-31; cf. Dan 1:1).

[130] Childs, *IOTS*, 614.

[131] Schlenke, 118; Collins, *Daniel*, 354;

[132] To be sure, the coherence of the chapter is stronger by means of this phrase— the word from Daniel begins when he confesses (9:3-4) and receives a response at the conclusion of the interpretation (9:23-27).

own decree.¹³³ Still others trace the "word" back to Jeremiah's prophecy in "the fourth year of Jehoiakim" (Jer 25:1).¹³⁴ In terms of these human decrees, Collins himself states, "the starting point is uncertain" and requires the interpreter to elaborate with chronological exactitude. An attachment to Jeremiah's prophecy is a possibility, due to the Jeremianic language throughout vv. 24-27 (see below); however, the seventy-years prophecy in Jeremiah does not speak of the restoration of Jerusalem. To which "word going out" is the messenger referring?

Reference to the "word going out" (יצא דבר) in 9:23 is the likeliest option, but this option comes with two important caveats. First, the theme of "word" is not an abstraction created *ex nihilo*, but progresses from Dan 1-6 into 7-12. The "word" in 9:23, 25 is one component of a pattern—דבר or the Aramaic מלה-in which a matter, question or circumstance confronts Daniel (1:20; 2:15). Visions or commands, even the "writing on the wall" (5:15), that Daniel received earlier in the book follow this pattern (2:4, 9, 23; 4:30). When the word or content was received, it required wisdom and understanding, not only to determine its meaning, but to assure its trustworthiness (2:9; 6:12). Language involving "word" (דבר,מלה), "interpretation" (פשר) or the variations of "decree" (פתגם, גזרה, טעם, דת) from earlier in the book correlates with the themes we find later in Dan 7-12. Such a connection follows if these revelations are meant to unveil the final Ruler, Yahweh, and the declarations implicit in His rulership.

Second, evidence suggests that the preceding *prayer* can function as the "word going forth." The multiplicity of the "word" throughout the book, the definition's connection to Daniel's vocation and the "sealing" of these words must all be taken into account when commenting on the "word going out" in 9:25. Viewing the prayer as a type of "word" may seem strange at first, but when we compare this occurrence to the occurrences throughout the book, we uncover a correlation between the "word" and the content of the visions: the "word" at the time of the "third year of Cyrus" (10:1, 11) or even the "book" (ספר) in which Daniel is to "keep the words (הדברים) secret" (12:4). In Dan 9, the prayer (9:3-19) takes the place of the content. The author is then asking the reader to consider the confession as such. The confession (vv. 3-19) and the eschatological imagery (vv. 24-27) are supposed to be read together.¹³⁵ Daniel's "word" recounts the story of Israel's sin as anchored in the LP, and it is the decree (vv. 24-27) that reveals how such a trajectory will end.

---

¹³³ Doukhan argues for one of three decrees from the book of Ezra: Cyrus (1:1-4), Darius (6:6-12) or Artaxerxes (7:12-26), which he leans toward in the end ("The Seventy Weeks of Daniel 9: An Exegetical Study," *AUSS* 17 [1979], 15).

¹³⁴ Montgomery, 391; Koch, *Das Buch Daniel*, 150.

¹³⁵ Again, joining Jeremiah, Leviticus, and the LP with 9:24-27 has always been implied by the shape of the chapter.

2.6. Identifying the "Anointed" Figures (מָשִׁיחַ)

With the "word going forth" at the beginning, these first seven weeks end with the rise of an "anointed" figure characterized as a "prince" (נָגִיד מָשִׁיחַ). Reference to an anointed "prince" (נָגִיד) confirms the suspicions of some interpreters, while baffling others. Those whose suspicions are confirmed read a clear reference to Epiphanes in ch. 8, with no small amount of help from 11:5.[136] Reference to an Israelite "prince" in 9:25 logically fits into the assumed Antiochene context. However, those baffled by the occurrence of "prince" in 9:25-26 have good reason to puzzle over the implications of locking down his identity. First, the term נָגִיד is not necessarily common to the OT, and out of the three instances it is used in Daniel, it occurs twice in 9:25-26. Also, whereas the closest variation of this figure—the "prince" (שַׂר) of the host" in 8:11—goes into more detail (comparatively speaking), no description is given of the anointed prince in 9:25 aside from being "cut off" in v. 26.

Rereading the Qumran material, we discover these sources circulate their own understanding of 9:25-27, but do so through the interconnectivity of related texts: in the case of "the anointed prince" (9:25), many Qumran readers looked to the messianic figure of Is 52:7 and 61:2.[137] This prince is also the one who "brings good news" (Is 52:7) and "proclaims the year of the Lord's favor" (Is 61:2). But even these scrolls reflect what Oegema calls a "many-sidedness" to their interpretation of the events in Dan 9:24-27.[138] Within the scrolls themselves is a shared diversity and tension stemming from a rich interpretive sophistication and a long history of volatile, socio-political upheaval (e.g. Seleucid/Ptolemaean priestly class, and later Sadducee, Hasidaean, Essene, Pharisaic and Hasmonean rulership).[139]

The *Melchizedek* scroll (11QMelch) also submits an interpretation of the "anointed" figure. The figure "is the anointed of the spirit, as Dan[iel] said [about him: 'Until an anointed, a prince, it is seven weeks' (Dan 9:25) and the messenger of] good who announces salvation is the one about whom it is written ['to comfort the [afflicted,' (Is 61:2) its interpretation] to instruct them in all the ages of the world."[140] The Qumran scribe not only links the anointed

---

[136] Adele Collins adds another reference to Antiochus IV Epiphanes as the "Prince of Greece (שַׂר־יָוָן) who is to come" (10:20) (*Cosmology*, 59). However, the long-standing tradition of princely figures relating to their respective angelic guardian makes such a reading difficult (10:13, 20-21; 12:1; cf. 8:11, 25). The reference is to the angelic being to which belongs a mysterious union between he and a specific leadership figure (cf. the prince of Tyre in Ezek 28:2). Goldingay sees some "recollection" of the King of Tyre by Daniel's use of נָגִיד and מָשִׁיחַ (*Daniel*, 232). Daniel emphasizes the identities of the angelic beings rather than the human figures to whom they are connected.

[137] Cf. *11QMelch*, Col. III, Frg. 4, Lines 17-25.

[138] Oegema, *Apocalyptic*, 28.

[139] Ibid.

[140] Lines 15-23. A connection to the initial scene of priestly consecration may be in view (cf. Lev 8:11), where Aaron "sprinkles" (נזה) the altar in order to "anoint" (מָשַׁח) the altar. This scene holds special significance for Dan 9:24-27 as well.

figure of 9:25 to a *pattern* of "anointed" figures, of which "Cyrus" (Is 52) is one iteration, but goes further by reconnecting Daniel's words to Is 52:7—the "good news" of the king of Zion's return.[141]

In the scroll of *Blessings* (1QSb), dated within the same bracket as pesher-Isaiah above (150-175 BCE), there is reference to a "prince of the community" who is also "anointed" (5.23-29; cf. Numbers 24; Jer 1:18, 5:14, Isa 49:2). Similar to the conferral of "servant" status, this coupling of "anointed prince" is a mantle that is transferrable and subject to disambiguation depending on the time, place, community and, ultimately, Yahweh's providence. Even if these communities (exilic "Israel," Essene) match the reference in 9:25 to a single leader, the dominant pattern—for which the canonical shape is responsible—welcomes subsequent interpretation. Figures, such as the anointed prince (9:25), belong within this pattern of governmental unrest.[142] Calling these leaders "anointed" does not break the pattern—rather, it is a descriptor that is well attested throughout the LP (Isa 45:1).

Attention to the context of the chapter, the whole book and proximate reception history (e.g. Qumran) all point to an alternative: the anointed figure is part of the large-scale pattern throughout the book of Daniel, namely, the rise and fall of human rulers in light of Yahweh's own impending rule.[143] Still, when we come to 9:24-27, the tone is darker and the *leitmotif* of monarchs claiming the Jewish faith (2:47; 3:28-29; 3:31-33; 4:34; 6:26-29) has dissolved.[144]

---

[141] Coming back to the lineage of servant, of which Daniel is a part, the Melchizedek scroll demonstrates how the mantle of servanthood is a transitional role. The role is dependent upon Yahweh's freedom and divine governmental architecture.

[142] Increasingly, the turmoil of the early first century BCE—first century CE called into question the occupational traits of the expected Messiah. Would he be a historical leader clothed as an eschatological figure (dominant before 100 BCE) or would he be "a prophet and (more often) a priest and/or king" (cf. Oegema, *Apocalyptic*, 27)? If he is one of the priesthood, we have Jason, Onias III or Onias IV. With regards to the identity of the figure in 9:25, both text and *history* inject their own dose of ambiguity.

[143] This pattern of governmental turbulence is both implicit and explicit within the book of Daniel. Implicitly, we see imperial reigns change hands at the book's key structural points (1:1; 5:1; 6:1, 28). Explicitly, the core statements of the book in Dan 2:20-23 and the dream of the statue (2:31-45) introduce the pattern in no uncertain terms. In Dan 7-12, the pattern continues: three human reigns followed by a fourth and final reign of upheaval (7:2-8; 8:3-25; 11:2-45). Like the relationship between Dan 2 and whole of Dan 1-6, so also Dan 7 functions as a "mission statement" for Dan 7-12.

[144] Schmid, *Old Testament*, 159-60. Schmid's *leitmotif* allows for a highly politicized reading that connects "thematically" to the messianic status of Cyrus in Is 45:1—this permits Schmid to reconstruct a shared tradition between Dan 1-6 (deemed Persian literature, 5th-4th BCE) and the work of Trito-Isaiah (160). Such "legends" (Dan 1-6), according to Schmid, may encourage certain thematic links (cf. Isa 45:1 and "name-declaration" in Psalms 145-147). However, one would expect such a *leitmotif* to permeate Dan 7-12—a text that is far more politically charged—yet, the text recasts the new government-powers in a different light. Schmid's argument may hold more weight in

Daniel 1-6 depicts how "God rules over his creation by means of the dominant empire at the time, which is responsible to him and that ... also acknowledges him as the sole God and ruler."[145] Daniel 7-12 intensifies the acknowledgement of Yahweh "as the sole God and ruler," but the human reigns are viewed as upstarts and increasingly adversarial to the presence of Yahweh's rule. Of course, this dark turn does not preclude God's intervention and guidance within the affairs of government (cf. 11:1-2).

2.7. Ambiguity within the Heptadic Units: "Seven and Sixty-Two Weeks"

Apart from the mysterious identity of the "anointed" figure, the rendering of 9:25 is another difficulty—the lack of punctuation leaves the text open to different chronologies: "Know therefore and understand that from the going out of the word to restore and build Jerusalem to the coming of an anointed one, a prince, there will be seven weeks and sixty-two weeks (ושבעים ששים ושנים שבעים שבעה) it will be built again with squares and moat, but in a troubled time."

Read like this, the verse may either separate the seven weeks from sixty-two weeks or keep both figures together: "seven weeks and sixty-two weeks" (69 weeks). With the phrase "after sixty-two weeks" (v. 26a), our initial move is to determine whether this block of weeks is its own unit apart from the seven prior weeks or if this phrase places us sixty-two weeks *into* a larger block of sixty-nine weeks. The OG author, for example, seems to clarify his position by fronting the figures in 9:26 and repeating the phrase again in 9:27. Of course, the multiplied sum of years in the OG attempts to align with Jesus' arrival and, perhaps, Theodotian (LXX2), who combines "seven and sixty-two weeks" until "he/it will return" (επιστρέψει). If one chooses to join the timeframes together, the reader can easily equate the figure from 9:25 with the "anointed" in 9:26, who follows the sixty-nine-week unit (cf. the Greek versions and NIV).

This syntactical ambiguity leaves us with a question: why is this portion of the breakdown divided in *this* way? Berner reads the 62 weeks as "der geschichtstheologisch motivierten *Binnengliederung*," outlining the march of time from the coming of an anointed figure (v. 25b), and the rebuilding of the "city," through the downfall of an anointed figure and city (v. 26), and, finally, up to the last week of the "covenant" (v. 27a). Presumably, the anointed prince plays his role "in a troubled time" (בצוק העתים; v. 25) and comes to a nondescript end. Interpreters slice the passage up to align with an assortment of political moments: Zerubbabel, the high priest Joshua (cf. Zech 4:14), or one from the line of Onias, and so on. Yet, the 62-week unit, though puzzling, remains straightforward in its overall execution—the majority of the seventy sevens follows the rise and fall of a royal figure, embroiled within war and nation-building, resulting in an inglorious demise.

7-12; however, his theme does not sufficiently track alongside the larger (shifting) pattern of government upheaval throughout the book.

[145] Schmid, *Old Testament*, 160.

As mentioned above in our understanding of 9:25-27, if we assign exact dates, figures and events to these blocks of heptadic time, we lose sight of Daniel's "kingdom perspective."[146] As with the chaotic forces behind and within the kingdoms prior (Dan 1-8), the author "dramatizes" Yahweh's kingdom-to-come and heightens the Sabbath-heptadic imagery in order to convey this amplification.[147] Similarly, Sumner notices a parallel between the presentation of the kingdoms in Dan 1-6 and the presentation of kingdoms in Daniel 9.[148] The message of 9:24-27 will inevitably gel with the overall message of the book of Daniel. As within the rise and fall of figures in 9:24-27, so also do we detect a correlation with the rising and falling of leaders and empires earlier in the book—to fill in the information that the text itself omits is an activity foreign to the grain of the theological message. The figure is not one historical referent nor is the construction *purely* symbolic as not to refer to anyone at any time, but refers, in reality, to the ascendant monarchs ruling human kingdoms.

Also, what of "Jerusalem" in this section of weeks? Over the course of the "seven weeks" (v. 25a) and the period of turmoil, namely "sixty-two weeks," the "restoration" (שׁוּב?) of Jerusalem arises in the background. For many readers, we need not look any further than Cyrus' edict (539 BCE) to determine the meaning of the construction (cf. 2 Chr 36:22-23; Ezra 1:1-4; Isa 44:24-28).[149] But, as shown above, the time-images as they stand do not accurately align the calculations with their respective events. Nevertheless, the task of restoring and rebuilding a destroyed "Jerusalem" is in view. The confluence of "Jerusalem" references in Dan 9—five out of ten in this chapter—is not by chance. The constant threat of destruction is an ever-present reality for Israel, hence the lament and repetition throughout Daniel's confession: "the desolations of *Jerusalem*" (v. 2), "the inhabitants of *Jerusalem*" (v. 7), a "great calamity ... against *Jerusalem*" (v. 12), God's "wrath" against "*Jerusalem*" (v. 16a), and "*Jerusalem* and your people" as a "byword" (v. 16c). The promise may be vague, but it stands alongside the promise to end sin (v. 24) and is, therefore, part of the same divine decree. We must remember the triadic construction (v. 24) is connected, both theologically and chronologically, with Daniel's "people" and "holy city" (v. 24a). One might say this "restoration" of Jerusalem (v. 25)—which includes Yahweh's saints—is an undercurrent of 9:24-27.

---

[146] VanGemeren, *Interpreting the Prophetic Word: An Introduction to the Prophetic Literature of the Old Testament* (Grand Rapids: Zondervan, 1996), 342.

[147] Ibid., 345.

[148] Wells and Sumner, *Daniel*, 98.

[149] For these same readers, the obvious starting point of the larger seventy sevens is the exile of 586 BCE. Collins shows the flaw in this logic: "Some scholars allow 586 B.C.E. as a possible starting point because the 'seven weeks' until the rebuilding of Jerusalem is then almost exact. The only capture of Jerusalem recorded in the Book of Daniel, however, is dated to the third year of Jehoiakim in Dan 1:1, and there is no mention of a destruction in 586 B.C.E." (*Daniel*, 355).

Restoring the city with "squares and moats" (רחב, חרוץ) is another strange feature in this building project. Goldingay feels these are distinct features of a "material" promise, and not just the stylized musings of a poet.[150] An actual restoration is envisioned. With the constant threat of foreign attack, one would expect reference to "walls" (cf. Neh 2:13, 4:7; Ezra 4:12-13, 16), especially in light of Jeremiah's pointed account: "The Chaldeans burned the king's house and the house of the people, and *broke down the walls* of Jerusalem" (39:8; cf. Lam 2:7). But when we read the sixty-two-week account of Jerusalem's accursed pattern of oppression and destruction, mention of a "square and moat" links to the demolition of a city. In Deut 13:16, Moses instructs Israel in the protocol meant for corrupt, idolatrous cities: once Israel locates all idol worshippers and contraband within the city, God's people must "gather all its spoil into the midst of its open square (רחב) and burn the city with all its spoil ... [I]t will be a heap forever. It will not be built again." In this image, the "square" is the center of a city's judgment and, ironically, the place where Israel was supposed to eliminate unrighteousness.[151] Prophets portray the "square" as the identifying mark of the city's true nature, in most instances acting as the place of mourning (Isa 59:14; Jer 5:1; cf. 49:26, 50:30; Amos 5:16). The condition of a city is determined by her streets and squares, whether it is in wisdom and folly (cf. Prov 1:20, 22:13, 26:13; Song 3:2) or general safety (cf. Zech 8:4-5).

In the end, we know the city "will be built again" (תשוב ונבנתה), shifting from the *hiphil* infinitive השיב ("restore") used earlier to the *qal* non-perfective תשוב ("again"). The author leaves the reader with a hint as to what to expect in these sixty-weeks: it is "in a troubled time" (בצוק העתים), or, the upheaval always abutting the restoration of the city and Israel herself. The description "distressing, troubling" (צוק) is not common and the *hiphil*-form seems to move from texts like Deut 28:53-57 and into the prophet Jeremiah, who borrows the scene from Deuteronomy (cf. Jer 19:9), and Isaiah (26:16; 29:2, 7; participial form, 51:13).[152] Although these earlier references in the LP are references to either the promise of exilic oppression or the realities of Exile, the occurrence in 9:25 is obscured by its terseness. The reader is left wondering how such an expanse of chaos and distress can be marked by such a short phrase—the only images and descriptions available are those common in the earlier canonical scriptures.

---

[150] Goldingay, *Daniel*, 261.

[151] Other references depict "the open square of the city" as the container for foreign or eschewed persons or items. In the narrative of the master and the servant in Judges 19, the "square" is the center of Gibeah, which is likened to Sodom and Gomorrah (vv. 15-24).

[152] Goldingay sees the construction mirroring the phrase "the stability of your times" (אמונת עתיך) in Isa 33:6 (*Daniel*, 261).

3. Daniel 9:26-27: The Conclusion to the Kingdom Pattern

3.1. Daniel 9:26

This verse begins after the conclusion of the sixty-two-week period, revisiting what may be the same "anointed" figure from the previous text.[153] The construction "an anointed one cut off and is nothing" (יכרת משיח ואין לו) is no less puzzling. Proponents of strong, historical parallelism squeeze this construction tightly for references that might shed light on the socio-political affairs of the time. Allusion to the assassination of Onias III is the usual suspect, but the act may also be the forced removal of Jason by Menelaus (172-71 BCE) in, what Koch terms, a "Zahlungsschwierigkeit."[154] For many who argue for a Christian predictive interpretation, this phrase strikes any doubt that the anointed one "cut off" is someone other than Jesus Christ.[155] However, to "cut off" (כרת) is general and implies any number of acts: death (Gen 9:11), starvation (Gen 41:36), separation from the community (Exod 8:9; 12:15), expulsion from the priestly office (1 Sam 2:33-36) or exile on a large scale (Ezek 25:7; 35:7). But with an individual (e.g. Onias III), many occurrences do, in fact, point to expulsion from a community as a viable option. Covenant violation is usually a factor, even operating as a word play in the *ratification* (כרת) of a covenant (2 Chr 7:18) or the punishment for violating the Sabbath (cf. Exod 31:14). This aspect can also involve the forming and breaking of the "strong covenant" (v. 27) found in the last half of the week as well as associations with the "prince of the covenant" (11:22) who is "swept away (in a flood)" (שטף; cf. 9:26). With this as an outcome, the text can accommodate either reference to *a non-Israelite or Israelite leader*, according to the covenant language. As Goldingay comments, "Talk of devastation, battle, and desolation (v 26) reflects the seriousness of the trouble brought to people, city, and temple by the combined force of heathen ruler(s) and usurper priest(s)."[156]

However, the image of "cut off" leaves too many possibilities on the table to confine the interpretation to a matter of covenant. If all of these references funnel into one person, then the one formerly "cut off" from a covenant in 9:26, in an ironic twist, forges his own covenant in 9:27. The ambiguous nature of the lexemes widens even more with the construction's relationship to ואין לו. The phrase ואין לו is peculiar and compounds the problem of matching a viable

---

[153] Goldingay rightly does not assume this "anointed" figure is the same one as in 9:25, since Daniel frequently uses anarthous constructions: "a vision, a prophet, a most sacred place [v 24]; a word, an anointed, a leader, a square, a moat [v 25]; an anointed, a leader, a people [v 26]; a covenant, a wing, an abomination, a conclusion, a desolate one [v 27]." He continues saying, "the effect is to contribute to the allusiveness appropriate to a vision, which cannot be resolved from within chap. 9 itself" (262).

[154] Koch, *Das Buch Daniel*, 142-43.

[155] Cf. Jerome, *Commentary on Daniel*; Leon Wood, *A Commentary on Daniel* (Grand Rapids: Eerdmans, 1973), 255; Doukhan, "Seventy Weeks," 18-21.

[156] Goldingay, *Daniel*, 261.

allusion to the text. Is the translation "not for himself" (KJV), "have nothing" (ESV), "disappear and vanish" (JPS), or, as Goldingay translates it, "will have neither the city nor the sanctuary"?[157] For those arguing for Onias III, connection to the loss of sanctuary and city implies "a reference to his displacement and withdrawal for safety to Daphne, near Antioch" (cf. 2 Macc 4).[158] But because of the terseness of the construction, there is not the detail necessary to come to any one conclusion. What is definitive: the leader will experience a fall according to Yahweh's decree. The theological point indicates any number of circumstances can befall an anointed leader, whether it is death, displacement, covenant expulsion (in the case of a high-priest, possibly) or the like.

Following the fall of the anointed leader, we witness the destruction (שחת) of the city and sanctuary (v. 26b). If we take the "city" to be the location and refuge for Israel, then the "people of the prince" work as a negative force opposing Yahweh and his people. The only other instance in which the term שחת is used in Daniel is 8:23-25 (cf. 11:17), where the final leader will be "exceedingly destructive (נפלאות ישחית)" and "destroy (ישחית) the mighty and the people of the holy ones." This point upsets interpretations that connect this "prince who is to come" (נגיד הבא) to the anointed prince in 9:25. Moreover, these "people of the prince" troubles those arguing for an Israelite leader since their allegiance appears to contradict Israel's own. The writer of the *Aramaic Apocalypse* (4Q246) possibly references this "people" as well as the "city." It also attaches a "kingdom" connotation to the people and the city: "they will rule several years over the earth and crush everything; a people will crush another people, and a city another city" (cf. Isa 19:2), "until the people of God" (cf. Dan 7:27) "arises and makes everyone rest from the sword" (cf. Isa 2:4; Mic. 4:3; Jer 14:13, 15). Even if we dismiss the nuance of "kingdom" that surrounds these elements, there is more to the people and the city first noticed.

The city (עיר) certainly takes on multiple nuances throughout the chapter. In 9:16, Daniel prays for "the city Jerusalem," but a flash of Zion-like characteristics illumines 9:18, which is a "city that is called by your name" (cf. Isa 60:14; 10:32; 33:20; 59:20) and "the holy hill of my God" (cf. Isa 10:32; 31:4). When we revisit the term in 9:24, the phrase enlarges to "your holy city" (עיר קדשך) and is followed by the enigmatic promise to "restore and build Jerusalem" (v. 25). It is a clear vision of a restored city, within which lies the temple-sanctuary and Daniel's "people" (v. 24). Combined with references to "your holy hill" or "the holy hill of my God," images of Mount Zion come into focus. Incredibly, the city in 9:24-27 is almost always paired with either the "people" (v. 24) or the "sanctuary" (v. 26). We read of the promise of Zion *without reference to or a vision of* Zion. The city-people-sanctuary complex imagined by Daniel is grand in scale, traversing any one depiction of physical Jerusalem through the ages, settling instead on the long-awaited "Jerusalem." The holy city may be con-

---

[157] Ibid., 226. See also Dan 11:19 for an expanded version of this construction.
[158] Ibid., 262.

quered and left desolate by oppressive rulers (cf. Dan 11:31), but it will also be rebuilt, even if only in its partial glory (cf. Ezra 3:12-13).¹⁵⁹

The final phrases in 9:26 slip quickly into obscurity. Even the first referent is indeterminate: "Its/his end (קֵץ) will come with a flood (בַשֶּׁטֶף)." Collins settles on the translation, "*his* end will be in a cataclysm," referring to Antiochus (cf. 11:45).¹⁶⁰ The ESV and JPS retain, "*Its* end will come," but the referent is still unclear. Is it the closest referent, namely, the ms subject of the participle (הבא), the "*people* (עַם) of the prince"? Or is "it" referring back to the הקדש of the first dual-construction in the clause, "the city (fs הָעִיר) and the *sanctuary* (ms הקדש)"? Conceptually, the phrase is just as vague: both the anointed leader *and* the city-sanctuary (יְשָׁחִית; v. 26b) suffer a type of destruction/downfall (יִכָּרֵת; v. 26a). The instrument is a flood (שֶׁטֶף). The term in its variations occurs only here in 9:26 and Dan 11:10, 22, 26 and 40. Still, these occurrences are hardly conclusive: the first instance tracks the "sons" of the "King of the South" sending armies that will "overflow" (שָׁטַף; 11:10), the second follows a non-royal "contemptible person" from before which "armies will be *utterly swept away* (הִשָּׁטֵף יִשָּׁטְפוּ)" (11:22, 26), and finally, the "King of the North" will attack "like a flood (וְשָׁטַף)" (11:40). Reading Dan 11 back into 9:26 not only overshadows the unique theological role of 9:24-27, but it also does not delimit our options to one figure (e.g. Antiochus), *contra* Collins.

A final, sweeping flood at "the end" insinuates war. However, the details are once again left at the periphery, leaving only an outline of possible events. With the ambiguity of the referent in 9:26c and the lack of extra terminology (e.g. armies, kings, names), the phrase could feasibly expand to mean the complete end or final war-like event. We also cannot be sure these phrases are events occurring *within* the span of the first sixty-nine weeks. The purpose of the decree appears to function *outside* of the flow of events, that is until the complete end arrives. It may be a reiteration or new angle on the word/decree initiating the larger section (חתך; 9:24).

This reading is more plausible when one includes the final clause of the verse: "until the end of war, desolations are decreed."¹⁶¹ As most commenta-

---

¹⁵⁹ We will see in 9:27 collects veiled references to the sanctuary (cf. 9:17, 26b, 27b) and concludes with a shocking truth: the end will come with a blessing (9:24) *and* a curse (9:27d). In an unexpected turn, the text moves away from the sanctuary-image to focus on the results of Sabbath rest and unrest; the city and people are included. Though veiled in Daniel, the importance of the sanctuary expands beyond 9:17 ("your sanctuary lies desolate"); e.g. Lam 5:18, 1 Macc 4:38. Such an expansion is another case of how historical events are used to amplify a larger, theological reality.

¹⁶⁰ Collins, 357. Collins' footnote on this phrasing is not very helpful: "Conservatives typically refer both passages to the Antichrist" (357n99). Though we need not claim reference to the Antichrist in 9:26, Collins fails to see that arguing for Antiochus offers little more explanation of the construction and what 9:24-27 is attempting to communicate.

¹⁶¹ In keeping with the ms format, the OG reads "and to the time of the end *he* will be fought from war."

tors point out, the construction "decreed" (נחרצת) is unique—the *niphal* participle of חרץ only appears in Dan 9:26, 11:36 and Is 10:23. But it is the construction's thematic relationship to Is 10:22-23 that truly informs our reading: "For though your people Israel are like the sand of the sea, only a remnant of them will return. *Complete destruction is decreed* (חרוץ כליון), *flooding* (שוטף) with righteousness. For the Lord God of hosts will make *a complete end* (כלה), as *decreed* (ונחרצה), in the midst of all the earth." The shared *niphal* participle נחרצת is an obvious link, but it is unlikely an ancient reader would miss the conglomeration of terms familiar to both Dan 9:24-27 and Isa 10:20-23.[162] Language related to the "end" is also shared between Isa 26:20 and Dan 11:36, particularly the "*indignation* (זעם)."[163] We, therefore, return to Daniel's interpretation of earlier scriptures and the theological message he not just "derives" from the prophecy, but *continues* from the traditions of Isa 10. Isaiah 10 begins with an indictment of those Assyrian rulers who "write iniquitous decrees" (vv. 1-2), transitioning to an indictment of Samaria (v. 10-11). In 10:15-20, we hear of a "remnant" that will endure great distress "in that day" (ביום ההוא; v. 20). The shift in Daniel seems to come by his inclusion of Israel *and the nations* in the end. By including this phrase, Daniel effectively dispels the expectation that Israel is still participating in the *exact same* process of restoration as projected in Lev 25-26. Daniel's interpreted vision expands on the restoration found at the end of Leviticus, and the restoration underlining Jer 25-33 (and now Isa 10:20-23), to include a pattern of oppression and "desolation" in the design.

3.2. Daniel 9:27

At the outset of the verse, we are waylaid again by ambiguity: who is the one making a strong or binding "covenant" (ברית)? Collins remains certain: whereas the "covenant" to which Dan 11:22, 28, 30 and 32 refers is a "holy covenant," this covenant in 9:27 is "the alliance of Epiphanes with the Hellenizing Jews."[164] Locating a "strong covenant" on a timeline of historical events,

---

[162] The apocalyptic images are adopted from Isa 10-11: these images range from the vast mountain-stone untouched by human hands (Dan 2:35; Isa 2:2, 11:6-9; cf. Mic 4:1) as well as the construction –כלה ונחרצה– in Dan 9:26-27, 11:36 (cf. Isa 10:22-23) (Henze, 284-5). Also see Dan 2:35 and Isa 41:15-16a, which share the same scene: the wind carries away the "chaff" (hills) and the "dust" (mountains/idols) from the "threshing floor." Also, the knowledge of God fills the earth (Dan 2:35; cf. Isa 11:9).

[163] In connection with "desolation" imagery, the conclusions of Isaiah (66:24) and Daniel (12:2) refer to an "object of horror" (דראון), an image found only in these passages. Again, this theological current runs through other apocalyptic texts ("the predetermined end" in 1QS IV.25). For a study on the relationship between Dan 12:2 and Isa 26:19 based on the "awakening" motif, see Daniel Bailey, "The Intertextual Relationship of Daniel 12:2 and Isaiah 26:19: Evidence from Qumran and the Greek Versions," *TynBul* 51.2 (2000): 305-8.

[164] Collins, *Daniel*, 357. The wording resembles a cultural device of "legal binding" used among a network of select comparative roots (the Hebrew הגביר, the Akkadian *dunnunu*, and the Aramaic תקף) (cf. Shalom Paul, "Gleanings from the Biblical and Tal-

whether second century or otherwise, is no easy task.[165] These options still do not reconcile the absence of a covenant mediator following the initial sixty-nine weeks—is it the first מָשִׁיחַ נָגִיד or the second מָשִׁיחַ before his demise?[166] Of course, the figure may also be a *prospective* mediator, separate from any previous reference, and preparing the way for a desolating force (v. 27d). It is also difficult to weigh either positive or negative effects of the covenant. Daniel 11:21-25 offers a short, narrative account of the patterns in 9:24-27, clearly covering the actions of "covenant"—from ruler to people—with shades of deceit and cunning (cf. 11:23-24). Nevertheless, to superimpose this narrative (11:20-25) upon the words of 9:26-27 disregards the contradictions separating the two accounts.[167] In 9:27, we are left only with a binding agreement between an unknown ruler and either a remnant (a *positive*, covenantal spin) or a typical majority of people (anarthous רבים; a *negative*, covenantal spin).[168] The "many" (רבים) may also be Daniel's people as a whole (vv. 19-20, 24), the "people of the prince" (v. 26), a *doomed* remnant leading into the Maccabean revolution (8:25; 11:14; cf. Is 10:20-23), those who "rise against the king of the south" or "the violent" (11:14), or the Danielic group known as the "many," who may turn to wisdom, righteousness or knowledge (12:2-4).

In the latter half of the final week, the same figure will "cease sacrifices and offerings" (יַשְׁבִּית זֶבַח וּמִנְחָה). The author turns from his normal wording for "end" (קֵץ, חתם, כלא), to "cease, rest" (שׁבת), a lexeme that follows directly after

---

mudic Lexica in Light of Akkadian," in *Mishnah le Nahum: Biblical and Other Studies Presented to Nahum M. Sarna in Honour of His 70th Birthday* [ed. Michael Fishbane and Marc Brettler; JSOTSup 154; Sheffield: JSOT, 1993], 242-56). Some also argue for a divine referent in the absence of a clear, human referent. Taking this route, Kline emphasizes the term גבד, normally a word for a prevailing party (הגביד), and may be included to describe the champion-like status of God as we find it in Is 10:21 (אל גביד) (see Meredith Kline, "The Covenant of the Seventieth Week," in *The Law and the Prophets: Old Testament Studies in Honor of Oswald T. Allis* [ed. J.H. Skilton; Nutley, N.J.: Presbyterian and Reformed, 1974], 466-67).

[165] Partial evidence of a particular, historical match is in 1 Macc 1:11, which reads, "Let us go and make a *covenant* with the Gentiles around us." This quotation does not escape the difficulty of the phrasing, but does add an element of reciprocity to the ratification.

[166] If an interpreter lumps together both figures, the difficulty remains since the anointed figure is "cut off and is no more" (9:26).

[167] To name a handful of examples, the "prince of the covenant" (11:22), which is ostensibly the covenant mediator of 9:27, falls prior to the rise of the King of South and is "swept away." If we follow the sequential sense of the heptadic images in 9:24-27, the forces of the "prince" rise up in parallel with a general "flood" of destruction. Given the amount of overlapping material in 9:27 and 11:20-27, a careful hermeneutic is necessary to determine the relationship between the two texts—more often than not, the texts are thrown together in an effort to reconstruct historical portraits.

[168] The narrative in Dan 11:20-25 supplements the notion of "many" (רבים) with the more detailed "small people-nation" (מְעַט־גּוֹי; 11:23).

the ב-שׁ in the heptadic construction השבוע. Even more striking is the marking of Sabbath as a "covenant forever" (ברית עולם) in Exod 31:16.[169] Using this conception of Sabbath and covenant as a context, it is possible to interpret Yahweh as the original covenant agent of 9:27—which has no clear human referent—and read the end of the sacrificial offerings as "rest" (שׁבת) enforced. Yet there is space enough within the expanse of divine agency to also have in view a human agent (cf. Cyrus in Is 45:1).

By now, the reader sees how this "final week" does not represent the last seven years of a time period, but a climax to the seventy sevens: "rest" (שׁבת; 27b) is being enacted forcefully upon *the people, city, temple and possibly all Levitical practices therein*, through a desolation or desolator.[170] It is revealed that the promised rest in Leviticus is taken from Israel and given to the "land," so to speak (cf. Lev 26:34-35). Yahweh's means of enforcement is a desolating force, which will itself suffer under God's original decree. This desolating force, whether it is a person ("desolator") or state of being ("desolation"), will itself end, כלה ("to finish").[171]

3.3. The Rise of the Desolating Force

An abrupt transition marks the second portion of 9:27. The reader pivots from a mysterious figure acting upon the institutions of Israel and covenant administration to the *dénoument* of the desolating force. Per standard practice for the author, the text continues underneath veiled references. The term כנף ("wing, the extreme end"), for example, is an unknown, non-descript location or object. Is it the wing or "corner of the altar" (JPS) or a stylized depiction of movement, as in "abominations will sweep in"? Adhering closely to the temple nuance, the OG and Theodotian simply replaces the word with ιερὸν ("temple, holy place"). Siding with the LXX rendering, Montgomery mixes the two nu-

---

[169] Additional time and space would permit us to track this "covenant" thread and the Sabbath thread together through the pertinent areas of tradition within the LP. As Schmid indicates, the "covenant theology" characterizing Isa 1, as but one example, draws from a genetic relationship to Leviticus-Deuteronomy and, thereby, "accentuates the 'Deuteronomistic' logic of 2 Kgs 25 (*Old Testament*, 162). The level to which Daniel is immersed in the Former and Latter Prophets cannot be stressed enough. Schmid also believes this passage is reflecting Isaianic thought, namely, a critique of sacrifice (Isa 1:10-15). The historical progression of the "end of sacrifice," according to Schmid, is likewise reflected in the Former Prophets: it is "an ongoing interpretation of the destruction of the temple and the removal of the cultic vessels (2 Kgs 25:8-12, 13-21)." The context of the holy vessels (כלי בית־האלהים) is by no means a coincidence given their presence at the beginning, middle and end of the book (Dan 1:2; 11:8; cf. 5:2-4). (cf. Num 18:3; 31:6; Josh 6:19; 1 Kgs 7:45-51).

[170] Daniel 9:24-27 places the final week in a specific context as a part of the "*runde Zahl*" (Porteous, *Das Buch Daniel*, 115).

[171] We notice how the word-choice returns to כלה, originating with the first כלה in 9:24b, "to *finish* the transgression," possibly to make a canopy or envelope that frames the two thoughts.

ances—the wing and the temple—arguing the phrase refers to a defiling object on the outside "pinnacle" of the temple.[172] Other translations render the whole phrase "wing of abominations" (ESV) or "overspreading of abominations" (KJV). The text itself does not commit to such a designation, using none of the nomenclature Daniel includes in the previous verses (הר־קדש,מקדש). It is a simple move, of course, to relocate the words of 9:17—"your sanctuary, which is desolate"—to the gaps in 9:27, but the interpreter would then diminish the scope of the desolating force that exceeds far beyond the walls of a temple. From a poetic angle, it appears the author is expressing the speed, scope, depth and, most of all, the *vehicle* (על כנף שקוצים) upon which the desolating force arrives.

The force itself, or "abomination of desolation" (שקוצים משמם), can translate into a number of titles.[173] Unlike 11:31 and 12:11, here we have the plural form of שקוץ lending to the complexity or vagueness of assigning a translation. Though the singular שקוץ is a concept found in many passages, the participle שמם or משמם is also difficult to translate. Lust renders the whole phrase, "the contemptuous deformation" using language similar to how one describes a profaning idol.[174] Including the term שקוץ, for example, may be reference to an abominable "statue or deity" (cf. "Molek," "Kemosh" and "Ashtoret" in 1 Kgs 11:5, 7; 2 Kgs 23:13). Ezekiel also compares "the detestable things (שקוץ) and abominations (תועבה)" to the idols of Egypt from which Israel could not depart (5:11; 7:20; 11:18; 20:8). Koch, Collins and others see an allusion in the form of a derogatory wordplay, the Phoenician sky deity Baal-*samen*—modifying שמם to

---

[172] Montgomery, 387.

[173] Cf. Lust, "Cult and Sacrifice in Daniel: The *Tamid* and the Abomination of Desolation" in *The Book of Daniel: Composition and Reception, Vol.2* (eds. John Collins and Peter W. Flint, Leiden: Brill, 2001), 671-88, here 685. He argues that the form of שקוצים in Dan 9:27 is not actually a plural noun, but a re-duplication carried over from the primary מ in the participle מְשֹׁמֵם. This would support his understanding of שקוץ as a singular "sacrifice," but not the numerous uses in other texts (Ezek 7:20; 11:21; 20:30; cf. 1 Kgs 11:5; 2 Kgs 23:13 for instances of the collective genitive). The use of the plural שקוצים in Dan 9:27 (*contra* Lust) appears to refer to "abominable acts" that vary in kind. One could argue for a substantival participle ("the desolator" or "appaller") similar to Dan 9:27c or even a typical, unspecified genitive ("of desolation"). Lust identifies משמם as Antiochus himself ("the Appaller"; 686-7); see also ESV, "the one who makes desolate." Hartman and DiLella believe the participle שמם is an intentional "mispronunciation" of the polel (משמם), derived from the plural noun שמים ("the heavens") (*The Book of Daniel* [AB 23; Garden City: Doubleday, 1978], 253). However, one alternative accounts for the relationship between שמם and שקוץ differently. Pairing משמם with an active force ("which causes desolation") corresponds well with the adjectival use in 9:17 (השמם) as well as the plural in 9:26 (שממות), according to Jeffrey A. Gibbs (*Jerusalem and Parousia: Jesus' Eschatological Discourse in Matthew's Gospel* [St. Louis: Concordia Academic, 2000] 184). Gibbs supports an active sense. When the phrase appears in 11:31 and 12:11, the singular "abomination" (שקוץ) is an instance of what "makes desolate."

[174] Lust, "Cult and Sacrifice," 675.

שָׁמַיִם ("sky, heavens")—or, the Syrian equivalent to *Zeus Olympios* (cf. 1 Macc 1:54; 2 Macc 6:1-2).[175] Maccabees, in possibly the earliest interpretation of the phrase, recounts "on the fifteenth day of Chislev, in the one-hundred-and-forty-fifth year, they raised a *desolating sacrilege* (βδέλυγμα ἐρημώσεως) upon the altar of burnt offering" (1 Macc 1:54). A similar account is in Josephus (cf. *Ant* 12.5.4 § 253). Such accounts reinforce Lust's thesis to a point, namely that the "the 'abomination of desolation' is a sacrifice imposed on the Jews as a replacement of the Tamid" (cf. 8:11-13).[176] Henze goes further, reading this as "a framed formula" (8:13; 9:27; cf. Is 64:9-10) with special reference to "the desecration of the temple" (Dan 11:31; 12:11; 1 Macc 1:54; 6:7; 2 Macc 6:2).[177] Goldingay defines "desolation" in this context as "national subservience to foreign powers" that converges at Antiochus Ephiphanes.[178]

However, the easy transitions between Dan 9:27, 11:31, 12:11, 1-2 Macc and other early accounts may tempt modern commentators to commit to an illegitimate transfer of meaning.[179] The ambiguity of the phrase in 9:27 does not justify this confirmation, as it might in, for example, other Danielic texts (cf. 8:11-13). Even the resources from which interpreters draw their conclusions disagree. Whereas Collins, following 1-2 Maccabees, sees a pagan altar or defiling sacrifice in the שקוצים משמם, Jerome's *Commentary* on Dan 11:31 claims Antiochus "set up an *image of Jupiter Olympius* in the temple at Jerusalem." Is the object a mockery of sacrifice, an idol or an appalling figure in 9:27? We only find this construction in 9:27—neither is it in 2 Macc 6:7 as one might expect. The mention of "unclean" (טמא) objects or practices is also not in Daniel,

---

[175] Such a connection, Koch notes, is a "Pfeiler der Makkabäerthese" (*Das Buch Daniel*, 136). See also Johan Lust, "Cult and Sacrifice," 677; Collins, *Daniel*, 357.

[176] Lust, 683.

[177] Henze, "Use of Scripture," 290; A. Collins combines earlier references and asserts that the defilement of the temple (cf. 8:13; 9:27) will last for "2300 evenings and mornings" (8:14) or a little over six years. At the half-week, the unit is cut in half (1150 days or 3 years), aligning with the implementation of Antiochus' policies in December 167 BCE—December 164 BCE (cf. 1 Macc 1:54; 4:52) (*Cosmology*, 59-60). Collins admits to the discrepancy between Daniel's chronology and modern dating, but reconciles the problem with an appeal to "prophecy after the fact" in order for Daniel to give an accurate portrayal of events.

[178] Goldingay, 232.

[179] Interpretations in 1-2 Macc, the Enoch scrolls and LXX Daniel contribute to the "desolator" personae in greater or lesser degrees. It stands to reason, however, that many of these texts adopt an undeveloped form of the "oppressive ruler" tradition and enhance it with names, dates, figures and historical features in order to crystallize an otherwise vague account. For example, Koch wonders if the "wicked branch" (ῥίζα ἁμαρτωλός) of 1 Macc 1:10 is a conglomeration of associations based on "the contemptible one" (נבזה) in Dan 11:21, as well as "the unjust and most villainous king" (βασιλεῖ ἀδίκῳ καὶ πονηροτάτῳ) in Dan 3:32 LXX ("Stages," 424). Koch is mostly interested in the cross-fertilization of Daniel-like events running between Maccabees, LXX Daniel and Enoch, resulting in the potential for different source-texts.

whereas all other literature supporting the historical references to the abomination of desolation (Jeremiah, Ezekiel, 1-2 Maccabees) frequently includes the idea.[180] Likely, the full force of these abominable desolations transcend the defilement of the altar—these forces represent a greater judgment originating in a nascent form through the traditions of Leviticus and Jeremiah or representative texts of the LP.

The shadowy figure behind these abominable acts or desolating force also transcends the defilement of the sanctuary. In Dan 8:13 the construction, "transgression that makes desolate," depicts a great and terrible event of catastrophic proportions.[181] The little horn begins to grow to become "as great as the prince of the host (שׂר־הצבא)" (8:11).[182] Is this the same Antiochene leader that removes the offering and overthrows the "sanctuary" (cf. 9:26 [?]) of the prince (8:11b-c)?[183] Even these accounts do not illustrate the historical specifics in any satisfactory manner. No single name is assigned to identify Antiochus Epiphanes IV –the silence is maintained on theological grounds.[184] Reading within the final form of Dan 9, the subject of Epiphanes IV is, at times, a sub-current running underneath other historical allusions (vv. 25-26; cf. 8:9-

---

[180] It is the primary reason, for example, that swine is not to be consumed (Lev 11:7) and stands as the image of revulsion and humiliation in Maccabean literature (cf. 2 Macc 6:7).

[181] Henze, "Use of Scripture," 290. Tracing the acts of Epiphanes throughout the text leads many to merge Dan 7-9 and 11. A conflation of this sort muddles the unique dynamics that are characteristic of Dan 9. However, associative activity running between Dan 7 and 8 is certainly plausible. Henze reads Daniel 8 as an "interpreted expansion" of ch. 7 (288) while Goldingay sees ch. 8 reaffirming the promise of ch. 7, albeit in "a worsening situation" (*Daniel*, 206-7); see also Holger Gzella, *Cosmic Battle and Political Conflict: Studies in Verbal Syntax and Contextual Interpretation of Daniel 8* (BibOr 47; Rome: Pontificio Istituto Biblico, 2003), 71-73.

[182] Some see the king in 8:23-25 as another iteration of the "beast" in 7:11-12, where his body is destroyed and burned while the remaining "beasts" scatter for "a season and a time" (7:12). Scholars working within the context of the events of 173-163 BCE, read both of these iterations as short narrative flashes of Antiochus IV Epiphanes (see Henze, "Use of Scripture," 289). These same interpreters fixate on 7:11-12 because after Epiphanes' sudden death in 163 BCE, he left only an infant son as heir (Antiochus V Eupator); therefore, the Seleucid Dynasty collapsed while a series of faction leaders fought to claim the throne.

[183] Those supporting a Seleucidian background see the "main offenses" of Antiochus IV beginning to unfold in Dan 8:10-12 (cf. Henze, 288).

[184] Childs reminds us that, "nowhere did the original author actually identify Antiochus by name with the evil one" (*IOTS*, 619). Carr accounts for the mysterious figure by appealing to a mistaken omission: "Even the book of Daniel, which probably was completed only decades before the Scriptural corpus was closed, was not updated to contain a correct prophecy of the death of Antiochus or anticipate the Hasmonean monarchy" (*Formation*, 166).

27, 11:2-45).[185] The last stages of the canonical process certainly permitted other interpretive voices—contemporary to the horrific exploits of the Seleucid ruler—to confirm Daniel's words regarding oppressive kingdoms were still true (cf. 2:20-23, 44). But where other second century apocalypses add more identifiable marks to Epiphanes' character, Daniel crafted a persona for the ruler out of various, biblical features and associations avoiding a single one-to-one association. As Koch explains, "Antiochus Epiphanes did not remain as the last enemy ... but became that enemy's *prefiguration*."[186] Childs sides with Koch on this point, identifying Antiochus as "representative of the ultimate enemy, but he himself was not the fulfillment of the visions."[187] The "indignation" (8:19) the exiles experience is only "a foreshadowing of the *final* period of indignation."[188]

3.4. The Decreed End of the Desolating Force

The rise and fall of the desolating force in 9:27 returns the reader to the baseline running throughout the book: the "universal horizon" and subversion of human rule in light of Yahweh's imminent rule.[189] We also return to Leviticus and Jeremiah, the starting points from where these traditions begin to expand and deepen. These textual associations between the LP and the language of 9:27c-d activates a number of canonical connections. First, we will look at the meaning of שמם (v. 27d) within the context of the book and the canon and, second, the relationship between the "decreed end" of the desolating force and earlier texts such as Leviticus, Deuteronomy and Jeremiah. First, we consider the sense of שמם (v. 27d). The syntax in the final clause is set up to anticipate a name of some sort (... נתך על), as Lust notes, but instead Daniel includes the qal-participle of שמם.[190] A reader usually finds a "person or persons upon whom 'wrath' or 'the end' is poured out, rather than an abstract notion

---

[185] Anatheia Portier-Young offers a detailed reconstruction of Antiochus Epiphanes' activities, going so far as to map his theological/political intentions throughout the book of Daniel. For Portier-Young, Epiphanes is more than a background figure in chs. 7-11, but a self-proclaimed divine in an elaborate power-play against the God of Israel. The words in Dan 2:20-23, which many recognize as the generative core of the book, is precisely the doxological faith-statement Epiphanes is attempting to uproot and destroy (*Apocalypse*, 180).

[186] Koch, "Daniel Among the Prophets," 127 (italics mine). Still, Koch notes this figural activity within the *prophetic* context of the book of Daniel, and not the context of the Writings.

[187] Childs, *IOTS*, 619.

[188] Ibid., 617.

[189] Unlike chs. 7-8 or 10-12, Daniel 9 breaks from, what Koch calls, "the characteristics of foreign world empires and the fate of their foremost rulers," and reverts focus back on to "the behavior and destiny of Israel" ("Stages," 422). The focus quickly shifts back to the universalization of human rule in v. 24 and synchronizes with the surrounding chapters when the reader comes to v. 27.

[190] Lust, 686.

such as 'desolation'" (cf. 2 Sam 21:10; Jer 42:18; Dan 9:11).[191] Nevertheless, we *do* find an "abstract concept" here in 9:27.

Daniel 9 focuses on a broad understanding of desolation (9:17-18, 26-27), unlike, for example, the clarifications supplied by 8:9-27 and 11:2-45. The *poel* participle in 9:27 (מְשֹׁמֵם) is generally considered a substantive, "the devastator, or alternatively the one who devastates" (*HALOT*). But the proper translation for the participles is only one difficulty that faces the interpreter in 9:27. Daniel 9:27 alone merges phrases from the preceding text in order to form what can only be described as a conglomeration of devastating effects. In 9:17-18, Daniel appeals to the "desolate" condition of the sanctuary,[192] followed by a general appeal to "our desolations" surrounding the "city" (v. 18). Daniel 9:26 appears to be a heightened pattern that makes sense of Daniel's concrete appeals in 9:17-18—a pattern including the images of Is 10:22-23 (cf. 28:22). The phrase, therefore, seems to toggle between describing a figure and describing a defiling event as the book unfolds (cf. 8:13).[193]

Second, the decreed end of the desolating force is a tradition rooted in Leviticus, Deuteronomy and Jeremiah.[194] Together, these clues point the reader

---

[191] Ibid. Lust concludes his argument by translating Mmv as a formal tag, "The Appaler," referring to Antiochus Epiphanes IV.

[192] Qumran scrolls also configure and re-configure how the relationship between "desolations/desolator" and the sanctuary is arranged. In 4Q174 (4QFlor), the "desolation" is a matter of exclusive holiness, since "strangers (זרים) will not again make it desolate (ישמוהו) as they desolated formerly (השמו בראישונה)" (Line 5). This may be an eschatological instance of Deut 23:2-3, but of interest is the reference to "a manmade sanctuary" (מקדש אדם; Line 6) that comes out of Exod 15:17-18. It is likely Essene frameworks delineated between the manmade sanctuary and a sanctuary "not made by human hands," so to speak. Following this logic, the notion of "desolation" as profanation of all things sacred *at a horizontal and vertical* dimension is noteworthy.

[193] It is also significant that the phrase "abomination of desolation" comes at the end of the passage. In Dan 8, the subject is the "transgression of desolation" (הפשע שמם), and narrates the rise of a powerful and cunning tyrant. Even the final line of 8:27 describes Daniel "appalled" (שמם), linking the traumatic experience of the vision to the collective trauma experienced by Israel (cf. 4:19). The next occurrence is in 9:27 with great emphasis on its desolating effects, albeit in a veiled description. Daniel 11:31 and 12:11 both take up the phrase "abomination that makes desolate" (שמם נתנו השקוץ משומם לתת שקוץ respectively); here, the phrase is reconfigured to portray the defilement event itself, just as in 8:27. Again, the presence of the phrase in 9:27 connects the text to its surrounding context (chs. 8, 10-12) and, yet, omits the details. One could see these descriptions in the veiled reference of 9:27 without reading the event/figure of 9:27 into 8:27, 11:31 or 12:11. These images are related but not equivalent.

[194] Land, Sabbath rest, people and obedience are the main ideas: Deut 28:37—"And you will be a *desolation* (לשמה), a proverb and a byword to all the peoples." Jeremiah 29:18b—"And they will be a horror to all the kingdoms of the earth, to be a curse, a *desolation* (ולשמה) a hissing and a reproach among all the nations where I have driven them." Jeremiah 25:11—"This whole land will be a waste, a *desolation* (לשמה)," serving Babylon for "seventy years" (25:11b).

back to the forewarning of Lev 26:31-34. The cities, land and sanctuary will be "desolate" (26:31-33), not just the altar and institution of sacrifice. The refrain, foretelling a "sevenfold" punishment (26:18, 20, 24, 28), becomes a reality since the people did not "listen" to God's commandments or prophets (esp. 26:14; Jer 23:16, 18). By these grim means, "Sabbath rest" comes (Lev 26:34) at the "determined end" (כלה; Dan 9:27; cf. 9:24 "לכלא הפשע"). But just as the desolating force hits with great speed and destruction, so also does the reversal come with quickly and powerfully. Desolation is revisited back onto the desolator (9:27).

When we investigate the background for such a reversal, we notice Jeremiah 16:18, which responds to the implicit question of Dan 9:27: "What wrong have we done?" and "What of the land?" Yahweh declares, in 16:18, "I will repay double their *iniquity* and their *sin* (עון; חטא), because they have corrupted my land with the carcasses of their *detestable* (שקוץ) things, and have filled my inheritance with their *abominations* (תועבה)." Jeremiah 32:34-35 and Ezekiel share and develop this relationship between the שקוץ and תועבה, linked by reference to destructive idols.[195] But Jer 16:18 adds another component. Both the land and God's "inheritance" are victims of abominable desolation, not through the fault of some unknown force, but through Israel's pervasive "sin and iniquity."[196] Of course, the framework in which these paradigms operate shifts slightly when we come to Daniel. The "land" is no longer what is (primarily) at stake, but Israel's standing before God. Moreover, the idolatry and "abominable" things with which Israel "desolated" their own land is trans-

---

[195] Jeremiah also takes the language of desolation further in his description of the "Destroyer" (שדד). The Destroyer leaves the people "ruined" (שדדנו; 4:13) and lays waste to the whole land (v. 20). Of course, this personification of ruin, which shares the same participial construction, is in oracles like Isaiah, where Moab is under the foot of the "destroyer" (שדד; cf. 15:1; 16:4). Jeremiah also uses the same personification as Isaiah, referring to the "destroyer of Moab" (48:8, 15, 20). The passive participle is even assigned to Israel at times, "the desolate one" (שדוד; Jer 4:30). Jeremiah, however, mentions the Destroyer (and its actions) the most—over half of the instances in both its finite and non-finite forms—and warns, "the Destroyer will come upon *every city* (כל־עיר)" and the surrounding plains and valleys (48:8). Additionally, Jeremiah later foresees the Destroyer "laying waste to Babylon" (51:55; cf. 51:48, 53), the original "destroyer" of the eastern peoples (49:28). Still, if Daniel is continuing this particular motif through the "Desolator" (משמם), he has changed it considerably. The poel of שמם, though it is from a reduplicated verb in close, semantic proximity to שדד, is still unique and is just as reminiscent of Lev 25-26 as it is the Jeremianic text. If we grant such a continuation of motif, then Daniel is purposefully enmeshing the title with multiple canonical contexts so that the reader is forced to draw from both sources to construct the visual.

[196] The act of "profaning" (חלל) occurs twice in the book of Daniel, with Dan 11:31 having the highest correlation to Jer 16:18. In this case, the leader "profanes" (חלל) the temple and fortress and substitutes the *tamid* with an "abomination that makes desolate" (השקוץ משומם) (Dan 11:31; cf. 9:17, 27).

formed—now, an "abominable" force will "desolate" Israel's sanctuary (a place that forbids idols).[197]

In comparing the earlier traditions and language of the LP with 9:27, we see how Daniel enlarges the stream of tradition to include more than what was expected. Explanations for how the latter days are to unfold take on a global appearance and the concept of "complete rest" advances on all timelines, all governments and the whole of creation. The canonical shape of Dan 9:24-27 translates the author's interpretation on a grand scale, where Yahweh "dealt with the powers of the world in their own history as they related to one another and Israel entered the picture only at the periphery with the coming of the kingship of God."[198] Israel is marginalized, Daniel argues, as a result of God's "indignation" (8:19)—an indignation not beginning in ch. 8, but at the beginning of the book with Nebuchadnezzar's siege (cf. 1:1).

To conclude this portion, a decreed end to the desolating force parallels the hope of a rebuilt "holy city" Jerusalem (v. 24), taking the reader back to the beginning of the interpretation. These parallels follow the non-linear imagery throughout vv. 24-27 and adduce a panorama in which these patterns, over the course of the three divisions of the seventy sevens, merge and weave in upon one another. Secondly, this abridged record of the seventy sevens (vv. 25-27) ends on a harsh note: Yahweh will "resolve" all abominable circumstances that leave His people and places desolate, but at great cost. In this presentation of the Eschaton, the portrait is not of a totally restored city or a people at rest, although such an image is within the wider, canonical portrait of the Hebrew canon (the "city," cf. Is 66:12-16; the "temple," cf. Ezek 48:12-13; the "people," cf. Jer 32:37-42). Daniel's interpretation of the revelation is grey and difficult to visualize, much like the path of post-exilic "Jerusalem."

We are also returning to the implied frame of 9:24-27, where the final movements of 9:24 appear to fit after v. 27 or after the fall of the desolator/desolation. The final actualization of these patterns in 9:24-27—fulfilling over the course of Yahweh's decreed plan—will reveal the fall of the ultimate human kingdom and the end of sin, all *in conjunction with* the advent of Yahweh's kingship. By carefully tailoring the account of the final days in this way, Daniel can hold taut the theological tension between *judgment* for Israel's conduct and blessed *rest* as promised through divine covenant. Not unlike the method of the Chronicler, Daniel's method draws out elements of "ontological continuity within Israel's history."[199] The decreed plan for the saints as well as

---

[197] Given additional time and space, one could trace the language of desolation from Jeremiah through, what Beckwith terms, the "canonical appendix" to the prophet, namely the book of Lamentations (341). In this text, we find a series of laments that gather the dark language of destruction and exile to itself and demonstrate a poetic expression of Jerusalem's demise. The "city of Zion," for example, is the object of "desolation" (שמם; 1:4; 5:18).

[198] Childs, *IOTS*, 615.

[199] Childs, *IOTS*, 651.

the "decreed end" of the final desolating force include *all* of Yahweh's people. The figuration of the desolator incorporates the plight of the faithful saints and "symbolically engages the community in ending desolation."[200] The category "symbol," in this context, does not mean a fiction, but an ongoing reality not constrained by a single figure or event. The character of God is both preserved and exalted; both justice and mercy take their course.

4. Conclusion

The final days, according to Daniel, will look more like the completion of a divine plan than the rest expected after the Levitical curse is lifted (cf. 26:40). The passage unveils the plan in terms of patterning—under the umbrella of a time-image "seventy sevens" which represents the fullness of time. To crystallize this point further, Childs combines Jeremiah's prophecy with the judgment incurred from Israel's disobedience of "the Law of Moses," asserting, "the land would lie fallow to make up for the sabbaths which have been disregarded."[201] Childs realizes there is no longer "land" for an Israelite to preserve. He is instead making a poignant, theological claim: disobeying Yahweh's law, in the shape of Sabbath rest, and disobedience to Yahweh's prophets, in the shape of idolatry, will result in a terrible recompense, in the shape of a final, "completion." From Leviticus to Jeremiah, the traditions of rest, land desolation and stewardship shift to a horizon of unrest, covenant violation, desolate "cities," and the exile from one land to another. Daniel relocates the pattern of restoration and destruction to a pattern of fulfilled sin-debt and the recurring rise/fall of human dominion. The figuration of the land's "rest" in Leviticus rolls onward, through Jeremiah's seventy-year prophecy and into Daniel's "seventy sevens." From there, we experience the patterns of Dan 9:24-27, wherein are glimpses of an eschatological clockwork. Just as the writer of the *Aramaic Apocalypse* (4Q246) relays, these patterns unfold for "the people of God" (cf. Dan 7:27) until Yahweh's presence "arises and makes *everyone* rest from the sword" (cf. Isa 2:4; Mic 4:3; Jer 14:13, 15). Rest, therefore, will be realized in either case.

---

[200] Willis, *Dissonance*, 124.

[201] Childs, *IOTS*, 617. The shaping process responsible for highlighting the redefinition of "rest" is more expansive than a redaction-criticism. Differences may be subtle, at first, but Childs separates these activities clearly: "The setting of canonical boundaries in exclusion of rival claims is different from the transformation of an ancient tradition to serve authoritatively in a new situation" ("Response," 53). Conflating these concepts may also lead to confusion between a canonical approach and an inner-biblical exegetical program. Foremost, however, is the ongoing confusion between a canonical approach and redaction criticism. Childs responds, "I have often made use of redactional criticism in studying the seams within the literature, but I have drawn such different implications from my analysis that I would distinguish my approach from that usually understood by that method" (53-54).

Of course, Daniel's widened vision of Yahweh's complete plan not only stretches forward, it also demonstrates to the reader that Yahweh's plan stretches *back*. Completion of God's intended rest was always within the blueprints of the created order. The *Ruhetag* paradigm originates in Creation (Gen 2:1-3), generating the feasts and commandments surrounding the Sabbath-heptadic pattern, and cannot be reduced to an insert based on a postexilic calendar.

Without disconnecting from the original motifs and patterns of the LP, the traditions shift to form a culmination of rest, no longer contingent on land and cities, but the *people or saints*—it is the "end of sin."[202] To state the shift in tradition this way is not to discount the truth of earlier eschatological claims (Isaiah, Jeremiah). It is critical to differentiate between the blessed rest envisioned in the LP and, as Anderson entitles the situation, a "completion of sins" or recall of standing debt.[203] Communities interpreting Daniel continually look to the end of sin and oppression *from within* the same "decreed plan" arching over the first audience(s).

---

[202] Even the Maccabean authors recognize such a promise. He fills in this ambiguity surrounding the "end of sin" by equating these final phrases with the message of Lev 26 and the final punishment of the nations: "I beg the readers of my book not to be disheartened by the calamities but to bear in mind that chastisements come not in order to destroy our race but in order to teach it. If the ungodly among us are not left long to themselves but speedily incur punishment, it is a sign of God's great goodness to us. With the other nations the Lord waits patiently, staying their punishment until they reach the full measure of their sins. Quite otherwise is His decree for us, in order that He should not have to punish us by calamity, He never deserts His people" (2 Macc 6:12-15).

[203] Anderson, *Sin*, 93; cf. Berner also concludes the seventy sevens anticipate a resolution for Israel's sin-debt, by accounting for them in "full measure."

CHAPTER 5
Ambiguity and Space

1. The Biblical Theological Dimension of Daniel 9:24-27

As we have seen in our exegetical treatment of Dan 9:24-27, a canonical approach supplies a number of unique, interpretive angles. But the canonical approach is not complete until the canonical shape takes its course through a two-testament witness. A complete, canonical reading of Dan 9:24-27 and its adjacent parts obliges the reader to inspect the text in its biblical theological context and inspect its potential for theological reflection. Such an inspection tends to be an afterthought or attachment to one's methodology. Better to see the biblical theological significance of the text as the outcome of a thoroughgoing canonical reading.[1]

The chapter divides into four parts: first, the implications of the text's canonical shape, namely, its style of openness. In this section, we will trace how interpretive possibilities create interpretive and confessional space for the purpose of including future generations of faithful readers. Second, considering the reception of Dan 9 in the NT (cf. Matt 24; Mark 13; Luke 21) allows us to engage a canonical example of a community's movement into the interpretive and confessional space of Dan 9:24-27. The third major section will coordinate the canonical shape of Dan 9:24-27 in the OT, the voice of NT, and join the witnesses together in order to locate Dan 9 within the two-testament canon. The fourth and final section continues from the context of the two-testament witness to a Christian reflection on the passage—Dan 9:24-27 as Christian scripture. Faithful readers, in Daniel's terms, are *wise* readers, who embody the patterns of Dan 9:24-27 (e.g. residing in a rest-less world, "discerning the times," occupying Daniel's penitential role).

---

[1] Unfortunately, we enter this area suffering a degree of academic hostility. Johann Gabler laid much of the foundation for arguments proposing a separation between biblical studies (a descriptive, historical discipline) and dogmatic theology (a philosophical, constructive discipline) (cf. Gerhard Hasel, "The Relationship Between Biblical Theology and Systematic Theology," *TrinJ* 5 [1984] 113-27; Magne Saebø, "Johann Philipp Gabler at the End of the Eighteenth Century: History and Theology," in *On the Way to Canon* [Sheffield: Sheffield Academic, 1998], 310-27; Childs, *BTONT*, 11).

1.1. Daniel's Expansion of Meaning: Preface to a Biblical-Theological Reading

Childs writes, "the canon functions truthfully and authoritatively in all its frailty."² By this, he does not mean scripture is brittle or subject to error, but is *subtle* in the various ways it makes its theological sense. Strategic vagueness—or leaving a meaning open-ended—is one of these modes. An in-depth reading of Dan 9:24-27 has already revealed points in which the text is not explained in full (the holiest object, the "anointed," the implied punctuation of 9:25, etc.), allowing for many interpretive possibilities.³

Most interpreters would not readily identify this openness as a trait of the final form. However, it is a powerful tool that enables the text to speak to more than one audience while honoring the proximity of the historical situation.⁴ Moreover, a vagueness in meaning is not regarded positively, often due to three misconceptions. The first misconception is that editorial comments and shaping are associated, almost exclusively, with the *addition* of text. But ambiguity is most effective when it omits text or broadens a term to be purposefully unspecific. Given the muted nature of this strategy, it is less of a hermeneutical tool and more of a feature recognized by the reader. Second, is a misconception that a text with multiple interpretive possibilities is an unintentional flaw, or the product of historical gaps in the knowledge of the author. Third, any literary feature that withholds data or subjects one to misunderstanding will generally attract a negative response. In the case of Daniel, this third misconception is particularly pressing—how can one ascertain the historical setting or collect facts gleaned from "between the lines" when beset by such gaps?

But what positive notes can we sound regarding Daniel's style of interpretive openness, so as to address these misconceptions? The resolution lies in the reader's understanding of the multi-faceted nature of the canonical shape. The canonical texts are not merely "transmissive, closed, and incapable of creativity and growth, but self-involving, open to the future, and dynamic."⁵ To encounter a text that forces the reader to understand and, yet, misunderstand is, as Childs puts it, the "nature of language."⁶ Among studies that champion a

---

² Childs, "Response," 55.

³ Even the newest commentary introduces Dan 9:24-27 with a characteristic obscure-ity: "The passage is notoriously difficult. It seems compressed, with a number of expressions used only here and of ambiguous meaning (Wells and Sumner, *Daniel*, 189).

⁴ Not all OT books share this aspect of the text—different texts are shaped in different ways.

⁵ Anthony Thiselton, "Canon, Community and Theological Construction," in *Canon and biblical Interpretation*, SHS 7 (eds. Craig Bartholomew and Anthony Thiselton; Grand Rapids: Zondervan, 2006), 27.

⁶ "Response to Reviewers," 52. Studies in literary convention and ambiguity provide a vocabulary for Daniel's practice of veiling details and events in chapter 9. David Aaron, Soon Peng Su and G.B. Caird give a limited, albeit illuminating survey of ambiguity and metaphor in the biblical canon (*Biblical Ambiguities: Metaphor, Semantics and Divine Imagery* [Leiden: Brill, 2001]; Caird, *The Language and Imagery of the Bible*

political agenda, for example, encountering Daniel's ambiguity may seem like an arbitrary maneuver. Childs answers plainly: at no time was the author "cloaking a political commentary with religious language."[7] Rather, the author writes with Yahweh's people in mind—a people making up many, many generations. In what follows, we will consider two spheres in which Daniel's style lends a helpful depth-dimension to an otherwise flat definition: (1) prediction and prophecy (2) history and opacity.

1.2. Prediction and Prophecy

Since an open-ended meaning is rarely characterized as a type of theological intention, predictions and end-time models will frequently operate on the assumption that a heightened *perspicuity* exists in Dan 7-12. Some have gone so far as to decode the book for hidden meaning within the letters themselves.[8] Absent an acceptance of Daniel's mysterious language, interpreters may unwittingly delve into an allegorical interpretation of the book: one would no longer connect texts, but make selective correspondences between current events and single-verse references.[9] To focus on the predictions of the first witness, according to Seitz, is to mine the Old Testament for its "resourcefulness" rather than its holistic importance.[10] The text of Daniel begins to function as a depository for modern-day correspondences.

[Grand Rapids: Eerdmans, 1980]; Su, *Lexical Ambiguity in Poetry* [London/New York: Longman, 1994]). Metaphorization is also a key component in Dan 9:24-29, with strong ties to ambiguity. Martien A. Halvorson-Taylor looks at the "metaphorization of exile" and how such metaphorization transitions from one exilic picture to another (e.g. Lev 26; Jer 25-29) (*Enduring Exile: The Metaphorization of Exile in the Hebrew Bible* [VTSup 141; Leiden: Brill, 2011]).

[7] Childs, *IOTS*, 620.

[8] Cf. Michael Drosnin, *The Bible Code* (New York: Touchstone, 1997); Grant Jeffrey, *The Mysterious Bible Codes* (Nashville: Word, 1998). Jeffrey believes the message of Daniel 9 is universally accessible through a code. He writes "the information encoded in the Bible can only be accurately interpreted after a historical event has actually occurred" (58). The presence of the encoded term, "Yeshua," for example, confirms that Jesus is the "messiah" referred to in 9:25 (97).

[9] Cf. T.C. Smith, *Reading the Signs: A Sensible Approach to Revelation and other Apocalyptic Writings* (Macon, Ga.: Smyth & Helwys, 1997); John Walvoord, *Daniel: The Key to Prophetic Revelation* (Chicago: Moody Press, 1971); Hal Lindsey, *The Late, Great Planet Earth* (Grand Rapids: Zondervan, 1970). In the early reception of Dan 7-12, it is worth noting that the predictive model was but one avenue of eschatological interpretation. M.H. Farris cites two different streams of prophetic reading, each with its own sub-categories: (1) Jerusalemic (fall of the anointed) and Christological (loss of the Messiah); (2) preterist (symbols signify present reality) and futurist (a prophecy of something "not yet"). On the extremes of these axes, one could plot something like contemporary prophetic interpretation (The Formative Interpretations of the Seventy Years of Daniel [Ph.D., University of Toronto, 1990], 317-29).

[10] Seitz, *Character*, 23.

As Childs affirms, it is this property throughout the canonical shape of the text that allows Daniel to speak "prophetically of the end of the age."[11] This text was "no prophecy-after-the-event," but was an interpretation "to confirm the earlier prophecy which he believed."[12] This belief in an "earlier prophecy" shows that Daniel's spectrum of prophetic activity is greater than a reference to one number or date cast far into the future. The prophetic word in question reaches back further than Dan 2:44-45 and even further than Jer 25:11-14. Once we anchor this prophetic word in a given text, the interpreter's task is still incomplete: what of the textual associations supporting the more explicit texts (cf. Gen 2:1-3)? We will not repeat previous arguments here, but it suffices to note how the entirety of the Old Testament canon is "prophetic," and no text is larger or smaller than another within the providential decree of Yahweh's purposes.

1.3. Apocalyptic and the Openness of the Text

It is also common to discuss Danielic prophecy in conjunction with its apocalyptic surroundings. Fervent debate continues over the parent forms of apocalyptic, whether these forms originate in the prophetic genre or from a school of wisdom.[13] Overemphasis on "apocalyptic" as a formal tag is an unfortunate byproduct, leading some scholars to view the exercise as a case of *"obscurum per obscurius."*[14] Still, a number of definitions are worth considering. On the one hand, wisdom has a firm place in the Danielic genre. Playing off of the prophecy/wisdom binary, a "fusion of two traditions" showcases this role: an emphasis on "revealed wisdom" and the sapiential tradition.[15] These tradi-

---

[11] Childs, *IOTS*, 619.

[12] Ibid., 618.

[13] Von Rad argues extensively for wisdom as the social and textual precedent for early Jewish apocalyptic (*Wisdom in Israel* [Nashville: Abingdon, 1972], 263-83). Though we cannot sufficiently engage these debates, it is preferable to see prophecy (see definition above) and wisdom working together, resulting in the distinctive style and features we find in biblical apocalyptic (Dan 7-12). Beckwith, for example, believes we should return to a simple tag, such as "Danielic" or "Enochic literature" instead of apocalyptic, which is cumbersome and suffers from a "paradoxical" definition based on "the latest expressions" (*OT Canon*, 344). Beckwith submits a definition of apocalyptic, but it is (intentionally) bare and unhelpful: "Apocalyptic is literature in which God reveals great secrets to a favored saint (such as Daniel or Enoch) or a prophet (such as John)" (345).

[14] Philip Davies, "Eschatology in the Book of Daniel," *JSOT* 17 (1980) 38. Davies believes a fixation on apocalyptic "has driven a wedge" between the tales (chs. 1-6) and the visions (chs. 7-12), thereby obscuring the "organic development" of the book (33).

[15] Oegema, *Apocalyptic*, 13. He points to three lenses through which much of apocalyptic scholarship studies the material: reception history, social setting and "intellectual history" (compares "cross-fertilization" and "common apocalyptic" markers). Collins' own definition of apocalyptic is equally opaque: "a genre of revelatory literature with a narrative framework, in which a revelation is mediated by an otherworldly being to a

tions combined allow for equal weight to be distributed to both surfaces. Still, the *prophetic* ingredient within apocalyptic cannot be overlooked. Oegema contributes a useful hybridization—apocalyptic is a prophetic-sapiential forge for the "creation of religious identity."[16] Sumner's conclusion, however, correctly anticipates our angle of approach: "No matter whether Daniel's roots are prophetic or wisdom related, or both, *the two now present, within the Old Testament canon, a framework of meaning* within which we can see the importance of Daniel's message about the one coming on the clouds in the end time."[17]

For our purposes in this section, we will briefly investigate the part "apocalyptic" plays in Daniel's style of ambiguity. The genre *itself* is obscure and, due to the nature of the material, is difficult to relate to any clear, literary parentage. Is it coincidence that an author, in guarding his text from historical reductionism, chooses a vehicle rife with images, terseness and hyper-natural circumstances? Some indeed feel Daniel's obscure, theological message is secondary to the political and scribal influences entangled within apocalyptic. In such cases, apocalyptic is the craft of social and political advocacy, bearing little influence on the theological meaning of the text. The openness of the text, it follows, is a *byproduct* of the byproduct. Sweeney, for example, claims that Daniel "has a blatantly political and nationalistic agenda which it conveys with religious language."[18] This assertion highlights the tenuous strands upon which an overly socio-political reading is balancing. How can such an agenda be conveyed "blatantly" if the *conveyance* is "religious language"? Sweeney misrepresents the accessibility of Daniel's "religious language" in ch. 9, insinuating that the language is clear and open to all manner of historical parallel. These difficulties seem to sprout from the assumption that apocalyptic occupies a compartment separate from theological expression.[19]

---

human recipient, disclosing a transcendent reality which is both temporal, insofar as it envisages eschatological salvation, and spatial insofar as it involves another, supernatural world" ("Apocalypse: The Morphology of a Genre" [*Semeia* 14; Atlanta: Society of Biblical Literature, 1979], 9). With a wellspring of scrolls, both deuterocanonical texts and pseudapigrapha flowing out of the second century BCE—second century CE, a genre quickly turned into a *movement*. Textual features of apocalyptic morphed into sociopolitical features of propaganda—ambiguity is seldom considered a fixture of apocalyptic texts.

[16] Oegema, *Apocalyptic*, 14.
[17] Wells and Sumner, *Daniel*, 105-06n13 (italics mine).
[18] Sweeney, "End of Eschatology," 124.
[19] "The complexity of Daniel," VanGemeren observes, "reflects the wisdom of God's plan of redemption. *God* holds the key to understanding the prophecy of Daniel" (*Interpreting*, 342, italics mine). Ultimately, the veiled transmission of Daniel's words is God's will and action rather than the outgrowth of a social construct or the response of the reader. Of interest, is the similarity between the historical precision of the text and the precision of doctrinal studies: "For a true statement to serve the truth of being," T.F. Torrance writes, "it must fall short of it, be revisable in the light of it, and not be mistaken for it, since it does not possess the truth in itself but in the reality it serves. Thus a

Given the priority of the canonical shape in the text, our first instinct must be to *reprioritize* Sweeney's sequence, assigning "apocalyptic" (or "Danielic," *pace* Beckwith) a servant status to the overall sense exerted by the text. Daniel 9, as with any other biblical apocalypse (cf. Isa 24-27), deserves its own discrete recognition or we risk imposing a formal (and foreign) category upon the context. Apocalyptic, therefore, serves as a vehicle in Dan 9:24-27 to transport both revelation and mystery, according to Childs:

> The apocalyptic visions of Daniel offer a witness distinct from the classic prophets of the Old Testament. This theological tension remains regardless of whether or not the book is assigned a position in the canon among the Prophets or the Writings. Daniel's radical stance calls into question all human endeavours of 'bringing in the kingdom' or of 'humanizing the structures of society.' Rather, this biblical witness challenges the faithful to be awake and ready for the unexpected intervention of God in wrapping up all of human history.[20]

1.4. The Importance of History

As Seitz comments on Childs' own approach to Daniel: "Having joined the two halves of the book, not on a prophecy-fulfillment model overly constrained by historicism but by attention to the dynamic of God's accomplishing word, *the way was also open to continue to see Daniel as scripture beyond the timetables at the end of the book and long after the details of Maccabean persecution were past and gone.*"[21] Though critical of some lines of contemporary, predictive, and referential reading, Seitz is not denying the historical realities throughout Daniel's message. Seitz is merely highlighting the trajectory of the canonical shape within, and not in spite of, its natural setting.[22] The natural, historical setting—when incorporating the larger canonical intention—refers to events from the past, present and future. A canonical approach to Dan 9:24-27 is not a-historical, but *all*-historical.

In no way do we jettison the *bemerkenswerte Geschichte* of Dan 9:24-27; in fact, the history particular to Daniel is necessary for investigating how, why and where the authors place sequential chronology in the background and sculpt the text into a "theochronological" unit. Such attention to history is a

---

dash of inadequacy is necessary for its precision" (*Reality & Evangelical Theology: The Realism of Christian Revelation* [Eugene: Wipf & Stock, 2003], 66). To restate this point, ambiguity can stand closer to the truth of statements, in some respects, than detailed reference.

[20] Childs, *IOTS*, 622.
[21] Seitz, *Figured Out*, 31-32.
[22] "A canonical reading does not domesticate history, but brings it into proper focus and proportion" (Seitz, "Prophetic Associations," 166).

feature of the canonical approach.[23] A scholar's first inclination may be to accuse the approach of obfuscation since—whether purposefully or inadvertently—it is *foiling* historical integrity. But this strategy serves a larger historiographical program, wherein the architect of the historical account supplies the "unifying thought" in which "time is construed as a whole."[24] Few interpretations of Dan 9:24-27 entertain ambiguity, especially if said interpretation largely depends upon historical allusion. History, instead, is being read through multiple lenses. Daniel does not just "give report" but is "interpreting history in the light of prophecy...not prophecy in the light of history."[25]

Finally, concealment of meaning is a mode by which a reader enters the text repeatedly and humbly. It is in imagery and how the author widens the possible meaning of words that causes the reader to have to reach for this reality, thereby exercising his or her interpretive faculties in the process.[26] Such non-referential language, particularly metaphor, is a model candidate in such a process, as observed in our exegesis of 9:24-27.[27] In Dan 9, the strategic

---

[23] Dennis Olson calls this feature the approaches' "historical confrontation with Ancient Israel" ("'Seeking' the Inexpressible Texture of Thy Word: A Practical Guide to Brevard Childs' Canonical Approach to Theological Exegesis," *PTR* 14.1 [2008] 53-68).

[24] Willis, 30. She re-contextualizes this idea in her study of Daniel, owing to the work of Paul Ricouer (*Time and Narrative* [trans. K. McLaughlin and D. Pellauer; Chicago: University of Chicago Press, 1984) and Carol Newsom ("Rhyme and Reason: The Historical Resumé in Israelite and Early Jewish Thought," in *Congress Volume Leiden 2004* [ed. A. Lemaire; Boston: Brill, 2006], 227).

[25] Childs, *IOTS*, 620. Prophecies constructed "in light of history" are abundant, as Sumner summarizes: "For historical reasons both Jews and Christians were, for the most part, stout preterists. Jews found the 'cutting off' in the tragic events of AD 70 or 135. Christians pointed to Jesus's death or the fall of Jerusalem as judgment upon that event (and in fulfillment of the Gospels' prediction). Futurist interpretations were the outliers: for example, on the Christian side when the Severan persecution inspired imminent expectations of the end (which needed to be dampened by Hippolytus), and on the Jewish side when Sabbatai Sevi made his failed messianic claims in the Middle Ages" (Wells and Sumner, *Daniel*, 190). Sumner echoes this notion of space, pointing to the "surplus of meaning in the original passage itself."

[26] In a general sense, Caird, 92, brings imagery and ambiguity together when speaking of "generalization" or "indeterminancy." Terms can be intentionally broad; however, Daniel's style of ambiguity aligns best with what Caird defines a "style of economy" (94). It is a narrative unfolding in its "starkest outline" and only mentions "decisive points." In the narrative, there is an unidentifiable time and place that "call for interpretation."

[27] Relating images and veiled language, Aaron observes two functions of ambiguity in metaphor: (1) "to establish possible meanings" and (2) to find the "limits of its implications" (*Biblical*, 2). To achieve these functions, the author and the reader require a "shared reading strategy" (20). This means that, "the successful decoding of a speaker's metaphors will be dependent upon the extent to which the speaker and his or her hearers share an interpretive strategy." He also wants to avoid the unhelpful binary of "literal" and "figurative" language, proposing "gradient" levels of judgment for ascertaining *how* metaphorical a text is. He writes, "the way variables influence changes along a meaning

vagueness is of a specific kind, neither wholly referential nor wholly non-referential. *Suspended* referentiality would be a more appropriate label. Childs, in his conclusions concerning obscurity and the shape of Dan 9, ends with the following:

> Therefore, the biblical writer used symbolic language, and spoke of 'times and seasons,' of the 'contemptible one,' of the 'transgression that makes desolate,' and of the 'little help." Regardless of how sure the interpretation of these figures may have seemed to the wise, nevertheless, they always required a translation. The vision itself remained veiled.[28]

The act of veiling texts—within a canonical shape—carries with it a theological reasoning: it is to exult the "*peculiar* relationship between the text and the people of God which is constitutive of canon."[29] Indeed, the relationship between the canonical shape of the Hebrew text and God's communication through scripture to successive generations is mystifying. As Driver puts it, "[T]he peculiar, textually-mediately relationship between God and his people begins well within the biblical period, Childs argues, in a series of decisions meant to become *binding on future generations of Israel.*"[30] Webster also directs our attention to the humble station of canon and its ability to "bind" future generations by holding together the dialectic of revelation and mystery:

> Neither revelation nor the canon abolish the mystery of God's freedom, which remains beyond codification. *Because* it is a function of *deus revelatus*, the canon is also a function of *deus absconditus*. Because in revelation God remains hidden—that is, because God's self-communication is his making present of the sheer incomprehensible gratuity of his being and act—a theological understanding of the canon must always be demarcated from an account of non-referential cultural norms.[31]

To encounter the interpretive possibilities woven into Dan 9:24-27 is also to encounter yet another facet of God's own mystery and revelatory character, both of which he divulges in his freedom, mercy and inclination to include the

---

continuum." One metaphor can be more intense than another (29). This gradient of figurative significance is parallel to a gradient of ambiguity (for example, strongly figurative parallels increase ambiguity); this is termed "the meaning continuum and the relative role of ambiguity" (112).

[28] Childs, *IOTS*, 621.
[29] Ibid., 75 (italics mine).
[30] Driver, *Brevard Childs*, 128, italics mine.
[31] Webster, *Word and Church*, 15.

faithful reader. The theological message and application of Dan 9:24-27 is just as much contingent on its strategically crafted presentation as the content within the text.

1.5. Creating Space and the Reception of Daniel 9:24-27

Whether the context shifted from Persian to Seleucid or Greek to Roman backgrounds, Daniel continued to be authoritative and identified as scripture, especially "as a true witness to the end of the age, which still lay in the future."[32] It is the presence of the interpretive possibilities in the text that frees the text from the constraints of antiquation or narrow to a single audience. Words, after all, are conveyances for "bridging space, time and other gaps of differentiation."[33] Opening the space up, through the widening of meaning and other strategies, keeps the text from sealing off future readers—it is "the manner in which the book was shaped in the canonical process" that "provides a critical check against the perennial danger of politicizing and trivializing its message."[34] Space is, in the case of Dan 9:24-27, a result of the author's style and shaping. Sweeney feels this ability to voice a message that reverberates through numerous generations is what makes Daniel "the quintessential eschatological book of the Hebrew Bible."[35] Daniel 9, therefore, is *more* than apocalyptic literature. This move to create space, as Driver argues, is a feature of "Scripture's unity," which "at both the exegetical level and the hermeneutical or theological level, admits a range of answers." Thus, the dynamic of space making is not only a literary phenomenon, but a theological essential.

We can trace a multitude of communities that occupy the space created by the complex, canonical shape of Daniel's text. To illustrate, Childs points to the work of 2 Esdras, wherein the reception of Dan 9:27 (cf. 8:13; 11:31; Matt 24:15) moves past its primary context. In the time of 2 Esdras, the "desolator" and the "fourth beast" as a whole is no longer identified with the Seleucid Empire or Epiphanes (12:10f), but the author is, nevertheless, "very well aware that his interpretation differs from that originally understood by Daniel when Esdras identifies the fourth beast with Rome."[36] Likewise, the author of 1-2 Maccabees

---

[32] Childs, *IOTS*, 619.

[33] Erhard Gerstenberger, "Canon Criticism and the Meaning of *Sitz im Leben*," in *Canon, Theology and Old Testament Interpretation* (ed. Gene Tucker et al.; Philadelphia: Fortress, 1988), 21. Christine Helmer also uses the same language to describe the essential characteristic of biblical theology, which "is to provide a bridge for two-way traffic between biblical exegesis and systematic theology's reflection on the subject matter" ("Biblical Theology: Bridge over Many Waters," *CurBS* 3 [2005] 169-96).

[34] Childs, *IOTS*, 622.

[35] Sweeney, "End of Eschatology," 123. Wellhausen calls this protraction in the Scriptures, an "elasticity of hope" ("Zur Apokalyptischen Literatur," *Skizzen und Vorarbeiten* 6 [1899]: 225-34).

[36] Childs, *IOTS*, 619.

does not *totally* equate the "abomination of desolation" (Dan 9:27) with the actions of Antiochus IV Epiphanes, namely the removal of the *Tamid*.[37]

The example of awaited "rest" is also framed to allow subsequent readerships to occupy its interpretive and theological parameters. Implicit to this space is the following question: How long before full rest comes to Israel (cf. Dan 12:13)? If this *is* the question, it makes sense to create an eschatological space for future generations to interpret or actualize their place in Daniel's episodic summary of rest and unrest. When we ask this same question from within Christ's church, we solidify the ontological bond we share with our Israelite recipients and recognize "space" as more than a trick of the wording. Seitz emphasizes the manner in which this eschatological (and ontological) space opens within the canonical scriptures, namely, "under figures and occupying that space *prepared* for such and extended understanding by virtue of the dynamic life of a personal God with his people."[38]

2. Daniel 9:24-27 in the Olivet Discourse

Recognizing interpretive space in Dan 9:24-27, Childs inquires, "How was it possible that the New Testament ... could interpret the visions of Daniel as foretelling events which still lay in the future?"[39] In what follows, we will outline and integrate the contribution of the NT witness—particularly, the Olivet Discourse (Matthew 24-25; Mark 13; Luke 21)—as it takes up Dan 9:24-27 and other texts.[40] The gospel writer bases much of Matthew 24-25 on the scaffolding provided by Dan 9:24-27 while still directing the reader to other parts of Daniel. Explicit use of the phrase "abomination of desolation" (cf. Dan 8:13; 9:27; 11:31) in Matt 24:15 is not the only connection tying this passage to Daniel.[41] Though we affirm a higher degree of continuity between these passages,

---

[37] Childs notices the effect of Daniel's eschatological space through the post-Maccabean context (*IOTS*, 619).

[38] Seitz, *Character*, 18.

[39] Childs, *IOTS*, 614.

[40] Interaction with the Gospel accounts will be limited to Matt 24-25 with the occasional reference to parallel accounts since the majority of associations appear in the discourse. That said, comparison with key points in Luke and Mark will help demonstrate Matthew's apparent interest in Daniel's text. One major example of this relationship is in Mark 13-14. Mark 13-14 associates the "Son of Man" with Dan 7:13– the only two independent quotations (13:26; 14:62)—but redirects this Danielic thread to the foreground, setting the Matthean emphasis on the canonical voice of Dan 9:24-27, to the background (cf. Craig Evans, "Daniel in the New Testament: Visions of God's Kingdom," in *The Book of Daniel: Composition and Reception, Volume II*, 490-527).

[41] Another possible connection is Dan 12:13 ("But go your way until the *end* [קֵץ] and you will *rest* [נוח] and will stand in your allotted place at the *end* [קֵץ] of days") and Matt 24:13 ("But the one who endures to the *end* [τέλος] will be *saved* [σῴζω]"). Of course, we cannot automatically span the bridge between languages and semantic differences, but the OG provides a potential window into the apostles' question, "what will be

however, there is also noticeable *discontinuity* woven into the NT appropriation of 9:24-27. As we will observe, discontinuity is a welcomed trait of those readerships that occupy the space of Dan 9:24-27, who thereby continue to validate the "word going forth" to Yahweh's decreed end.

2.1. Persecution of the Faithful Saints

Both Yahweh's "saints" and Christ's "elect" are subject to persecution (Dan 7:25; 11:33-36; 12:3, 10, 13; Matt 24:4-9, 22). Here, it is not Dan 9:24-27 to which Matthew is alluding, but the unfolding narrative of Dan 7-12. True, the reference to the "abomination of desolation" links Matthew to Dan 8:13, 9:27, 11:31 and 12:13; however, the plot of Matt 24-25 follows all of the "waypoints" that mark Dan 7-12. Blomberg describes the associations, stating, "a constellation of allusions rather than an actual quotation seems to be a more accurate description of Matthew's form."[42] In Dan 11, a portion of the chapter is devoted to a brief narrative not unlike what we find in Matt 24:

> And the wise among the people will make many understand, though for some days they will stumble by sword and flame, by captivity and plunder. When they stumble, they will receive a little help. And many will join themselves to them with flattery, and some of the wise will stumble, so that they may be refined, purified, and made white, until the time of the end, for it still awaits the appointed time. And the king will do as he wills. He will exalt himself and magnify himself above every god, and will speak astonishing things against the God of gods. He will prosper until the indignation is accomplished; for what is decreed will be done (Dan 11:33-36)

> But go your way until the end. And you will rest and you will stand in your allotted place at the end of days (Dan 12:13)

> For many will come in my name, saying 'I am the Christ,' and they will lead many astray. And you will hear of wars and rumors of wars. See that you are not alarmed, for this must take place, but the end is not yet. For nation will rise against nation, and kingdom against kingdom, and there will be famines and earthquakes in various places. All these are but the beginning of the birth pains. Then they will deliver you up to tribulation and put you to death, and you will be hated by all nations for my name's sake. And then many will

---

the sign…of the *end* (συντέλεια) of the age" (Matt 24:3): "And you will go, for there are yet days and hours until the fulfillment of the *consummation* (συντέλεια). And you will rest and will rise upon your glory at the *consummation* (συντέλεια) of days" (Dan 12:13 LXX). Matthew's discourse augments the end of days to include the consummation under Christ.

[42] Craig Blomberg, "Matthew," in *Commentary on the New Testament Use of the Old Testament* (ed. G.K. Beale; Grand Rapids: Baker Academic, 2007), **86-87**.

fall away and betray one another and hate one another. And many
false prophets will arise and lead many astray. And because of law-
lessness will be increased, the love of many will grow cold. But the
one who endures to the end will be saved (Matt 24:4-13)

Like Dan 11, Matt 24 is adopting a narrative that naturally grows from an immersive reading of 9:24-27. These related narratives are not unlike detailed photographs taken from within the vague landscape of Daniel's interpretation (9:24-27).

The authors of Dan 11 and Matt 24-25, though centuries apart, both appeared to have been applying the framework of 9:24-27 at some point, identifying *persecution* as one of the common threads. Oppression enters through flattery and deceit (Dan 11:35-36; Matt 24:4, 12) before chaos spreads through catastrophe and warfare (Dan 11:33-34; Matt 24:5-6), at a time when it is "kingdom against kingdom" (Dan 7:23-24; Matt 24:7; cf. Is 19:2). Persecution as never before witnessed will befall God's elect saints, a point communicated by both passages (Dan 9:12; 12:1 [esp. θ']; Matt 24:21). Both authors employ images of cosmic upheaval to convey the incredible events, both containing physical and spiritual implications (Dan 7:2; 12:3; Matt 24:29).[43] In the end, those who patiently endure will be "delivered," a notion with many possible nuances (Dan 12:13; Matt 24:13). Even here, it is more accurate to associate these images as "conceptual parallels" rather "than even a formal echo."[44]

2.2. The Mantle of Wisdom

Like Daniel, readers are instructed throughout the passage to take up the mantle of wisdom in the midst of persecution. The mantle of wisdom of which the book of Daniel is so concerned (9:22-23; cf. 2:20; 12:10) is detectable in the Gospel account, but transformed. The emphasis on *discernment* in Matt 24-25 is not only greater, but of a specific quality (cf. 24:4-5, 11, 24). We already know wisdom is characteristic of the persecuted (cf. Dan 11:33-36; 12:2, 10-13)—those who suffer for Christ are also those who "discern" and take a wise path (cf. Matt 24:4-9). The instruction moves from non-deception (πλανάω) to readiness (ἕτοιμος), being awake (γρηγορέω) and wisdom (φρόνιμος) in the face of Christ's imminent return (24:42-44; 25:13). It is true, the angelic messenger instructs Daniel to "know and understand" (vv. 22-23, 25) the *same canonical*

---

[43] The "convulsion of the heavens" is a standard convention for describing such turmoil in Jewish eschatology (Ezek 32:7-8; *2 Esd.* 5:4; *1 En.* 80:4; *As. Mos.* 10:5; cf. Blomberg, 88).

[44] Blomberg, 89. As with any of these continuities, there are also distinctions unique to the Gospel account. For example, Matthew likens these tribulations to "birth pains," implying that Christ's return will bring something new in His glorious train. The identity of the Son of Man who will inherit the final kingdom is disambiguated: Christ is and will be king (Matt 24:27, 30; Dan 7:13-14) and the persecuted saints will be restored (Dan 7:27; 11:35; 12:1-3; Matt 24:13).

patterns as the reader who must "be aware" and discerning in Matt 24-25. Specifics, such as the pursuit of true and false Christ-figures (24:5), are exclusive to the NT account, but the rise and fall of kingdoms (24:7) as well as the linchpin event of the "abomination of desolation" (24:15) locate Matt 24-25 well within the canonical boundaries of Daniel's Sabbath-heptadic pattern while the Gospel account retains its own details, emphases and theological concerns.

Wisdom is also the common denominator in both Daniel and Matthew's exhortation for discerning the "end" (24:45; 25:1-9). Among such hermeneutical obstacles as ambiguity or difficult translations, both canonical witnesses agree, the most formidable impasse is the knowledge of the precise time of Jesus' return: "But concerning that day and hour no one knows, not even the angels of heaven nor the Son, but the Father only" (24:36). The finality of Jesus' statement should give us pause when treating the timetables in Dan 9:24-27 as a forensic matter of history. It is an unfortunate, but astute, observation by Sumner, who writes, "the human mind has often sought to know 'when shall these things be' (12:6; cf. Matt. 24:3) in terms of a human timetable."[45] Even the Matthean account maintains a tension, in which the exhortation to be watchful is held taut with the inability to know the "day and hour" of the Son of Man's coming (24:27).

Again, the final day is paramount in Matthew's discourse, but the question of Daniel's timeframe is not entirely ignored. "We are told," Sumner writes, "that it is out of mercy that God has shortened the days (24:22), for otherwise no one could have survived. As some in the history of Daniel's interpretation pointed out, this cutting short may mean that the number schemes offered by Daniel have been changed, out of mercy, by God himself."[46] Sumner's evaluation aligns well with the potential interpretive force inherent to the seventy sevens in Dan 9:24. The time frame is coordinated with God's merciful plan in which oppressive rulers operate for a time—as per the sin-debt discussed above—but are ultimately supplanted by Yahweh's promised rule. To lock down the "day and the hour" (Matt 24:36) of the final day is to interpret in error, according to the Gospel writer, and ignores "a salutary warning against excessive interest in this aspect of Daniel to the exclusion of its larger purpose."[47]

Interpreters of the NT account are urged to include an "emphasis on the virtue of watchfulness"[48] just as interpreters of Daniel are to wrestle with and locate themselves in the imagery of 9:24-27.[49] One is not conflated into the

---

[45] Childs, *IOTS*, 622.
[46] Wells and Sumner, *Daniel*, 111.
[47] Ibid.
[48] Ibid.
[49] It is not by chance the book of Daniel ends with the salvation and vindication of the "wise" (12:3-10). We find a group of scenes that form into a portrait of wise character. The portrait is left without a resolution and anticipates an ending from its canonical position.

other; both deliver their own message. Watchfulness is certainly implicit in Dan 7-12, but, as is the pattern with space making, the reception of this same teaching in the Gospel account is partly explicit and partly implicit. The line of biblical writers, bound by the character and actions of the one Triune God, "pointed to the end of the world in order to call forth *a faithful testimony* from the people of God."[50]

2.3. The "Abomination of Desolation" (βδέλυγμα τῆς ἐρημώσεως)

We will not retrace our steps through the exegesis of 9:27, but we will consider Matthew's use of the phrase through Dan 8-11. Our first reaction may be to link Matt 24:15 exclusively to one of the references in Daniel (9:27, 8:13 or 11:31); however, the association is more complex. Certainly the wording, if not the concept, of Daniel's "abomination that makes desolate" or desolating force is present in Matt 24:15 (cf. Mark 13:14). But, as Collins correctly identifies, the phrase and its nuances are "part of an eschatological tableau" related now to the destruction of Jerusalem by the Romans.[51] To say the Matthean account is offering a *total* explanation of the desolating force in Dan 9:27 is inaccurate. By this time, Antiochus' figuration has left its mark, but the Gospels' interpretation and inclusion of the Danielic text is still valid, authoritative and instructive. There is space enough for the New Testament to track Daniel's prophetic message, and so, "if Antiochus did not prove to be the Old Testament Antichrist and the kingdom of God was not ushered in with his death, then for the canonical editors it was not the prophecy which was at fault, *but the earlier identification with those specific historical events.*"[52] Illustrating this point, Josephus writes concerning Dan 9:27, "These misfortunes our nation did in fact come to experience under Antiochus Epiphanes, just as Daniel many years before saw and wrote that they would happen."[53] Still, Josephus does not see a complete fulfillment of these events in either the Seleucid ruler or the fall of Jerusalem to the Romans.[54] As Childs alludes, it is too simplistic to claim each community receiving 9:24-27 is applying the entirety of the passage's theological sense to the crisis of its day. With that, we can see why Matthew leaves the reader with no more than a quick snippet of the construction βδέλυγμα τῆς ἐρημώσεως and a note for the reader "to understand" (νοέω; 24:15).

Here, attention to the parallel accounts (Mark 13:14; Luke 21:20) delivers fascinating results that will help articulate Matthew's use of the construction. Studies have long noted the seeming fluid personae of the "abomination of desolation" throughout the Gospel accounts. Mark 13:14 reads, "But when you see the abomination of desolation *standing where he should not be* (ἑστηκότα ὅπου οὐ δεῖ)." This account includes detail to create a personification—

---

[50] Childs, *IOTS*, 622 (italics original).
[51] Collins, *Daniel*, 358.
[52] Childs, *IOTS*, 620.
[53] Josephus, *Ant.* 10:276.
[54] Ibid.; Adler, "Apocalyptic Survey," 216.

common to the participial form of ἵστημι—of the "abomination of desolation." Alternatively, Luke 21:20 equates βδέλυγμα τῆς ἐρημώσεως with "Jerusalem" because "its *desolation* (ἐρήμωσις) has come near." Matthew 24:15 broadens the notion and describes "the abomination of desolation ... standing/erected (ἑστός) in the holy place," implying a human figure (cf. Matt 18:2; John 8:3; Acts 22:30), object (cf. Mark 3:24; 7:9; Rom 3:31) or power (cf. Acts 7:60; Rom 10:3; Heb 10:9), and, yet, avoiding any specificity.[55] Each instance of the construction is brief and not in agreement, with an additional clue in Matthew and Mark: "let the reader understand." This vague wording obligates the interpreter to reach for the Danielic backstory. If reference to the βδέλυγμα τῆς ἐρημώσεως was self-evident as an ostensive reference, we would not expect a call for further study. The canonical shape of Dan 9:24-27 continues, therefore, through the Gospel accounts and remains in expectation, not fulfillment.

2.4. Discontinuities Between Dan 9:24-27 and Matthew 24-25

The first notable discontinuity is the expansion from Israel and "Jerusalem" (Dan 9:3-19, 24) to the "righteous" apart from Israel (Matt 24:30; 25:10-12, 27-28). Although Daniel's text also affects people-groups outside of Israel, it is Jesus' discourse that voices the universalization of God's people (Israel and non-Israel) in the eschatological timeline. It is also likely this new dimension, veiled in the OT, is an outward movement of the larger, salvific plan. Considering Dan 12:1, a connection offered by Sumner, we can include a parallel aspect to Matthew's account of salvation: "And there will be a time of trouble, such as never has been since there was a nation until that time. But at that time your people will be delivered, everyone whose name will be found written in the book." This passage provides ample room (and motivation) to include the Gentile masses within those "delivered," or, as the OG augments, "exalted" (ὑψωθήσεται). Since both pictures of the great disaster are fitted together (Dan 12:1//Matt 24:21), a similar picture of salvation follows close behind: "the incomparable distress of Dan 12:1 will accompany this disaster (Matt 24:21)" until the "fulfillment of Dan 7:13-14."[56]

The strongest discontinuity is the unmistakable absence of Daniel's Sabbath-heptadic chronology, including the emphasis on the completed "end" of

---

[55] The genitive construction has an array of possibilities, either "epexegetical" or "genitive of apposition" (cf. Daniel Wallace, *Greek Grammar: Beyond the Basics, An Exegetical Syntax of the New Testament* [Grand Rapids: Zondervan, 1996], 95). Friedrich Blass and Albert Debrunner lean towards a genitive of *purpose* (*A Greek Grammar of the New Testament and Other Early Christian Literature* [Chicago: Chicago University Press, 1961], 166). In addition to the vague syntax, C.F.D. Moule writes this regarding the phrase: "This is so immensely versatile and hard-working a case that anything like an exhaustive catalogue of its uses would be only confusing and unnecessarily dull" (*An Idiom Book of New Testament Greek* [Cambridge: Cambridge University Press, 1982], 37).

[56] Wells and Sumner, *Daniel*, 110.

Yahweh's plan to eliminate Israel's sin-debt once and for all. Instead of illustrating how sin will end and transgressions will be covered (Dan 9:24), the NT discourse ends with the love and care of the "stranger" (25:35-46). Those who clothed, fed and cared for the stranger are the "righteous" (25:37) that "inherit the Kingdom" (25:34)—in part, this is what it means to "be awake" and prepare for the Son of Man. It is a puzzling (and surprising) answer to the question "How will we know it is you?" To be sure, we can detect hints of a heptadic background in the "shadows" of the discourse, but, in Christ's account of these events, the reader is swept into the final day of the "end" (συντέλεια/τέλος; 24:3, 6, 13-14)—the "end," here, is decidedly a series of moments in line with Christ's return. Whereas Daniel concludes his interpretation with the final act of the desolating force (9:27b-d), Matthew seems to focus in on the ambiguous space between the coming of the desolation and the fall of the desolating force. It is the "coming of the Son of Man" that truly finishes this chapter of the saints' story.

We conclude the section by reiterating how the NT reception of Dan 9:24-27, and other Daniel passages, is a critical link in the unfolding *Nachleben* of Dan 9. The canonical book of Daniel speaks with an OT voice *and* a two-testament voice. Echoing this truth from the standpoint of 9:24-27, we see "a kind of fit," Sumner observes, "between this passage in Daniel and the story of the events leading to the death of Jesus, where a mysterious messianic claim is conjoined to a symbolic end to sacrifice and a prediction of the coming disaster."[57] In the Gospel accounts, Daniel's "decreed end" moves into a declaration that Christ, the Son of Man, marks the end. Alongside the culmination, the discernment of the saints remains on the foreground of these passages, albeit in different senses.

Describing "the story of the events" in broad terms, as Sumner does, seems to capture the canonical prospect of Dan 9:24-27 and Matthew's own reception of the text, wherein he himself only utilizes the *skeleton* of Daniel's interpretation (cf. 9:2, 24-27). This utilization allows Matthew (and other accounts) to project its own voice and even generate its own riddles, mysteries, questions and disambiguation.[58] Quotation and ostensive reference are not the gatekeepers guarding our entrance into the New Testament. This point is proven by the broader and multifaceted system of association running between Daniel and Matthew. Rather, it is through a "hermeneutical reserve" of texts and the ontological relationship in the two-testaments.[59]

---

[57] Wells and Sumner, *Daniel*, 190.

[58] Matthew 24-25 leaves the reader with a flood of images as well as questions: What does the "great tribulation" entail (24:21)? How do we interpret 24:29, which reads, "Immediately after the tribulation of those days the sun will be darkened, and the moon will not give its light, and the stars will fall from heaven, and the powers of the heavens will be shaken?" These Gospel accounts, it seems, do not intend to resolve or add detail to the apocalyptic imagery.

[59] Wells and Sumner, 110.

3. Daniel 9:24-27 and the Character of Two-Testament Scripture

Before we set Dan 9:24-27 in its two-testament context, we must first elaborate on two tenets that uphold the canonical character of Christian scripture. The first tenet: interpreting an OT text in light of a two-testament witness is not just an ecclesial practice imposed from outside the text. Neither is appealing to the witness of both testaments an addendum or even a method *ad extra* attached in order to appease certain doctrinal claims. The Old and New Testaments themselves were not joined simply by "a mature Christian confession" or receive "a continual final set of chapters appended."[60]

The second crucial tenet of the canonical approach is that Christian interpretation of an OT passage does not stop at its NT appropriation. Put another way, the vehicle by which we speak of the OT as Christian Scripture is not reducible to *Vetus Testamentum en Novo receptum* ("how OT is received through the NT"), which, as with the example of Mark 13 and Matthew 24, is only one cross-section of the OT's scriptural significance.[61] Rather than a full-stop at the end of one tradition history, the reality of the New Testament witness adds "a kind of layered historical reference" which is "first in Jeremiah, then in Daniel itself, and again when the passage is read *in light of* the passion narratives."[62] The NT voice does not drown out the voice of the OT. It is worth remembering, as Seitz comments, that the "'New Testament' scriptural authority was given its logic and its material form with reference to the Scriptures as first received by the church."[63] Reducing the relationship between the OT and NT to a matter of cross-reference is only a "species" of scriptural interpretation.

In affirming these two tenets, a two-testament reading of Daniel 9 becomes the next, natural step in the canonical approach. The NT, therefore, is "the threshold and not the hearth" moving in accordance and conformity with the Old Testament.[64] Methods for which the canonical approach is often mistaken see the transition from one testament to another as an exchange of traditions placed in sharp, discernible relief (*Nachdunkelung*) or as the theological consequence of "form-critical exegesis."[65] Just as in the comments above, the

---

[60] Seitz, *Character*, 19.

[61] Seitz continues to define what he means by "OT *per se*": "'Unto itself' in the context of concern for the character of Christian Scripture is a theological category in the first instance, based upon the historical witness of OT as canon. The OT has a salvation-historical dimension, *but that dimension is by no means the chief way to understand the Scriptures of Israel as a Christian witness*" (*Character*, 21; italics mine).

[62] Wells and Sumner, *Daniel*, 190. The emphasis on "in light of" is necessary and is an appropriate preposition for communicating the layered sense of the New Testament reading of Daniel.

[63] Seitz, *Character*, 17.

[64] Ibid., 24.

[65] Cf. Hermann Gunkel, *Creation and Chaos in the Primeval Era and the Eschaton: A Religio-Historical Study of Genesis 1 and Revelation 12* (trans. K. William Whitney

NT reception of Dan 9:24-27 does not claim a full and final resolution to the Danielic text. The discrete voice of the Old Testament (also the "OT per se" or "OT unto itself") refers to its ability to "speak Christianly."[66] A discrete reading *is* indeed a two-testament reading, albeit one that rests on "the very fact that the Christian canon treasures a portion of the scripture in which the name of Jesus is not mentioned," which is "an initial warrant for seeking another theological option."[67] To perceive God in Daniel is not "an historical anachronism," but "a consciously Christian understanding of the continuing, authoritative function of the Old Testament for the Church."[68]

Refocusing on the contributions of the NT reception of Daniel, we now have an opportunity to include the unique contribution of Dan 9:24-27 for the purposes of a thick, biblical theological description. After accounting for the trajectories of both testaments, "the seventy years of exile end only at the Resurrection-Ascension and on the last day and that the interpretation of the texts in the canon *has to be held open yet wider* in hope of these events."[69] This wider space held open for the faithful readers and interpreters within the church begin to view Daniel as "an exemplar of Christian prayer" and *not only* a penitent representative of confessing Israel.[70] A wider space also recasts the role of the Gentiles within the sin-debt narrative discussed above. In the transition from loss of land or end of exile into complete rest or "the end of sin," Sumner reminds us that the "repossession of the land is dependent on Israel's sin, but the return, brought about in the defeat of the Gentiles can take place when *their* sin has reached the requisite measure to merit dispossession."[71] Redemption is another example of the contribution of the OT making its Trinitarian sense in conjunction with the NT. Commonly understood to be individ-

---

Jr.; Grand Rapids/Cambridge: Eerdmans, 2006); Koch, *The Growth of the Biblical Tradition: The Form-Critical Method* (trans. S.M. Culpritt; London: A&C Black, 1967), 110.

[66] This ability to speak with a Christian voice in *both* directions (unlike *Heilsgeschichte*), with equal weight bestowed upon each testament, is a distinctive feature of canonical biblical theology (Childs, *BTONT*, 16-18).

[67] Ibid., *OT Theology*, 30.

[68] Ibid.

[69] Wells and Sumner, *Daniel*, 186.

[70] Ibid., 187.

[71] Ibid.; cf. Anderson, *Sin*, 79. Of course, our place on the continuum of faith communities is not the same as plotting a position along the axis of tradition history—a deficient type of interpretation that "makes the Bible look like us and like the way we do theology." Israel is typological foreshadowing of the NT church, but not equated to it. The NT church is similar and different, continuous and, yet, discontinuous. Seitz answers the question as to why we not only occupy a different chronological space than Israel, but a qualitative space: "the very thing that makes us unlike the people within the Bible is the existence of the Bible itself, a full literary canon, *which we have in a form and scope no one there had*" ("The Old Testament as Abiding Theological Witness: Inscripting a Theological Curriculum," in *Word Without End: The Old Testament as Abiding Theological Witness* [Waco, Tx.: Baylor University Press, 2004], 3-12, here 7.).

ual and spiritual, the OT witness, through the medium of Dan 9:24-27, incorporates the community as well as the physical aspects of the "time to come." According to this understanding, Messianic expectation, in the context of a canonical approach, looks somewhat different between testaments. Our figural position aligns us with the same community, the same Triune God, and the same expectation. To be sure, figuration means, "for those who confess the Lordship of Jesus Christ there is an immediate morphological fit."[72]

4. Daniel 9:24-27 and the Rule of Faith

The rule of faith is indeed "the most central plank in canonical figuration."[73] Far from being a dogmatic extra—as if the rule could be *separated* from Christian scripture—it is "the historically shaped canon of scripture, in its two discrete witnesses" and "a christological rule of faith that in the church, by the action of the Holy Spirit, accrues textual authority."[74] As we discovered in our analysis of the character of two-testament scripture, Daniel 9:24-27 is indeed part of a "second witness to the work of God in Christ." But what primer do we use to communicate this truth? Awareness of *how* the OT speaks to the subject matter of the NT is vital. The rule, far from being an antique of the early church, is binding on the Christian reader and, likewise, "binds" the two testaments together. It exists because "God is known."[75] Because such a rule is contingent on the reality of God, it is more than a metanarrative,[76] tradition or a simple feature of communal use.[77] Rather than being an extra-textual overlay, it creates "interpretive relationship *within* the scriptures."[78] With regard to the text-subject matter relationship, the rule is "a hypothesis for reading" the Scriptures in their "coherent order and inherently relational character."[79]

The rule of faith has implications for the ongoing reception of Dan 9. Critical scholars contend that the only reason for the church's validation of texts

---

[72] C. Kavin Rowe, "The Doctrine of God is a Hermeneutic: The *Biblical Theology* of Brevard S. Childs," in *The Bible as Christian Scripture* (ed. Christopher Seitz; Atlanta: SBL, 2013), 382.

[73] Driver, *Brevard Childs*, 249.

[74] Ibid., "Childs and the Canon or Rule of Faith," in *The Bible as Christian Scripture*, 248.

[75] Childs, *OT Theology*, 29.

[76] cf. Paul Blowers, "The Regula Fidei and the Narrative Character of Early Christian Faith," *ProEccl* 16 (1999): 199-228.

[77] cf. Craig Allert, *A High View of Scripture? The Authority of the Bible and the Formation of the New Testament Canon* (Grand Rapids: Baker, 2007); see also William Abraham, *Canon and Criterion in Christian Theology: From the Fathers to Feminism* (New York: Oxford University Press, 1998); cf. David Kelsey, *The Uses of Scripture in Recent Theology* (Philadelphia: Fortress, 1975).

[78] Leonard Finn, "Reflections on the Rule of Faith," in *The Bible as Christian Scripture*, 221-42, here 222.

[79] Ibid., 232.

such as Dan 9:24-27 is to implant apocalyptic symbols and Christocentric references into the original meaning. This would allow early Christian interpreters to substitute Israel's context for their own. But this is hardly the case. The rule of faith was always operative for the church—it applies to the whole of Christian scripture while respecting its diverse literary forms (i.e. Jewish apocalyptic).[80] Childs, for example, is quick to chase this argument for the "oneness of scripture's scope" with the stipulation that this rule is "not a rival to the multiple voices within the canon."[81] The rule's foremost operation is to provide "the critical norm by which to *test* the truth of its reception."[82] Contexts and "hard" texts are not glossed over but met with rigor and patience. The God who reveals does so by including a "givenness" to the Scriptures, not an invitation to infuse meaning into a foreign context.

Using "completion" in Dan 9:24-27 as an example, the rule of faith dictates that the Creator God has elected Gentiles in the same manner as Israel—in a figure—granting endurance and "readiness" in the face of tribulation (cf. Matt 24:43), wisdom through the saints' embodiment of Christ (cf. 1 Cor 2:7; Eph 1:8, 17; Col 2:3) and grace in the face of judgment (cf. 1 Pet 1:6-9; Rev 13:9-10). Seitz sums up these points: "A typological reading of the Old Testament post historical criticism releases one particular slice of the past—God's ways with Israel—as forever contemporaneous, even to the extent of guiding and directing the church and *figurally displaying her future*."[83] "Completion," in light of this Trinitarian sense, dons new shades of meaning. A ruled reading of Dan 9:24-27, therefore, includes the salvific hand of Jesus Christ covering His Church at the "end," but, since Christ is also Yahweh the Creator God (central strut upholding the rule of faith), we cannot forget His plan for a "decreed end" (cf. 9:26) which entails judgment, desolation and the rise/fall of oppressive regimes.[84]

With this rule in mind, we can also see the mystery set forth by Dan 9:24-27, in its smaller area of effect, expands to become a "great mystery," as Ori-

---

[80] There is some debate as to the material form of the rule: one side argues for an intimate relationship between the scriptures and the *canon et regula fidei* (cf. Webster, *Word*, 9-46) while the other side argues for an abstract network of creeds, affirmations and sacraments (cf. Allert, *A High View?* 83). Driver responds, saying "it is altogether unlikely that the church's two-testament canon should have no relation whatsoever to its canon et regula fidei in the period before questions of the New Testament's scope were settled. Allert's hiatus between two ancient canons, paralleling the modern hiatus between scripture and canon, is almost the reductio ad absurdum of a widespread definition" ("Childs and the Canon," 275).

[81] Childs, *BTONT*, 719-25.

[82] Ibid., 66.

[83] Seitz, "Abiding Witness," 10.

[84] Irenaeus' own notion of the "end in Christ" is a good example of a seasoned reader of Scripture implementing the rule of faith to produce a faithful reading of the text. Irenaeus described Christ joining the end of time with the beginning ("recapitulation") thereby "encompassing within himself fully the entire experience of Israel and the Church" (cf. *Against Heresies*, III.21.10-23.8).

gen puts it, in which the ligaments of the biblical-theological narrative are made brighter in Christ, yet *still* sparse in detail (cf. Matt 24:27, 43). Christ, according to the rule, is also the Revealer God or "the revealer of mysteries" (Dan 2:47). How does this simple point transform our reading of 9:24-27? The area of effect, inevitably, will increase and exceed a one-to-one association between Jesus and the "anointed one" in Dan 9:25-26. Is it not also possible to see the Triune God as the foundation to the new "city" (9:24; Rev 21:2-3) as well as the "Holiest" (cf. Rev 16:5)? Once we integrate (or recognize?) the rule of faith into our OT readings, the presence of Christ in the inner-workings of Dan 9:24-27 is no longer out of the question. Irenaeus summarizes this activity nicely: "the Logos was active in the life of Israel, from creation to election to law-giving to cult to prayer and praise to prophetic word to final promise, because the only Son was of one being with the Father."[85] Such an understanding of the Triune God in Scripture and interpretation lends credence to a deeper and wider place for Christ in 9:24-27 and does not reduce the figure to a single reference (e.g. the "anointed" figure).

In sum, a canonical approach to Dan 9:24-27 is not complete until we communicate the text's Christian character. To speak of this OT passage's Christian character, as Seitz defines, is "to keep the character of its subject matter at the center and so to seek to honor the economic priority of the first witness by allowing its literal sense to connect with what the first witness strains to say more fully about the character of the One God, confessed as revealed in the subject matter of the second: God in Christ Jesus."[86] By way of analogy, we might compare this truth to a dense, centralized mass, where ruled readings of Dan 9:24-27 are likened to objects orbiting this mass. The objects are pulled toward this core by the masses' gravitational field (e.g. the rule of faith). The result or cumulative effect is the identification of Dan 9:24-27 as Christian scripture.

---

[85] Ibid., *On the Apostolic Preaching* (trans. John Behr; Crestwood, N.Y.: St. Vladimir's Seminary Press, 1997), 18. Augustine's words echo Irenaeus in stating how Jesus Christ is *latent* in the Old Testament and *patent* in the New Testament.

[86] Seitz, *Character*, 25.

CHAPTER 6
Conclusion

1. Daniel 9:24-27 as Christian Scripture

Above, we called the two-testament reading of Dan 9:24-27 an organic step, and not an organic *endpoint*. The reason for this distinction: a canonical approach also includes theological reflection on the Christian scriptures. As with biblical theology, we cannot account for the whole canonical approach until the role of Christian reflection is honored. Based on the subject matter of the canon, theological reflection imparts an ongoing practice of exegesis, meditation, application and textual discernment. This reflection is also an ever-strengthening cycle for the Christian reader, as he or she enters the world outside Scripture, embodying the word of God, and then returning to the canonical Scriptures to be sharpened and refreshed. It is with this reason in mind that Childs writes, "the understanding of the purpose of God in his deeds is therefore inextricably tied to the condition of the one viewing God's works."[1]

Applying this hermeneutically, we are constantly reengaging a text such as Dan 9:24-27 with new, keener eyes and responding with an increased sense (or presence) of the subject matter. Such a move does not mean an absence of or separation from earlier points of theological expression (e.g. virtues of a ruled reading), but, rather, a fitting articulation of all the previous areas named thus far. Once we configure these pieces and follow the canonical course of Dan 9:24-27, at least two practices arise which bear upon our own contemporary readership: (a) an interpretive and confessional space plotted out for the reader and (b) the exercise of "wisdom and discernment."

1.1. Space Enough for the Reader

Arguing that the extent of Daniel's theological voice reaches only as far as a sociological reaction to Hellenism is to argue for the *opposite* of an interpretive space. We may call this interpretive confinement. Reducing the text to one historical moment reduces interpretive space to one readership and, it follows, disregards the theological questions inherent to a canonical shape. Shrinking the space to one historical instance is "theologically inadmissible"

---

[1] Childs, *OT Theology*, 47.

and tends "to undercut the *seriousness* of the biblical witness."[2] This word, "seriousness," is a working indicator of the reader's posture toward the text and *from* the text. The meaningfulness of Scripture extends from its theological shape and its existence as God's chosen means of revelation. At the same time, this seriousness demarcates Scripture as a book "set apart" from other books. Space occupied by the Christian interpreter is not an abstract idea borne by the theories of literary criticism. Instead, this space is carefully "furnished" by the textual rationale of the Christian faith, overlaying both the real world and, in thinking after C.S. Lewis, the reality that is even "more real" than the first.[3]

Our space in the text of Dan 9:24-27 also asks us to acknowledge a "Christian account of time," according to Sumner, which "is not laid upon the text but grows out from it and the canon as a whole."[4] Two-testament Christians are "saints of the Most High" (Dan 7:18) and "in Christ" (Rom 3:23; 1 Cor 1:2). Accounting for the "end of sin" and the patterns that circulate within the seventy sevens, how do two-testament Christians interpret time with the recognition that Jesus Christ is primary in the completion of sin and sin-debt? We cannot reduce our answer to a single statement or resolution; however, we can affirm four "supports," crafted by Sumner, to help us confront the question:

> The answer to the 'when' question must be first the death, resurrection, and ascension of Jesus in fulfillment of the prophets; then, second the end of time that those events anticipate. Third, it must be the continuous flow of events of human history, which are not simply blotted out or leveled by the event of Christ. Fourth, within that flow, the answer to 'when' questions must include special times when, as it were, human history has bumped up against the final tribulation more directly than others. For all times are not the same; some convey that Christological-eschatological reality behind and ahead of all history more powerfully than others.[5]

Not unlike genetically inherited traits, the reader's space, in "the continuous flow of human history," confronts the same mysteries as the OT and NT audiences. As contemporary interpreters we are called to discern our own versions of kingdom upheaval and power struggles between embattled peoples. We are

---

[2] Childs, *IOTS* 621. It is primarily for this opportunity—to engage in theological reflection on God's Word—that Childs pushed against "easy diachronic reconstructions" that "fracture the witness as a whole" (*OT Theology*, 11; cf. Mark Gignilliat, *A Brief History of Old Testament Criticism: From Benedict Spinoza to Brevard Childs* [Grand Rapids: Zondervan, 2012], 156-7).

[3] Lewis' story, *The Great Divorce*, falls back on the theme of a "more real" reality into which those of us participating in our present reality cannot enter or experience (3d ed.; New York: HarperOne, 2001).

[4] Wells and Sumner, *Daniel*, 113.

[5] Ibid.

also called to think about the dire experience of "exile." Instincts passed on by modern schools of OT thought would resist the implication that present-day readers are part of Daniel's Sabbath-heptadic panorama. When Daniel realizes the end of Israel's trouble is not seventy years but seventy sevens, it is only from our vantage point, after the completion of the two-testament canon, that we can behold the space required for our participation in exile and rest. "The hearer," Sumner explains, "is in some sort of exile of his or her own, is called to fall into the ascended Christ's train, and must confront his or her own death and judgment."[6]

1.2. "Wisdom and Discernment" from the Reader

Just as Daniel and the subsequent architects of the text were charged with "wisdom and discernment," so also are we charged with wise reading and wise *living*. This application to the interpreter is ingredient to the canonical approach.[7] Like the inspired hand(s) that shaped Dan 9, we look to our scriptural predecessors and step into a stream of interpretive history that "arose from a profoundly theological sense of the function of prophecy which was continually illuminated through the continuing reinterpretation of scripture."[8] This type of interpretation discourages our tendency to "proceed in stages within a fixed sequence."[9] Casting the form of interpretive space in to a step-by-step process would disable the many moving parts holding together figuration, mystery and wisdom. Wisdom marks an interpreter who is within the canonical, interpretive and confessional space constructed by God's providential hand. Wise interpretation, therefore, is not a vestigial bit sewn on to the end of an exegetical study.[10]

A wise reader's engagement with an eschatological text, particularly a text shaped by openness, also means this engagement is not a "final step" or the end of our task, but is, as Childs states, an "ongoing study."[11] Neither is the task merely academic or a preface to a more energetic, spiritual experience, as Childs observes:

> The true expositor of the Christian Scriptures is the one who awaits in anticipation toward becoming the interpreted rather than the in-

---

[6] Ibid., 116.

[7] Rowe comments on Childs' *BTONT*, saying "for Childs, multileveled interpretation is but a contemporary rendition of ancient hermeneutical wisdom: all Bible reading is faith seeking understanding" ("Doctrine of God," 166; cf. Childs, 86).

[8] Childs, *IOTS*, 618.

[9] Ibid., *BTONT*, 381.

[10] Cf. Markus Bockmuehl, "Bible versus Theology: Is 'Theological Interpretation' the Answer?" *Nova et Vetera* 9.1 (2011) 27-47. He reminds us how German higher criticism reduced the Bible to "any other book" (33-34). Rather, Bockmuehl rightly states, "the true use of interpretation is to get rid of interpretation" (34).

[11] Childs, *BTONT*, 381.

> terpreter. The very divine reality which the interpreter serves to grasp, is the very One who grasps the interpreter. The Christian doctrine of the role of the Holy Spirit is not a hermeneutical principle, but that divine reality itself who makes understanding of God possible.[12]

The divinely inspired text of Dan 9 is "aretegenic" (virtue-producing) and calls the reader to exercise wisdom in the midst of cultural or "kingdom" shifts. Like Daniel and his friends in chs. 1-6, the message of God beckons the faithful to be "countercultural."[13] Indeed, that is one way in which apocalyptic pressures the reader: a challenge "to the captivity of our own cultural assumptions."[14]

Sumner also discusses the impact such a text would have on a faithful church, noting "that the whole of scripture speaks to the whole of human history, but some churches whose circumstances resemble Daniel's suffering may have a 'preferential option' in its interpretation."[15] Surely, certain communities may resonate with the patterns of 9:25-27 more than others. Discernment is a mighty tool in desperate times. But even in the midst of the storms and tumult through which these communities must navigate, events occur in a discernible pattern, not in predictable detail. We are released from predicting the future (cf. Dan 12:9), as both the OT and NT make clear, and called, instead, to discern *in hope*. The Danielic revelation "is not intended to further speculation but to encourage perseverance in faith, hope and love. It is to inspire confident hope in the final establishment of the everlasting kingdom of God."[16]

Coming into contact with the theological reality of Dan 9:24-27 is precisely what makes the message of Daniel "a living theological, content, present in spite of all the cultural differences."[17] It is the interpreter's link to the Word—which is both ontological and *textual*—that locates us within the promise and peril of Dan 9:24-27. Our place in this storyline demands we take care in our study of the end-times and not subtract from such a glorious hope by giving into our predilection for cheap talk concerning the last days. Eschatology, Daniel show us, is a richer enterprise than this. Far from being a panorama of current or future affairs and symbolism, enduring the "end" is about the *character* of the faithful saint. What is central to such a profile? It is wisdom and understanding (1:17; 2:48; 5:11-14; 10:12, 22), humility (10:12), endurance

---

[12] Ibid., 86-87.

[13] VanGemeren, *Interpreting*, 341. As VanGemeren reminds us, "the canonical message of Daniel encourages hope in the establishment of his kingdom while living in a real world ruled by power politics, egomaniacs, jealousy and greed" (344).

[14] Wells and Sumner, *Daniel*, 113.

[15] Ibid., 100.

[16] VanGemeren, *Interpreting*, 342.

[17] Childs, "Allegory and Typology within Biblical Interpretation," in *The Bible as Christian Scripture*, 300.

(10:11, 18-19; 12:13), a "fear of the Lord" (3:12; 10:7-9), contrition (9:3, 18-20) and integrity (6:3; 9:23; 12:3, 13).

The figure of Daniel is the key example and, in truth, the reader's proxy (10:2-21). In Dan 10, the entire passage is devoted to Daniel's spiritual and bodily condition and oddly devoid of visionary content. A physical, emotional, mental and spiritual toll has been taken. Though most of the faithful saints do not receive visions in this way, interpreters are still invited to imitate Daniel's immovable character and to reflect upon the seriousness, solemnity and hope necessary to process Yahweh's divine decrees. Daniel, we will recall, is an occupant of interpretive space, as is the reader, and one who carries the title "servant." Granting we occupy this "shared space" with the wise man, Daniel, it is possible to hear the words of 12:13 spoken to us, the interpreter: "Now go your way until the end and you will *rest* (נוח) and will stand in your allotted place at the end of days."[18]

2. Conclusion

A canonical approach to Dan 9:24-27 lets us revisit old questions with new lenses. As a result, our study generates *new* questions: In what way does Daniel transform a message of rest to a "decree of completeness"? Does Dan 9 convey more than eschatological content? What type of reading do we uncover when the shape of Dan 9:24-27 has a voice? What role does Daniel play apart from "author" (cf. 9:3-19)? How does the book fit in the canon *theologically*, with respect to Torah and the subsequent Prophets? In what way do contemporary readers enter Dan 9:24-27 while honoring the message of the whole book? Each chapter of this study builds on these questions, mounts ample evidence and moves the interpreter- if not slowly and steadily—into a better location from which to engage Dan 9:24-27 than he or she previously stood.

Chapter 1 begins the study with a survey of the field of Daniel literature. For the purposes of this thesis, however, both the commentary and *methodology* of the contributing work are necessary for exposing the various limbs of, what can only be called, a "family tree" in Daniel research. On this tree, various hermeneutical judgments can and do create problems and are responsible for some of the missteps along the path of present-day research. Moreover, the review includes a variety of Daniel studies so as not to reduce the project to a debate between conservative and non-conservative parties.

---

[18] Readers of Dan 12 cannot afford to miss where the chapter—and consequently, the book—leaves off. Daniel is told to "shut up the book and seal the words until the time of the end" (12:4). With these revelations sealed, the final act of wisdom by Daniel (and the reader) is to exclaim, "But I did not understand ... O my lord, what will be the outcome of these things?" (12:8). The charge to exercise wisdom resounds long after the book is over. Texts and interpretations in Daniel are still intended for the "wise who understand" (12:10) and "who would wait for the time appointed in God's calendar" (Childs, *IOTS*, 620).

Chapter 2 outlines the methodology by defining key terms such as "canon" and "canonical." To display the proper dimensions of these terms, we compare and contrast alternative canonical methods. In the end, a canonical approach to Dan 9:24-27 emphasizes the text's ability to make theological sense through its given shape. This theological sense is not bound by a single, historical situation—it moves beyond it while still connected to it.

Chapter 3 pulls in the context from surrounding passages, particularly Daniel's confession (9:3-19). The interpretation of 9:24-27 undoubtedly hearkens back to Jeremiah's "seventy years," but the Sabbath-heptadic traditions composing Jer 25-29 and Dan 9 look back even further. Leviticus 25-26:40-41 introduces a full-orbed understanding of Israel's Sabbath and intimates a promise of rest with a warning of desolation. Having these threads braided together, along with the canonical arrangement of the LP, reveals just how much Daniel has made this stream of traditions his own in vv. 24-27.

Chapter 4 enters into 9:24-27. "Seventy sevens" are a time image crafted from the canonical shape of the LP. Foregrounding the passage is a "decree": sin will end and all that the Prophets spoke of will come to pass. Until such a time is realized, Israel's exilic life will be governed by the rise and fall of human kingdoms. Each set of weeks represents a piece of the structure's overall pattern and each episode can accommodate any number of Persian, Jewish, Greek, Ptolemaic or Seleucid figures. Because, as Childs reiterates about the canonical shape of Daniel, "this is what canon means—the book continues truthfully to instruct and to admonish the people of God in the crisis of faith."[19]

Chapter 5 develops the course of this passage's canonical shape. By means of Daniel's style of widening patterns, Dan 9:24-27 opens up an interpretive and confessional space for future communities of faith. The NT reception of these texts is a waypoint within this space. The themes, language and motifs of Daniel 7-12 are recontextualized in the Gospels, offering a snapshot (not a complete picture) of Christ as the culminating figure and "end." But the theological force of the two-testament canon does not end there. A canonical approach demonstrates how Daniel's culminating rest is not a random idea in the midst of clamorous traditions, but a point located on a coherent narrative bound by the shared subject matter of two-testaments:

> [T]he oneness of scripture's scope is not a rival to the multiple voices within he canon, but a constant pointer, much like a ship's compass, fixing on a single goal, in spite of the many and various ways of God (Hb. 1.1), toward which the believer is drawn ... the recognition of the one scope of Scripture, which is Jesus Christ, does not function to restrict the full range of the biblical voices. It does not

---

[19] Ibid., 622.

abstract the message, or seek to replace coat of many colors with a seamless garment of grey.[20]

Chapter 6 concludes the study by marking out the space occupied by the present-day reader. A canonical approach to Dan 9:24-27 causes faithful interpreters to see themselves within the one people of God, discerning the times as Israel is to discern, enduring trials as Israel is to endure and to find complete rest as Israel is called to find complete rest. We are responsible for gaining wisdom and exercising discernment in the midst of crisis, anticipating (but not predicting) to the extent that God's people can prepare and equip themselves. "This biblical witness," Childs writes, "challenges the faithful to be awake and ready for the unexpected intervention of God in wrapping up all of human history."[21]

---

[20] Ibid., *BTONT*, 725.
[21] Ibid., *IOTS*, 622.

Appendix
The Dual-Location of the Book of Daniel

Another layer of theological and canonical context to consider is the multiple locations in which the book of Daniel is situated. Daniel is a good example of how various orders exert their theological force – it occupies a space in both the Prophets (LXX-family) and the Writings (MT-family). Most scholars maintain Daniel is part of the Writings based on the closing of the prophetic corpus or after the death of the fifth century BCE prophet, Malachi.[1] The question is, as Koch voices, "[I]s it really certain that he wanted to be a prophet in the first place and that the intended circle of his readers did indeed view him as such a figure?"[2] Within Daniel scholarship, there has yet to be an extensive treatment of how Daniel functions within the Hebrew and Greek canons. When a study comes within the orbit of this subject, the argument will tend to veer in either the direction of dating/authorship or politics and scripturalization. But by neglecting the complex relationship between Daniel and canon, we neglect a context that can shed light on a variety of thorny issues inherent to the book (e.g. genre, audience, politics, theology). What then is so significant about Daniel's canonical position?

Within the understanding of canon outlined above – namely, canon as a functional context, not a static expression of ecclesial debate – it is possible to read the placement(s) of Daniel as an intentional move, allowing both positions to illuminate features within the book that would otherwise go unnoticed. Sailhamer situates Daniel in the Prophets and not the Writings while claiming that, "both in content and chronology, Daniel is suited for either position."[3] In like manner, Julius Steinberg, in an astute observation, concludes that the two positions of Daniel suggest an intertextual relationship: "Für beide Positionen von Daniel können textinterne Argumente in Anschlag gebracht werden. Sowohl eine Platzierung des Buches unter den Propheten als auch eine Platzierung ausserhalb dieser Gruppe kann textintern gerechtfertigt werden. Die 'griechische' Einstufung ist daher nicht

---

[1] Hartman and DiLella, *Book of Daniel*, 9-10.
[2] Koch, "Is Daniel Also Among the Prophets?," 119.
[3] Sailhamer, "Daniel," in *NIV Compact Bible Commentary* (Grand Rapids: Zondervan, 1999), 396.

zwangsläufig die bessere."⁴ Donn Morgan weighs the duality of Daniel's witness: "On the one hand, Daniel, through his name and actions, stands with Joseph and the prophets. On the other hand, Daniel as a sage represents the authoritative post-exilic scribal tradition through which the meaning of Torah and the Prophets is given."⁵ He continues by noting how "the visionary Book of Daniel points backward to the basic scriptures, Torah and Prophets, and forward to the ongoing process of interpretation."⁶ These conclusions note the many layers underneath Daniel's place in the canon: the comparable and incomparable message of Daniel and the Prophets, a genre that is both apocalyptic and yet non-apocalyptic, the multiple historical markers ranging from Persia to Greece, and a penchant for teaching wisdom *and* the prophetic hope.⁷

Relegating Daniel to a closed and fixed position in one corpus of the MT canon creates at least two major difficulties in such a model. First, analyzing Daniel according to its fixity simplifies the historical picture of Daniel's compilation. The book contains both prophetic *and* sapiential elements. Challenges include transitions in genre (chs. 1-6; 7-12), transitions in language (1:1-2:3, 8:1-12:13 in Hebrew; 2:4b-7:28 in Aramaic) and a thematic bracket of "wisdom" at both ends of the text (1:4, 17-20; 12:3, 10). Variations of the book show traces of intentional shaping at the beginning and end of the text. We find this activity – albeit for different theological reasons – in the additions of the Greek texts of Theodotian, which adds an introduction and conclusion to the book, whereas the OG adds two additional chapters to the conclusion.⁸ Second, by grouping the Writings with all other non-Mosaic books (simply, "the Prophets"), whether as an expansion or a separate group of *ad hoc* texts, the position of interpretation afforded Daniel is neglected. This illustration demonstrates that "canon does not simply perform the formal function of separating the books that are authoritative from others that are not, but is the rule that delineates the area in which the church hears the Word of God."⁹

---

⁴ Steinberg, *Die Ketuvim*, 130.
⁵ Morgan, *Between Text and Community: The 'Writings' in Canonical Interpretation* (Minneapolis: Augsburg Fortress, 2007), 49.
⁶ Ibid., 49.
⁷ Very little is known about the intentions behind moving Daniel from one position to another and even less about whether such intentions were theological, cultural or societal. Koch, in his impactful article "Is Daniel Among the Prophets," concludes that Daniel's relocation to the Writings in the MT was a move from "prophecy" (Christian appropriation) to "mere pedagogy" (Jewish re-appropriation) (119). Beckwith, arguing the opposite point, finds the Christian appropriation of the book through its full acceptance of *the Septuagintal additions* to be for "the purpose of edification," and not only to convey prophecy (Beckwith, *OT Canon*, 341).
⁸ Beckwith, *OT Canon*, 339. The configuration coordinates well with the MT, where chapter 1 (the beginning) and 12 (the end) frame a nucleus of wisdom, thereby creating a potential context for how the book might be read.
⁹ Childs, *Biblical Theology in Crisis*, 99.

To conclude, the dual-location of Daniel within the canons is not a product of unintended circumstances or an accident of whatever community happened to be reading the book, but a function of the book's shaping and final form. The book of Daniel is shaped in such a way as to maintain an open-ended receptivity with prophetic books and the Writings. This is quite different from saying Daniel was shaped to fit in either a set fixed corpus of the Prophets or a set, fixed corpus of the Writings. Hermeneutically, this affirmation entails "working theologically within the narrow and wider forms of the canon in search for both the truth and the catholicity of the biblical witness to the church and the world."[10] A canonical approach to the book of Daniel will not rule out the possibility that the text's placement in various orders holds a theological significance. By appealing to a dual-location, however, we do not commit to, what Childs calls, "an expedient compromise in the name of ecumenicity," but "a genuine theological grappling with the issues which is prepared to test the strengths and weaknesses of both traditional positions."[11]

---

[10] Ibid., 67.
[11] Ibid., 66.

Bibliography

Aaron, David. *Biblical Ambiguities: Metaphor, Semantics and Divine Imagery*. Brill Reference Library of Ancient Judaism 4. Leiden: Brill, 2001.

Abegg, Martin. "The Calendar at Qumran." Pages 145-72 in *Judaism in Late Antiquity, Volume 1*. Edited by Alan Avery-Peck and Jacob Neusner. Leiden: Brill, 2001.

Abou-Chaar, Iskandar. "Rereading Isaiah 40-55 as 'Project Launcher' for the Books of the Law and the Prophets." Pages 101-128 in *Festschrift in Honor of Professor Paul Nadim Tarazi, Volume 1: Studies in the Old Testament*. Edited by Nicolae Roddy. New York: Peter Lang, 2013.

Abraham, William. *Canon and Criterion in Christian Theology: From the Fathers to Feminism*. New York: Oxford University Press, 1998.

Ackroyd, Peter. "Two Old Testament Historical Problems of the Early Persian Period." *Journal of Near Eastern Studies* 17.1 (1958): 13-27.

Adams, Jim. *The Performative Nature and Function of Isaiah 40-55*. Journal for the Study of the Old Testament Supplements 448. New York: T&T Clark, 2006.

Adler, William. "The Apocalyptic Survey of History Adapted by Christians: Daniel's Prophecy of 70 Weeks." Pages 201-238 in *The Jewish Apocalyptic Heritage in Early Christianity*. Edited by James C. VanderKam. Assen: Royal Van Gorcum, 1996.

Allert, Craig. *A High View of Scripture? The Authority of the Bible and the Formation of the New Testament Canon*. Grand Rapids: Baker, 2007.

Alter, Robert. *The Art of Biblical Narrative*. New York: Basic Books, 1981.

Anderson, Robert. *The Coming Prince*. London: Hodder, 1881.

Anderson, Gary. *Sin: A History*. New Haven: Yale University Press, 2009.

Athas, George. "In Search of the Seventy 'Weeks.'" *Journal of Hellenic Studies* 9 (2009) 2-20.

Auberlen, Carl A. *The Prophecies of Daniel and the Revelation of St. John*. Translated by Adolph Saphir. Edinburgh: T&T Clark, 1856.

Auwers, J.M. and H.J. De Jonge eds. *The Biblical Canons*. Leuven: Leuven University Press, 2003.

Bailey, Daniel. "The Intertextual Relationship of Daniel 12:2 and Isaiah 26:19: Evidence from Qumran and the Greek Versions." *Tyndale Bulletin* 51.2 (2000): 305-308.

Baker, David L. *Two Testaments, One Bible: A Study of the Theological Relationship Between the Old & New Testaments*. Downers Grove: IVP, 1991.

Barker, Kit. "Speech Act Theory, Dual Authorship, and Canonical Hermeneutics: Making Sense of Sensus Plenior." *Journal of Theological Interpretation* 3.2 (2009): 227-239.

Barr, James. *The Concept of Biblical Theology: An Old Testament Perspective*. Minneapolis: Augsburg Fortress, 1999.

———. "Unity: Within the Canon or After the Canon." Pages 151-158 in *One Scripture or Many? Canon from Biblical, Theological and Philosophical Perspectives*. Edited by Christine Helmer. Oxford: Oxford University Press, 2004.

Barrera, Julio Trebolle. "Origins of a Tripartite Old Testament Canon." Pages 129-145 in *The Canon Debate*. Edited by Lee McDonald. Peabody: Hendrickson, 1995.

Barton, John and Michael Wolter eds. *Die Einheit der Schrift und die Vielfalt des Kanons*. Berlin: De Gruyter, 2003.

———. "Intertextuality and the 'Final Form' of the Text." Pages 33-38 in *Congress Volume: Oslo 1998*. Edited by A. Lemaire. Supplements to Vetus Testamentum 80. Leiden: Brill, 1995.

———. "What is a Book? Modern Exegesis and the Literary Conventions of Ancient Israel." Pages 1-14 in *Intertextuality in Ugarit and Israel*. Edited by Johannes de Moor. Leiden: Brill, 1998.

———. *The Old Testament: Canon, Literature and Theology: Collected Essays of John Barton*. Society for Old Testament Studies Monograph Series. Aldershot: Ashgate, 2007.

———. *Reading the Old Testament: Method in Biblical Study*. Louisville: John Knox, 1984.

Baum, Armin D. "Revelatory Experience and Pseudapigraphical Attribution in Early Jewish Apocalypses." *Bulletin of Biblical Research* 21.1 (2011): 65-92.

Beal, Timothy. "Intertextuality." Pages 128-30 in *Handbook of Postmodern Biblical Interpretation*. Edited by A. Adams. St. Louis: Chalice, 2000.

Beale, G. K. *The Use of Daniel in Jewish Apocalyptic and in the Revelation of St. John*. Lanham: University Press of America, 1984.

Beckwith, Roger. *Calendar, Chronology and Worship: Studies in Ancient Judaism and Early Christianity*. Leiden: Brill, 2005.

———. "Daniel 9 and the Date of the Messiah's Coming in Essene, Hellenistic, Pharisaic, Zealot and Early Christian Computation." *Revue de Qumran* 10 (1979-81): 167-202.

———. "Early Traces of the Book of Daniel." *Tyndale Bulletin* 53.1 (2002): 74-82.

———. "A Modern Theory of Old Testament Canon," *Vetus Testamentum* 41.4 (1991): 385-95.

———. "The Significance of the Calendar for Interpreting Essene Chronology and Eschatology." *Revue de Qumran* 10 (1979-81): 167-202.

Beferle, Stefan. "The Book of Daniel and Its Social Setting." Pages 205-28 in *The Book of Daniel: Composition and Reception, Vol. 1*. Edited by John Collins and Peter Flint. Leiden: Brill, 2002.

Behr, John. *The Way to Nicaea: Formation of Christian Theology, Volume 1*. New York: St. Vladimir's Seminary Press, 2001.

Beldman, David. "Literary Approaches and Old Testament Interpretation." Pages 67-95 in *Hearing the Old Testament: Listening for God's Address*. Edited by Craig Bartholomew and David Beldman. Grand Rapids: Eerdmans, 2012.

Bergsma, John S. *The Jubilee from Leviticus to Qumran*. Supplement to Vetus Testamentum 115. Leiden: Brill, 2007.

———. "The Persian Period as Pentitential Era: The 'Exegetical Logic' of Daniel 9.1-27." Pages 50-64 in *Exile and Restoration Revisited: Essays on the Babylonian and Persian Periods in Memory of Peter R. Ackroyd*. Edited by Gary N. Knoppers and Lester L. Grabbe. New York: T&T Clark, 2009.

Berner, Christoph. "The Heptadic Chronologies of Testament of Levi 16-17 and Their Sources," *Journal for the Study of the Old Testament Pseudapigrapha* 22.1 (2012): 40-52.

———. *Jahre, Jahrwochen und Jubiläen: Heptadische Geschichtskonzeptionen im Antiken Judentum*. Edited by John Barton and Reinhard Kratz. Beihefte zur Zeitschrift für die alttestamentliche Wissenschaft 363. Berlin: De Gruyter, 2006.

Bernstein, Moshe. "Scriptures: Quotations and Use." Pages 839-42 in *The Encyclopedia of the Dead Sea Scrolls*. Edited by L.H. Schiffman and J.C. Vanderkam. 2 vols. Oxford: Oxford University Press, 2000.

Bickerman, Ernest. *Der Gott der Makkabeer*. Berlin: Schocken, 1937.

Blass, Friedrich and Albert Debrunner. *A Greek Grammar of the New Testament and Other Early Christian Literature*. Chicago: Chicago University Press, 1961.

Blenkinsopp, Joseph. *Isaiah 40-55*. Anchor Bible 19A. New York: Doubleday, 2000.

———. *Prophecy and Canon: A Contribution to the Study of Jewish Origins*. Notre Dame: University of Notre Dame Press, 1977.

Blomberg, Craig. "Matthew." Pages 1-110 in *Commentary on the New Testament Use of the Old Testament*. Edited by D.A. Carson and G.K. Beale. Grand Rapids: Baker Academic, 2007.

Blowers, Paul. "The Regula Fidei and the Narrative Character of Early Christian Faith." *Pro Ecclesia* 16 (1999): 199-228.

Bockmuehl, Markus. "Bible versus Theology: Is 'Theological Interpretation' the Answer?" *Nova et Vetera* 9.1 (2011): 27-47.

———. *Revelation and Mystery: In Ancient Judaism and Pauline Christianity*. Eugene: Wipf and Stock, 1990.

Boda, Mark. "Biblical Theology and Old Testament Interpretation." Pages 122-153 in *Hearing the Old Testament: Listening to God's Address*. Edited by Craig Bartholomew and David Beldman. Grand Rapids: Eerdmans, 2012.

Boyarin, Daniel. "Inner Biblical Ambiguity, Intertextuality and the Dialectic of Midrash: The Waters of Marah." *Prooftexts* 10 (1990): 29-48.

Brooke, George. "The 'Apocalyptic' Community, the Matrix of the Teacher and Rewriting Scripture." Pages 37-53 in *Authoritative Scriptures in Ancient Judaism*. Supplements to the Journal for the Study of Judaism 141. Edited by M. Popovic. Leiden/Boston: Brill, 2010.

Broyles, Craig. "Traditions, Intertextuality and Canon." Pages 145-75 in *Interpreting the Old Testament: A Guide for Exegesis*. Edited by Craig Broyles. Grand Rapids: Baker, 2001.

Bruce, F.F. *Biblical Exegesis in the Qumran Texts*. London: Tyndale, 1959.

Buhl, Frants. *Canon and Text of the Old Testament*. Edinburgh: T&T Clark, 1892.

Burer, Michael. *Divine Sabbath Work*. Winona Lake, Ind.: Eisenbrauns, 2012.

Caird, G.B. *The Language and Imagery of the Bible*. Grand Rapids: Eerdmans, 1980.

Cargounis, C.C. "History and Supra-History: Daniel and the Four Empires." Pages 387-97 in *The Book of Daniel in Light of New Findings*. Bibliotheca ephemeridum theologicarum lovaniensium 106. Edited by A.S. van der Woude. Leuven: Leuven University Press, 1993.

Carr, David. *The Formation of the Hebrew Bible: A New Reconstruction*. Oxford: Oxford University Press, 2011.

———. "The Many Uses of Intertextuality in Biblical Studies: Actual and Potential." Pages 505-36 in *Congress Volume: Helsinki 2010*. Edited by Marti Nissinen. Vetus Testamentum Supplements 148. Leiden: Brill, 2010.

———. *Writing on the Tablet of the Heart: Origins of Scripture and Literature*. Oxford: Oxford University Press, 2005.

Chapman, Stephen. "The Canon Debate: What It Is and Why It Matters." *Journal of Theological Interpretation* 4.2 (2010): 273-294.

———. "Imaginative Readings of Scripture and Theological Interpretation." Pages 409-421 in *Out of Egypt: Biblical Theology and Biblical Interpretation*. Edited by Craig Bartholomew. Scripture and Hermeneutics Series 5. Grand Rapids: Zondervan, 2006.

———. *The Law and the Prophets: A Study in Old Testament Canon Formation*. Forschungen zum Alten Tesament 27. Tübingen: Mohr Siebeck, 2000.

———. "The Old Testament Canon and its Authority for the Christian Church." *Ex Auditu* 19 (2003): 125-48.

Charlesworth, James H., ed. *The Old Testament Pseudapigrapha: Volume 1, Apocalyptic Literature and Testaments*. Peabody: Hendrickson, 2009.

Chazon, Esther. "Is Divrei ha-Meorot a Sectarian Prayer?" Pages 3-17 in *The Dead Sea Scrolls: Forty Years of Research*. Edited by Devorah Dimant. Leiden: Brill, 1992.

Childs, Brevard. "Allegory and Typology within Biblical Interpretation." Pages 299-310 in *The Bible as Christian Scripture*. Edited by Christopher Seitz; Atlanta: SBL, 2013.

———. *Biblical Theology in Crisis*. Philadelphia: Westminster, 1970.

———. *Biblical Theology of the Old and New Testaments: Theological Reflection on the Christian Bible*. Minneapolis: Augsburg Fortress, 1992.

———. "Biblische Theologie und christlicher Kanon." Pages 13-27 in *Zum Problem des biblischen Kanons*. Edited by Ingo Baldermann et al. *Jahrbruch für Biblische Theologie* 3. Neukirchen-Vluyn: Neukirchener, 1988.

———. "The Canonical Shape of the Prophetic Literature." *Interpretation* 32.1 (1978) 46-55.

———. "Critique of Recent Intertextual Canonical Interpretation." *Zeitschrift für die alttestamentliche Wissenschaft* 115 (2003): 173-84.

———. *Introduction to the Old Testament as Scripture*. Philadelphia: Fortress, 1979.

———. *Isaiah*. Old Testament Library. Louisville: Westminster John Knox, 2001.

———. "Midrash and the Old Testament." Pages 47-59 in *Understanding the Sacred Text: Essays in Honor of Morton S. Enslin on the Hebrew Bible and Christian Beginnings*. Edited by John Reumann. Valley Forge: Judson, 1972.

———. *Old Testament Theology in a Canonical Context*. Philadelphia: Fortress, 1985.

———. "Response to Reviewers of Introduction to the Old Testament as Scripture." *Journal for the Study of Old Testament* 16 (1980): 52-60.

———. "Speech-Act Theory and Biblical Interpretation." *Scottish Journal of Theology* 58.4 (2005): 375-392.

Clements, Ronald. *Old Testament Prophecy: From Oracles to Canon.* Louisville: Westminster John Knox, 1996.
Coggins, Richard, and Anthony Phillips, eds. *Israel's Prophetic Tradition: Essays in Honour of Peter Ackroyd.* Cambridge: Cambridge University Press, 1982.
Collins, Adele. *Cosmology and Eschatology in Jewish and Christian Apocalyptic. Journal of the Study of the Old Testament Supplement* 50. Edited John Collins. Leiden: Brill, 1996.
Collins, John. "Apocalypse: The Morphology of a Genre." *Semeia* 14. Atlanta: Society of Biblical Literature, 1979.
_____. "Apocalyptic Genre and Mythic Allusions in Daniel." *Journal for the Study of the Old Testament* 21 (1981): 83-100.
_____. "Canon, Canonization." Pages 460-463 in *The Eerdmans Dictionary of Early Judaism.* Edited by John J. Collins and Daniel C. Harlow. Grand Rapids: Eerdmans, 2010.
_____. "Changing Scripture." Pages 23-45 in *Changes in Scripture: Rewriting and Interpreting Authoritative Traditions in the Second Temple Period.* Edited by Hanne von Weissenberg and Marko Marttila. Beihefte zur Zeitschrift für die alttestamentliche Wissenschaft 419. Berlin/New York: De Gruyter, 2011.
_____. "Current Issues in the Study of Daniel." Pages 1-15 in *The Book of Daniel: Composition and Reception, Volume 1.* Edited by John Collins and Peter Flint. Leiden: Brill, 2002.
_____. *Daniel.* Hermeneia. Minneapolis: Augsburg Fortress, 1993.
_____. "Inspiration or Illusion: Biblical Theology and the Book of Daniel." *Ex Auditu* 6 (1990) 30-38.
_____. "The Jewish Apocalypses." *Semeia* 14 (1979): 1-20.
_____. "The Meaning of 'the End' in the Book of Daniel." Pages 91-98 in *Of Scribes and Scrolls: Essays in Honor of John Strugnell.* Edited by H. Attridge, J.J. Collins and T.H. Tobin. Lanham: University Press of America, 1990.
Collins, Yarbro. *Cosmology and Eschatology in Jewish and Christian Apocalypticism.* Edited by John Collins and G.E. Nickelsburg. Journal for the Study of the Old Testament Supplements 50. Leiden: Brill, 1996.
Cornhill, C.H. "Die siebzig Jahrwochen Daniels." *Theologische Studien und Skizzen aus Ostpreussen* 2 (1889): 1-32.
Crawford, Sidnie White. "Understanding the Textual History of the Hebrew Bible: A New Proposal." Pages 60-69 in *The Hebrew Bible in Light of the Dead Sea Scrolls.* Edited by Nóra Dávid and Armin Lange. Göttingen: Vandenhoeck & Ruprecht, 2012.
Davies, Philip. "Eschatology in the Book of Daniel." *Journal for the Study of the Old Testament* 17 (1980): 33-53.
_____. "The Jewish Scriptural Canon in Cultural Perspective." Pages 36-52 in *The Canon Debate.* Edited by Lee McDonald and James Sanders. Peabody: Hendrickson, 2002.
Day, John. "Wisdom and Daniel." Pages 161-69 in *Wisdom in Ancient Israel.* Cambridge: Cambridge University Press, 1995.
De Hulster, Izaak. "Imagination: A Hermeneutical Tool for the Study of the Hebrew Bible." *Biblical Interpretation* 18 (2010): 114-36.

De Jong, M.J. "Why Jeremiah is Not Among the Prophets: An Analysis of the Terms נביא and נביאם in the Book of Jeremiah." *Journal for the Study of the Old Testament* 35.4 (2011): 483-510.

De Long, Kindalee Pfremmer. "Daniel and the Narrative Integrity of his Prayer in Chapter 9." Pages 219-49 in *A Teacher for All Generations: Essays in Honor of James C. VanderKam, Volume One*. Leiden: Brill, 2012.

Dempster, Stephen. "Canons to the Right and Canons on the Left: Finding a Resolution in the Canon Debate." *Journal of Evangelical Theological Society* 52.1 (2009): 47-77.

―――. "An 'Extraordinary Fact': Torah and Temple and the Contours of the Hebrew Canon, Part 1." *Tyndale Bulletin* 48.1 (1997): 23-56.

―――. "An 'Extraordinary Fact': Torah and Temple and the Contours of the Hebrew Canon, Part 2." *Tyndale Bulletin* 48.1 (1997): 191-218.

―――. "The Prophets, the Canon and a Canonical Approach." Pages 293-329 in *Canon and Biblical Interpretation*. Scripture and Hermeneutics Series 7. Edited by Craig Bartholomew and Anthony Thiselton. Grand Rapids: Zondervan, 2006.

―――. "Torah, Torah, Torah: The Emergence of the Tripartite Canon." Pages 87-128 in *Exploring the Origins of the Bible: Canon Formation in Historical, Literary, and Theological Perspective*. Edited by Craig Evans and Emmanuel Tov. Grand Rapids: Baker, 2008.

Dequeker, Luc. "King Darius and the Prophecy of Seventy Weeks Daniel 9." Pages 187-210 in *The Book of Daniel in Light of New Findings*. Edited by A.S. van der Woude. Bibliotheca ephemeridum theologicarum lovaniensium 106. Leuven: Peeters, 1993.

Dimant, Divorah. "The Seventy Weeks Chronology (Dan 9,24-27) in the Light of New Qumranic Texts." Pages 57-76 in *The Book of Daniel in the Light of New Findings*. Edited by A.S. van der Woude. Bibliotheca ephemeridum theologicarum lovaniensium 106. Leuven: Leuven University Press, 1993.

DiTommaso, Lorenzo. "4QPseudo-Daniel $^{A-B}$ (4Q243-4Q244) and the Book of Daniel." *Dead Sea Discoveries* 12.2 (2005): 101-133.

―――. *The Book of Daniel and the Apocryphal Daniel Literature*. Leiden: Brill, 2005.

Doukhan, Jacques. *Daniel: The Vision of the End*. Berrien Springs, Mich.: Andrews University, 1987.

Draisma, Sipka, ed. *Intertextuality in Biblical Writings: Essays in Honor of Basvan Iersel*. Kampen: J.H. Kok, 1989.

Driver, Daniel. *Brevard Childs: Biblical Theologian: For the Church's One Bible*. Grand Rapids: Baker Academic, 2010.

Driver, G.R. "Isaiah 52:13-53:12: The Servant of the Lord." Pages 90-105 in *In Memoriam Paul Kahle*. Edited by M. Black and G. Fohler. Beihefte zur Zeitschrift für die alttestamentliche Wissenschaft 103. Berlin: Töpelmann, 1968.

―――. "Sacred Numbers and Round Figures." Pages 62-90 in *Promise and Fulfillment: Essays Presented to Professor S.H. Hooke*. Edited by F.F. Bruce. Edingburgh: T&T Clark, 1963.

Drosnin, Michael. *The Bible Code*. New York: Touchstone, 1997.

Doukhan, Jacques. "The Seventy Weeks of Daniel 9: An Exegetical Study." *Andrews University Seminary Studies* 17 (1979): 1-22.

Dunn, Geoffrey. "Tertullian and Daniel 9:24-27: A Patristic Interpretation of a Prophetic Time-Frame." *Zeitschrift für Antikes Christentum* 6 (2009): 330- 44.

Ellis, E. Earle. *The Old Testament in Early Christianity: Canon and Interpretation in the Light of Modern Research*. Eugene: Wipf and Stock, 2003.

Endres, J C. *Biblical Interpretation in the Book of Jubilees*. Catholic Biblical Quarterly Monograph Series 18. Washington: The Catholic Biblical Association of America, 1987.

Erho, Ted. "Historical-Allusional Dating and the Similitudes of Enoch." *Journal of Biblical Literature* 130.3 (2011): 493-511.

Eshel, Esther. "Possible Sources of Daniel." Pages 387-94 in *The Book of Daniel: Composition and Reception, Volume 2*. Edited by John J. Collins and Peter W. Flint. Leiden: Brill, 2001.

Eshel, Hanan. "4Q390, the 490-Year Prophecy, and the Calendrical History of Second Temple Period." Pages 102-110 in *Enoch and Qumran Origins*. Grand Rapids: Eerdmans, 2005.

_____. "The Roots of the Hasmonean Revolt: The Reign of Antiochus IV." Pages 13-27 in *The Dead Sea Scrolls and the Hasmonean State*. Grand Rapids: Eerdmans: Yad Ben-Zvi, 2008.

Eslinger, Lyle. "Inner-biblical Exegesis and Inner-Biblical Allusion: The Question of Category." *Vetus Testamentum* 42.1 (1992): 47-58.

Evans, Craig. "Daniel in the New Testament: Visions of God's Kingdom." Pages 490-527 in *The Book of Daniel: Composition and Reception, Volume 2*. Edited by John J. Collins and Peter W. Flint. Leiden: Brill, 2001.

_____. and Emanuel Tov eds. *Exploring the Origins of the Bible: Canon Formation in Historical, Literary, and Theological Perspective*. Grand Rapids: Baker Academic, 2008.

Falk, Daniel. "Qumran Prayer Texts and the Temple." Pages 106-26 in *Sapiential, Liturgical and Poetical Texts from Qumran – Oslo, 1998*. Leiden: Brill, 2000.

_____. "Scriptural Inspiration for Penitential Prayer in the Dead Sea Scrolls." Pages 127-57 in *Seeking the Favor of God, Volume 2: The Development of Penitential Prayer in Second Temple Judaism*. Edited by Mark Boda and Daniel Falk. Atlanta: Society of Biblical Literature, 2007.

Farris, M.H. *The Formative Interpretations of the Seventy Years of Daniel*. PhD. Dissertation. University of Toronto, 1990.

Fewell, Danna N., ed. *Reading Between Texts: Intertextuality and the Hebrew Bible*. Louisville: Westminster John Knox, 1992.

Finn, Leonard. "Reflections on the Rule of Faith." Pages 221-42 in *The Bible as Christian Scripture*. Edited by Christopher Seitz; Atlanta: SBL, 2013.

Fishbane, Michael. *Biblical Interpretation in Ancient Israel*. Oxford: Clarendon, 1985.

_____. "From Scribalism to Rabbinism: Perspectives on the Emergence of Classical Judaism." Pages 64-80 in *The Garments of Torah: Essays in Biblical Hermeneutics*. Bloomington: Indiana University Press, 1989.

_____. "Law to Canon: Some Ideal-Typical Stages of Development." Pages 65-86 in *Minḥah Le-Naḥum: Biblical and Other Studies Presented to Nahum M. Sarna in Honour of His 70th Birthday*. Edited by Marc Zvi Brettler and Michael Fishbane. Continuum International, 1993.

_____. "Revelation and Tradition: Aspects of Inner-biblical Exegesis." *Journal of Biblical Literature* 99.3 (1980): 343-361.

_____. "Types of Biblical Intertextuality." Pages 39-44 in *Congress Volume: Oslo 1998*. Edited by A. Lemaire. Supplements to Vetus Testamentum 80. Leiden: Brill, 1995.

Fitzmeyer, Joseph. "Further Light on Melchizedek from Qumran Cave 11." *Journal of Biblical Literature* 86 (1976): 25-41.

_____. "The Use of Explicit Old Testament Quotations in Qumran Literature and the New Testament." Pages 3-58 in *The Semitic Background of the New Testament*. Grand Rapids: Eerdmans, 1997.

Flint, Peter. "The Daniel Tradition at Qumran." Pages 329-67 in *The Book of Daniel: Composition and Reception, Volume 2*. Edited by John J. Collins and Peter W. Flint. Leiden: Brill, 2001.

Ford, Desmond. *The Abomination of Desolation in Biblical Eschatology*. Washington, D.C: University Press of America, 1979.

_____. *Daniel*. Nashville, Tenn.: Southern, 1978.

France, R.T. *Jesus and the Old Testament: His Application of Old Testament Passages to Himself and His Mission*. London: Tyndale, 1971.

Gammie, John G. "The Classification, Stages of Growth, and Changing Intentions in the Book of Daniel." *Journal of Biblical Literature* 95.2 (1976): 191-204.

_____. "A Journey through Danielic Spaces: The Book of Daniel in the Theology and Piety of the Christian Community." *Interpretation* 39 (1985): 144-56.

Geertz, Clifford. *The Interpretation of Cultures*. New York: Basic, 1973.

Gentry, Peter. "Daniel's Seventy Weeks and the New Exodus." *Southern Baptist Journal of Theology* 14.1 (2010): 26-44.

Gerstenberger, Erhard. "Canon Criticism and the Meaning of *Sitz im Leben*." Pages 20-31 in *Canon, Theology and Old Testament Interpretation*. Edited by Gene Tucker. Philadelphia: Fortress, 1988.

Gese, Hartmut. "Die Bedeutung der Krise unter Antiochus IV: Epiphanes für die Apokalyptik des Danielbuches." *Zeitschrift für Theologie und Kirche* 80 (1983): 373-88.

Gibbs, Jeffrey A. *Jerusalem and Parousia: Jesus' Eschatological Discourse in Matthew's Gospel*. St. Louis: Concordia Academic, 2000.

Gignilliat, Mark. *A Brief History of Old Testament Criticism: From Benedict Spinoza to Brevard Childs*. Grand Rapids: Zondervan, 2012.

Gilbert, Maurice. "La Prière de Daniel: Dn 9, 4-19." *Revue théologique de Louvain* (1972): 284-310.

Ginsberg, H.C. *Studies in Daniel*. New York: Jewish Theological Seminary of America, 1948.

Goldingay, John. *Daniel*. Word Biblical Commentary 30. Edited by David A. Hubbard and Glenn W. Barker. Nashville: Thomas Nelson, 1989.

_____. "Story, Vision, Interpretation: Literary Approaches to Daniel." Pages 295-313 in *The Book of Daniel in the Light of New Findings*. Edited by A.S. van der Woude. Bibliotheca ephemeridum theologicarum lovaniensium 106. Leuven: Leuven University Press, 1993.

Goldstein, J.A. *1 Maccabees*. Anchor Bible 41. Garden City: Doubleday, 1976.

Goppelt, L. *Typos: The Typological Interpretation of the Old Testament in the New*. Grand Rapids: Eerdmans, 1982.

Goswell, Greg. "The Temple Theme in the Book of Daniel." *Journal of the Evangelical Theological Society* 55.3 (2012): 509-520.
Grabbe, Lester L. "The End of the Desolations of Jerusalem": From Jeremiah's 70 Years to Daniel's 70 Weeks of Years." Pages 67-72 in *Early Jewish and Christian Exegesis.* Edited by Craig A. Evans. Atlanta: Scholars Press, 1987.
_____. "Fundamentalism and Scholarship: The Case of Daniel." Pages 133-52 in *Scripture: Meaning and Method: Essays Presented to Anthony Tyrrell Hanson.* Edited by Barry P. Thompson. Hull: Hull University Press, 1987.
_____. "The Seventy-Weeks Prophecy (Daniel 9:24-27) in Early Jewish Interpretation." Pages 595-611 in *Die Fragmente der Vorsokratiker, Band 1.* Edited by Hermann Diels. Berlin: Weidmannsche Buchhandlung, 1954.
Grelot, P. "Soixante-dix Semaines d'Annees" *Biblica* 50 (1969) 169-86.
Guillort, J. *Cultural Capital: The Problem of Literary Canon Formation.* Chicago: University of Chicago Press, 1993.
Gunkel, Hermann. *Creation and Chaos in the Primeval Era and the Eschaton: A Religio-Historical Study of Genesis 1 and Revelation 12.* Translated by K. William Whitney Jr. Grand Rapids/Cambridge: Eerdmans, 2006.
Gzella, Holger. *Cosmic Battle and Political Conflict: Studies in Verbal Syntax and Contextual Interpretation of Daniel 8.* Biblica et orientalia 47. Rome: Pontificio Istituto Biblico, 2003.
Hahn, Scott. *Kinship by Covenant: A Canonical Approach to the Fulfillment of God's Saving Promises.* New Haven: Yale University Press, 2009.
Halvorson-Taylor, Martien A. *Enduring Exile: The Metaphorization of Exile in the Hebrew Bible.* Vetus Testamentum Supplements 141. Leiden: Brill, 2011.
Hartman, Louis F., and Alexander A. DiLella. *The Book of Daniel.* Anchor Bible 23. Garden City: Doubleday, 1978.
Hasel, Gerhard. "The Hebrew Masculine Plural for "Weeks" in the Expression "Seventy Weeks" in Daniel 9:24." *Andrews University Seminary Studies* 31 (1993): 105-118.
_____. "Interpretations of the Chronology of the Seventy Weeks." Pages 13-63 in *70 Weeks, Leviticus, Nature of Prophecy: Daniel and Revelation Committee Series 3.* Edited by Frank Holbrook. Washington D.C.: Review and Herald Publishers, 1986.
_____. "The Relationship Between Biblical Theology and Systematic Theology," *Trinity Journal* 5 (1984): 113-27.
Hector, Avalos. "Daniel 9:24-25 and Mesopotamian Temple Rededications." *Journal of Biblical Literature* 117 (1998): 507-11.
Hehn, Johannes. *Siebenzahl und Sabbat bei den Babyloniern und im Alten Testament.* Leitziger Semitistische Studien 2. Leipzig: Zentralantiquariat der DDR, 1968.
Helmer, Christine. "Biblical Theology: Bridge over Many Waters." *Currents in Research: Biblical Studies* 3 (2005): 169-96.
Helmer, Christine, and Christof Landmesser eds. *One Scripture or Many? Canon from Biblical, Theological and Philosophical Perspectives.* Oxford: Oxford University Press, 2004.
_____. "Transhistorical Unity of the New Testament Canon from Philosophical, Exegetical, and Systematic-Theological Perspectives." Pages 13-50 in *One Scripture or Many? Canon from Biblical, Theological and Philosophical Per-*

spectives. Edited by Christine Helmer and Christof Landmesser. Oxford: Oxford University Press, 2004.

Hempel, Charlotte and Judith Lieu, eds. *Biblical Traditions in Transmission: Essays in Honour of Michael Knibb*. Leiden: Brill, 2006.

Henze, Matthias. "4 Ezra and 2 Baruch: Literary Composition and Oral Performance in First-Century Apocalyptic Literature." *Journal of Biblical Literature* 131.1 (2012): 181-200.

_____. "4QApocryphon of Jeremiah C and 4QPseudo-Ezekiel: Two 'Historical' Apocalypses." Pages 25-42 in *Prophecy after the Prophets? The Contribution of the Dead Sea Scrolls to the Understanding of Biblical and Extra-Biblical Prophecy*. Edited by Kristin De Troyer and Armin Lange. Leuven: Peeters, 2009.

_____. *Biblical Interpretation in Qumran*. Grand Rapids: Eerdmans, 2005.

_____. "The Use of Scripture in the Book of Daniel." Pages 279-305 in *A Companion to Biblical Interpretation in Early Judaism*. Edited by Matthias Henze; Grand Rapids: Eerdmans, 2011.

Hess, Richard. "The Seventy Sevens of Daniel 9: A Timetable for the Future?" *Bulletin for Biblical Research* 21.3 (2011): 315-330.

Hoehner, H.W. "Daniel's Seventy Weeks and New Testament Chronology." *Biblioteca Sacra* 132 (1975): 47-65.

Hogeterp, Albert. "Daniel and the Qumran Daniel Cycle: Observations on 4QFour Kingdoms $^{A\text{-}B}$ (4Q552-553)." Pages 173-91 in *Authoritative Scriptures in Ancient Judaism*. Supplements to the Journal for the Study of Judaism 141. Edited by M. Popovic. Leiden: Brill, 2010.

Holladay, William. *Jeremiah 1*. Hermeneia. Minneapolis: Fortress, 1986.

Irenaeus. *On the Apostolic Preaching*. Translated by John Behr. Crestwood, N.Y.: St. Vladimir's Seminary Press, 1997.

Janowski, Bernd. "Die 'Kleine Biblia': Zur Bedeutung der Psalmen für eine Theologie des Alten Testaments." Pages 381-420 in *Der Psalter in Judentum und Christentum*. Edited by Erich Zenger. Freiburg: Herder, 1998.

Jeffrey, Grant. *The Mysterious Bible Codes*. Nashville: Word, 1998.

Jeremiah, David. *What in the World is Going On? 10 Prophetic Clues You Cannot Afford to Ignore*. Nashville: Thomas Nelson, 2008.

Johnston, Robert. "The Sabbath as Metaphor in the Second Century C.E." *Andrews University Seminary Studies* 49.2 (2011): 321-335.

Jones, Bruce William. "The Prayer in Daniel IX." *Vetus Testamentum* 18 (1968): 488-493.

Kalafian, Michael. *The Prophecy of the Seventy Weeks of the Book of Daniel: A Critical Review of the Prophecy as Viewed by Three Major Theological Interpretations and the Impact of the Book of Daniel on Christology*. Lanham: University Press of America, 1999.

Kelsey, David. *The Uses of Scripture in Recent Theology*. Philadelphia: Fortress, 1975.

Kline, Meredith. "The Covenant of the Seventieth Week." Pages 452-69 in *The Law and the Prophets: Old Testament Studies in Honor of Oswald T. Allis*. Edited by J.H. Skilton. Nutley, N.J.: Presbyterian and Reformed, 1974.

Knibb, Michael. "The Book of Daniel in Its Context." Pages 16-36 in *The Book of Daniel: Composition and Reception, Volume.1*. Edited by John J. Collins and Peter W. Flint. Leiden: Brill, 2001.

_____. "Reflections on the Status of the Early Enochic Writings." Pages 143-54 in *Authoritative Scriptures in Ancient Judaism*. Supplements to the Journal for the Study of Judaism 141. Edited by M. Popovic.Leiden/ Boston: Brill, 2010.

_____. "'You are Indeed Wiser than Daniel': Reflections on the Character of the Book of Daniel." Pages 399-411 in *The Book of Daniel in the Light of New Findings*. Edited by A.S. van der Woude. Bibliotheca ephemeridum theologicarum lovaniensium 106. Leuven: Leuven University Press, 1993.

Knoppers, Gary N. and Lester L. Grabbe eds. *Exile and Restoration Revisited: Essays on the Babylonian and Persian Periods in Memory of Peter R. Ackroyd*. New York: &T Clark, 2009.

Koch, Klaus. *Das Buch Daniel*. Erträge der Forschung 144. Darmstadt: Wissenschaftliche Buchgesellschaft, 1980.

_____. "Das Profetenschweigen des deuteronomistischen Geschichtswerks." Pages 115-128 in *Die Botschaft und die Boten: Festschrift für H.W. Wolff*. Edited by Jorg Jeremias. Neukirchen-Vluyn: Neukirchen-Verlag, 1981.

_____. "Deuterokanonische Zusätze zum Danielbuch." Alter Orient und Altes Testament 38 1.2. Neukirchen-Vluyn: Neukirchener Verlag, 1987.

_____. "Die mysteriösen Zahlen der judäischen Könige und die apokalyptischen Jahrwochen." *Vetus Testamentum* 28 (1978): 433-41.

_____. "Is Daniel Also Among the Prophets?" *Interpretation* 39 (1985): 117-30.

_____. *The Growth of the Biblical Tradition: The Form-Critical Method*. Translated by S.M. Culpritt. London: A&C Black, 1967.

_____. *The Rediscovery of Apocalyptic* in *Studies in Biblical Theology*. Second Series 22. Translated by Margaret Kohl. Naperville, Ill.: Alec R. Allenson Inc., 1972.

_____. "Sabbatstruktur der Geschichte." *Zeitschrift für die alttestamentliche Wissenschaft* 95 (1983): 403-30.

_____. "Stages in the Canonization of the Book of Daniel." Pages 421-46 in *The Book of Daniel: Composition and Reception, Volume 2*. Edited by John Collins and Peter Flint. Boston: Brill, 2002.

_____. "Vom profetischen zum apokalyptischen Visionsbericht." Pages 387-411 in *Apocalypticism in the Mediterranean World and the Near East: Proceedings of the International Colloquium on Apocalypticism, Uppsala, August 12-17, 1979*. Tübingen: Mohr Siebeck, 1983.

Koorevaar, Hendrik. *A Structural Canonical Approach for a Theology of the Old Testament, Version 3.2*. Leuven: Evangelische Theologische Faculteit, 2000.

Kratz, Reinhard. *Das Judentum im Zeitalter des Zweiten Tempels, Kleine Schriften I*. Tübingen: Mohr Siebeck, 2013.

_____. "Die Visionen des Daniel." Pages 219-36 in *Schriftauslegung in der Schrift: Festschrift für Odil Hannes Steck zu seinem 65. Geburtstag*. Edited by Reinhard Kratz. Beheifte zur Zeitschrift für die alttestamentliche Wissenschaft 300. Berlin: De Gruyter, 2000.

Kristeva, Julia. *Desire in Language: A Semiotic Approach to Literature and Art*. Translated by Thomas Gora. New York: Columbia University Press, 1980.

_____. *Revolution in Poetic Language*. Translated by Margaret Waller. New York: Columbia University Press, 1984.

Kugel, James. "The Bible's Earliest Interpreters." *Proof* 7 (1987): 275-96.

Laato, Antti. "The Seventy Yearweeks in the Book of Daniel." *Zeitschrift für die alttestamentliche Wissenschaft* 102 (1990): 212-225.

Lacocque, André. *The Book of Daniel*. Translated by David Pellauer. Atlanta: John Knox, 1979.

———. "The Liturgical Prayer in Daniel 9." *Hebrew Union College Annual* 47 (1976): 119-142.

La Haye, Tim and Jerry Jenkins. *Are We Living in the End Times? Current Events Foretold in Scripture... And What They Mean*. Wheaton, Ill.: Tyndale, 1999.

Lamaire, André and Magne Saebø. *Congress Volume: Oslo 1998*. Vetus Testamentum Supplement 80. Leiden: Brill, 2000.

Lang, B. "The 'Writings': A Hellenistic Literary Canon in the Hebrew Bible." Pages 41-65 in *Canonization and Decanonization: Papers presented to the International Conference of the Leiden Institute for the Study of Religions*. Edited by Arij van der Kooij and Karel van der Toorn. Leiden: Brill, 1998.

Lange, Armin and Matthias Weingold. *Biblical Quotations and Allusions in Second Temple Jewish Literature*. Journal of Ancient Judaism Supplements 5. Göttingen: Vandenhoeck and Ruprecht, 2011.

———. "From Literature to Scripture: The Unity and Plurality of the Hebrew Scriptures in Light of the Qumran Library." Pages 51-107 in *One Scripture or Many? Canon from Biblical, Theological, and Philosophical Perspectives*. Edited byChristine Helmer and Christine Landmesser. Oxford: Oxford University Press, 2004.

Laurentin, André. "Weattah-Kainun." *Biblica* 45 (1964): 190-97.

Leiman, Sid. *The Canonization of the Hebrew Scriptures: The Talmudic and Midrashic Evidence*. Hamden: Archon, 1976.

Leuchter, Mark. "The Manumission Laws in Leviticus and Deuteronomy: The Jeremiah Connection." *Journal of Biblical Literature* 127.4 (2008): 635-653.

Levine, Baruch. "The Language of Holiness: Perceptions of the Sacred in the Hebrew Bible." Pages 241-55 in *Backgrounds for the Bible*. Edited by Michael P. O'Connor and David Noel Freedman. Winona Lake, In.: Eisenbrauns, 1987.

Lewis, C.S. *The Great Divorce*. 3d ed. New York: HarperOne, 2001.

Lindsey, Hal. *The Late, Great Planet Earth*. Grand Rapids: Zondervan, 1970.

Liverani, Mario. "The Chronology of the Biblical Fairy-Tale." Pages 73-88 in *The Historian and the Bible: Essays in Honor of Lester Grabbe*. Edited by Philip Davies. Journal of the Study of the Old Testament Supplements 530. New York: T&T Clark, 2010.

Lucas, Ernest. *Daniel*. Apollos Old Testament Commentary 20. Downers Grove: IVP, 2002.

Luckenbill, Daniel. "The Black Stone of Esarhaddon." *American Journal of Semitic Languages and Literature* 41 (1924-25): 165-73.

Lurie, David. "A New Interpretation of Daniel's 'Sevens' and the Chronology of the Seventy 'Sevens.'" *Journal of the Evangleical Theological Society* 33.3 (1990): 303-309.

Lust, Johan. "Cult and Sacrifice in Daniel: The Tamid and the Abomination of Desolation." Pages 671-88 in *The Book of Daniel: Composition and Reception, Volume 2*. Edited by John Collins and Peter W. Flint. Leiden: Brill, 2001.

Lyons, William John. *Canon and Exegesis: Canonical Praxis and the Sodom Narrative*. Journal for the Study of the Old Testament Supplements 352. Sheffield: Sheffield Academic, 2002.

Mason, Rex. "The Treatment of Earlier Biblical Themes in the Book of Daniel." Pages 81-100 in *Perspectives on the Hebrew Bible: Essays in Honor of Walter J. Harrelson*. Edited by James L. Crenshaw. Macon: Mercer University Press, 1988.

McComiskey, Douglas. "Exile and Restoration from Exile in the Scriptural Quotations and Allusions of Jesus." *Journal of the Evangelical Theological Society* 54.1 (2010): 673-96.

McComiskey, Thomas E. "The Seventy 'Weeks' of Daniel against the Background of Ancient Near Eastern Literature." *Westminster Theological Journal* 47 (1985): 18-45.

McDonald, Lee ed. *The Canon Debate: On the Origins and the Formation of the Bible*. Peabody: Hendrickson, 2002.

_____. *The Formation of the Christian Biblical Canon*. Peabody: Hendrickson, 1995.

McFall, Leslie. "Do the Sixty-Nine Weeks of Daniel Date the Messianic Mission of Nehemiah or Jesus?" *Journal of Evangelical Theological Society* 52.4 (2009): 673-718.

Meadowcroft, Tim. "Exploring the Dismal Swamp: The Identity of the Anointed One in Daniel 9:24-27." *Journal of Biblical Literature* 120.3 (2001): 429-49.

Mertens, Alfred. *Das Buch Daniel im Lichte der Texte vom Toten Meer*. Stuttgarter Biblische Monographien 12. Würzburg: Echter Verlag, 1971.

Metzger, Bruce. *The Canon of the New Testament: Its Origin, Development, and Significance*. Oxford: Oxford University Press, 1997.

Miano, David. *Shadow on the Steps: Time Measurement in Ancient Israel*. Atlanta: Society of Biblical Literature, 2010.

Milgrom, Jacob. *Cult and Conscience: The Asham and the Priestly Doctrine of Repentance*. Leiden: Brill, 1976.

Miller, J.E. "The Redaction of Daniel." *Journal for the Study of the Old Testament* 52 (1991): 115-24.

Miller, J.W. *The Origins of the Bible: Rethinking Canon History*. New York: Paulist, 1994.

Montgomery, James. *A Critical and Exegetical Commentary on the Book of Daniel*. 3rd ed. Edingburgh: T&T Clark, 1959.

Morgan, Donn. *Between Text and Community: The "Writings" in Canonical Interpretation*. Minneapolis: Augsburg Fortress, 2000.

Morgan, Thaïs. "The Space of Intertextuality." Pages 30-38 in *Intertextuality and Contemporary American Fiction*. Edited by Patrick O'Donnell and Robert Con Davis. Baltimore: John Hopkins University Press, 1989.

Moule, C.F.D. *An Idiom Book of New Testament Greek*. Cambridge: Cambridge University Press, 1982.

Müller, H. "קדש qds helig." Pages 589-609 in *Theologisches Handwörterbuch zum Alten Testament*. Edited by Ernst Jenni and Claus Westermann. Munich: Chr. Kalser, 1984.

Naiman, Hindy. "Interpretation as Primordial Writing: Jubilees and Its Authority Conferring Strategies." *Journal for the Study of Judaism* 30 (1999): 379-410.

Newman, R.C. "Daniel's Seventy Weeks and the Old Testament Sabbath-Year Cycle." *Journal of the Evangelical Theological Society* 16 (1973): 229-34.

Newsom, Carol. "Rhyme and Reason: The Historical Resumé in Israelite and Early Jewish Thought." Pages 293-310 in *Congress Volume Leiden 2004*. Edited by A. Lemaire. Boston: Brill, 2006.

Nielsen, Kristen. "Intertextuality and Biblical Scholarship." Pages 17-32 in *Congress Volume: Oslo 1998*. Edited by A. Lemaire. Supplements to Vetus Testamentum 80. Leiden: Brill, 1995.

Niditch, Susan. *The Symbolic Vision in Biblical Tradition*. Harvard Semitic Monographs 30. Chico: Scholars Press, 1983.

Nissinen, Marti. "Pesharim as Divination, Qumran Exegesis, Omen Interpretation and Literary Prophecy." Pages 43-60 in *Prophecy after the Prophets? The Contribution of the Dead Sea Scrolls to the Understanding of Biblical and Extra-Biblical Prophecy*. Edited by K.D. Troyer and Armin Lange. Contributions to Biblical Exegesis and Theology 52. Leuven: Peeters, 2009.

Noble, Paul. *The Canonical Approach: A Critical Reconstruction of the Hermeneutics of Brevard S. Childs*. Leiden: Brill, 1995.

Nogalski, James. "Intertextuality and the Twelve." Pages 102-124 in *Forming Prophetic Literature: Essays on Isaiah and the Twelve in Honor of John D.W. Watts*. Journal for the Study of the Old Testament Supplements 235. Edited by J.W. Watts and Paul House. Sheffield: Sheffield Academic, 1996.

Noth, Martin. *The Deuteronomistic History*. Translated by J.A. Clines. Journal for the Study of the Old Testament Supplement 15. Sheffield: JSOT Press, 1981.

Oegema, Gerbern. *Apocalyptic Interpretation of the Bible: Apocalypticism and Biblical Interpretation in Early Judaism, the Apostle Paul, the Historical Jesus, and their Reception History*. London: T&T Clark, 2012.

Olson, Dennis. "'Seeking' the Inexpressible Texture of Thy Word: A Practical Guide to Brevard Childs' Canonical Approach to Theological Exegesis." *Princeton Theological Review* 14.1 (2008): 53-68.

Paul, Shalom. "Gleanings from the Biblical and Talmudic Lexica in Light of Akkadian." Pages 242-56 in *Mishnah le Nahum: Biblical and Other Studies Presented to Nahum M. Sarna in Honour of His 70th Birthday*. Edited by Michael Fishbane and Marc Brettler. Journal for the Study of the Old Testament Supplement 154. Sheffield: JSOT, 1993.

Payne, J.B. "The Goal of Daniel's Seventy Weeks." *Journal of the Evangelical Theological Society* 21 (1978): 97-115.

Plöger, Otto. *Das Buch Daniel*. Kommentar zum Alten Testament 18. Stuttgart: Gütersloher Verlagshaus Gerd Mohn, 1965.

Porteous, Norman. *Das Buch Daniel*. Das Alte Testament Deutsch 23. Göttingen: Vandenhoeck & Ruprecht, 1985.

Porter, Paul A. *Metaphors and Monsters: A Literary Critical Study of Daniel 7 and 8*. Coniectanea Biblica: Old Testament Studies 20. Uppsala: CWK Gleerup, 1983.

Portier-Young, Anathea. *Apocalypse Against Empire: Theologies of Resistance in Early Judaism*. Grand Rapids: Eerdmans, 2011.

Poythress, Vern. "Hermeneutical Factors in Determining the Beginning of the Seventy Weeks (Daniel 9:25)." *Trinity Journal* 6 (1985): 131-49.

Provan, Iain. "Canons to the Left of Him: Brevard Childs, His Critics, and the Future of Old Testament Theology." *Scottish Journal of Theology* 50 (1997): 1-38.

_____. *In the Stable with the Dwarves: Testimony, Interpretation, Faith and the History of Israel.* Vancouver: Regent College Publishing, 1998.

Puech, E. "Notes sur le manuscript de X1QMelkisedeq." *Revue de Qumran* 12 (1987): 483-513.

Pusey, E.B. *Daniel the Prophet.* New York: Funk and Wagnalis, 1865.

Pyper, Hugh. "Reading in the Dark: Zechariah, Daniel and the Difficulty of Scripture." *Journal for the Study of the Old Testament* 294 (2005): 485-504.

Radner, Ephraim. "Doctrine, Destiny and the Figure of History." Pages 46-67 in *Reclaiming Faith.* Edited by Ephraim Radner and George Sumner; Grand Rapids: Eerdmans, 1993.

Redditt, Paul. "The Community Behind the Book of Daniel: Challenges, Hopes, Values and Its View of God." *Perspectives in Religious Studies* 36.3 (2009): 321-39.

_____. "Daniel 9: Its Structure and Meaning." *Catholic Biblical Quarterly* 62 (2000): 236-49.

_____. "Daniel's Position in the Tanach, the LXX-Vulgate, and the Protestant Canon." *Old Testament Essays* 23 (2010): 178-93.

Rendtorff, Rolf. *The Canonical Hebrew Bible: A Theology of the Old Testament.* Leiden: DEO, 2005.

Reno, Rusty R. "Biblical Theology and Theological Exegesis." Pages 385-408 in *Out of Egypt: Biblical Theology and Biblical Interpretation.* Edited by Craig Bartholomew et al. Grand Rapids: Zondervan, 2006.

Ricoeur, Paul. *The Rule of Metaphor: Multidisciplinary Studies of the Creation of Meaning in Language.* Translated by Robert Czerny. University of Toronto Romance Series 37. Toronto: University of Toronto Press, 1977.

_____. *Time and Narrative.* Translated by K. McLaughlin and D. Pellauer. Chicago: University of Chicago Press, 1984.

Riffaterre, Michael. *Semiotics of Poetry.* Bloomington: Indiana University Press, 1978.

Rigger, Hansjörg. *Siebzig Siebener: Die 'Jahrwochenprophetie' in Dan 9.* Trierer Theologische Studien 57. Trier: Paulinus, 1997.

Rogers, Jessie. "Searching for Daniel in 1 Corinthians: Methodological Considerations." Paper presented at the annual meeting of the SBL. San Francisco, Calif., November 21, 2011.

Roh, Se Young. "Creation and Redemption in Priestly Theology." Ph.D. diss. Drew University, 1992.

Rose, Walter. "Messianic Expectations in the Old Testament." *In die Skriflig* 35.2 (2001): 275-88.

Rowe, C. Kavin. "The Doctrine of God is a Hermeneutic: The *Biblical Theology* of Brevard S. Childs." Pages 155-172 in *The Bible as Christian Scripture.* Edited by Christopher Seitz. Atlanta: SBL, 2013.

Rowley, H.H. "The Unity of the Book of Daniel." Pages 235-268 in *The Servant of the Lord and Other Essays on the Old Testament.* London: Athlone, 1952.

Ryle, Herbert E. *The Canon of the Old Testament: An Essay on the Gradual Growth and Formation of the Hebrew Canon of Scripture.* 2d ed. London: Macmillan and Co., 1904.

Sæbø, Magne. *On the Way to Canon.* Sheffield: Sheffield Academic, 1998.

Sailhamer, John. "Biblical Theology and the Composition of the Hebrew Bible." Pages 25-36 in *Biblical Theology: Retrospect & Prospect*. Edited by Scott J. Hafemann. Grand Rapids: InterVarsity, 2002.

———. "Daniel." Pages 445-558 in *NIV Compact Bible Commentary*. Grand Rapids: Zondervan, 1999.

———. *Introduction to Old Testament Theology: A Canonical Approach*. Grand Rapids: Zondervan, 1995.

Sanders, James. *Torah and Canon*. Philadelphia: Augsburg/Fortress, 1972.

———. "What's Up Now? Renewal of an Important Investigation." Pages 1-7 in *Jewish and Christian Scriptures: The Function of 'Canonical' and 'Non-Canonical' Religious Texts*. London: T&T Clark, 2010.

Scalise, Charles. *Hermeneutics as Theological Prolegomena: A Canonical Approach*. Macon: Mercer University Press, 1994.

Scheetz, Jordan. *The Concept of Canonical Intertextuality and the Book of Daniel*. Eugene: Pickwick, 2011.

Schlenke, Barbara. "Verantwortung angesichts des Endes Das Gebet des Daniel in Dan 9,4-20." Pages 105-123 in *Juda und Jerusalem in der Seleukidenzeit*. Edited by Ulrich Dahmen and Johannes Schnocks. Göttingen: Bonn University Press, 2010.

Schmid, Konrad. "Innerbiblische Schriftauslegung: Aspekte der Forschungsgeschichte." Pages 1-22 in *Schriftauslegung in der Schrift: Festschrift für Odil Hannes Steck zu seinem 65. Geburtstag*. Edited by Reinhard G. Kratz. Beiheffte zur Zeitschrift für die alttestamentliche Wissenschaft 300. Berlin: De Gruyter, 2000.

———. *The Old Testament: A Literary History*. Translated by Linda Maloney. Minneapolis: Fortress, 2012.

Scholz, Stefan. "Kanones in Theologie, Literaturwissenschaften und Kulturwissenschaften. Einführende Bemerkungen zur Kanonforschung der Neuzeit und Moderne." Pages 33-38 in *Kanon in Konstruktion und Dekonstruktion: Kanonisierungsprozesse religiöser Texte von der Antike bis zur Gegenwart, Ein Handbuch*. Edited by Eve Becker and Stefan Scholz. Berlin/Boston: De Gruyter, 2012.

Schultz, Richard. *In Search of a Quotation: Verbal Parallels in the Prophets*. Journal for the Study of the Old Testament: Supplement Series 180. Sheffield: Sheffield University, 1999.

———. "Intertextuality, Canon, and 'Undecidability': Understanding Isaiah's 'New Heavens and New Earth' (Isaiah 65:17-25)." *Bulletin for Biblical Research* 20.1 (2010): 19-38.

Seeligman, I.L. "Voraussetzungen des Midraschexegese." *Studia in Veteris Testamenti pseudepigraphica* 1 (1953): 50-81.

Segert, Stanislav. "Poetic Structures in the Hebrew Sections of the Book of Daniel." Pages 261-76 in *Solving Riddles and Untying Knots*. Edited by Jonas C. Greenfield. Winona Lake, In.: Eisenbrauns, 1995.

Seidl, Theodor. "Die 70 Jahrwochen des Daniel in der Deutung der Peschitta, Dan 9,24-27: Analyse - Vergleich - Bewertung." Pages 335-347 in *Lingua Restituta Orientalis*. Edited by Regine Schulz. Wiesbaden: Otto Harrassowitz Verlag, 1990.

Seitz, Christopher. "The Canonical Approach and Theological Interpretation." Pages 59-110 in *Canon and Biblical Interpretation*. Scripture and Hermeneutics Series 7. Edited by Craig Bartholomew and Anthony Thiselton. Grand Rapids: Zondervan, 2006.

———. *The Character of Christian Scripture: The Significance of a Two-Testament Bible*. Grand Rapids: Baker, 2011.

———. *Figured Out: Typology and Providence in Christian Scripture*. Lousiville: Westminster John Knox, 2001.

———. *The Goodly Fellowship of the Prophets: The Achievement of Association in Canon Formation*. Grand Rapids: Baker, 2009.

———. "The Old Testament as Abiding Theological Witness: Inscripting a Theological Curriculum." Pages 3-12 in *Word Without End: The Old Testament as Abiding Theological Witness*. Waco: Baylor University Press, 2004.

———. "Prophetic Associations." Pages 156-66 in *Thus Says the Lord: Essays on the Former and Latter Prophets in Honor of Robert R. Wilson*. Edited by John J. Ahn and Stephen Cook. London: T&T Clark, 2009.

———. *Prophecy and Hermeneutics: Toward a New Introduction to the Prophets*. Studies in Theological Interpretation. Grand Rapids: Baker, 2007.

———. "Scripture Becomes Religion(s): The Theological Crisis of Serious Biblical Interpretation in the Twentieth Century." Pages 13-33 in *Figured Out: Typology and Providence in Christian Scripture*. Louisville: Westminster John Knox, 2001.

Shea, William. "Darius the Mede: An Update." *Andrews University Seminary Studies* 20.3 (1982): 229-47.

———. "The Prophecy of Daniel 9:24-27." Pages 75-118 in *70 Weeks, Leviticus, Nature of Prophecy*. Edited by Frank Holbrook. Washington, D.C.: Biblical Research Institute, 1986.

Sheppard, Gerald. "Biblical Wisdom Literature at the End of the Modern Age." Pages 369-98 in *Congress Volume: Oslo 1998*. Edited by A. Lemaire. Supplements to Vetus Testamentum 80. Leiden: Brill, 1995.

———. "Canonization: Hearing the Voice of the Same God Through Historically Dissimilar Traditions." *Interpretation* 36 (1982): 21-33.

———. *The Future of the Bible: Beyond Liberalism and Literalism*. Toronto: United Church, 1990.

———. "Theology of the Book of Psalms." *Interpretation* 46 (1992): 143-55.

Smith, J.S. *Reading the Signs: A Sensible Approach to Revelation and other Apocalyptic Writings*. Macon: Smyth & Helwys, 1997.

Smith, J.Z. "Canons, Catalogues and Classic." Pages 300-307 in *Canonization and Decanonization: Papers presented to the International Conference of the Leiden Institute for the Study of Religions*. Edited by Arij van der Kooij and Karel van der Toorn. Leiden: Brill, 1998.

Sommer, Benjamin. "Exegesis, Allusion and Intertextuality in the Hebrew Bible: A Response to Lyle Eslinger." *Vetus Testamentum* 46 (1996) 486-87.

———. "Inner-biblical Interpretation." Pages 1819-25 in *The Jewish Study Bible*. Edited by Adele Berlin and Marc Brettler. Oxford: Oxford University Press, 2004.

———. *A Prophet Reads Scripture: Allusions in Isaiah 40-55*. Stanford: Stanford University Press, 1998.

———. "Psalm 1 and the Canonical Shape of Jewish Scripture." Pages 199-221 in *Jewish Bible Theology: Perspectives and Case Studies*. Edited by Isaac Kalimi. Winona Lake, In.: Eisenbrauns, 2012.

———. "The Scroll of Isaiah as Jewish Scripture, Or, Why Jews Don't Read Books." Pages 225-242 in *SBL 1996 Seminar Papers*. Atlanta: Scholars Press, 1996.

Steinberg, Julius. *Die Ketuvim - ihr Aufbau und ihre Botschaft* in the Bonner Biblische Beiträge Band 152. Edited by Frank Lothar-Hossfeld and Rudolf Hoppe. Hamburg: Philo, 2006.

Steck, Odil Hannes. *Israel und das gewaltsame Geschick der Propheten: Untersuchungen zur Überlieferung des deuteronomistischen Geschichtsbildes im Alten Testament, Spätjudentum und Urchristentum*. Wissenschaftliche Monographien zum Alten und Neuen Testament 23. Neukirchen-Vluyn: Neukirchener Verlag, 1967.

———. *Die Prophetenbücher und ihr theologisches Zeugnis: Wege der Nachfrage und Fährten zur Antwort*. Tübingen: Mohr Siebeck, 1996.

Steins, Georg. "Kanon und Anamnese: Auf dem Weg zu einer Neuen Biblischen Theologie." Pages 110-129 in *Der Bibelkanon in der Bibelauslegung: Methodenreflexionen und Beispielexegesen*. Edited by Egbert Ballhorn and Georg Steins. Stuttgart: Kohlhammer, 2007.

———. "Kanonisch-intertextuelle Bibellektüre – My Way." Pages 55-68 in *Intertextualität: Perspektiven auf ein interdisziplinäres Arbeitsfeld*. Edited by Karin Herrmann and Sanra Hübenthal. Aacken: Shaker, 2007.

Stone, Michael. *Ancient Judaism: New Visions and Views*. Grand Rapids: Eerdmans, 2011.

———. *Features of the Eschatology of IV Ezra*. Harvard Semitic Studies 35. Atlanta: Scholars Press, 1989.

Stone, Tim. "The Compilational History of the Megilloth: Canon, Contoured Intertextuality and Meaning in the Writings." Ph.D. diss., St. Andrews University, 2010.

Strickert, F.M. "Damascus Document VII, 10-20 and Qumran Messianic Expectation." *Revue de Qumran* 47 (1986): 327-50.

Su, Soon Peng. *Lexical Ambiguity in Poetry*. London/New York: Longman, 1994.

Sundberg, Albert. *The Old Testament of the Early Church*. Harvard Theological Studies 20. Cambridge: Oxford University Press/ Harvard University Press, 1964.

Swanson, T.N. "The Closing of the Collection of Holy Scripture: A Study in the History of the Canonization of the Old Testament." Ph.D. diss., Vanderbilt University, 1970.

Sweeney, Marvin. "The End of Eschatology in Daniel? Theological and Socio-Political Ramifications of the Changing Contexts of Interpretation." *Biblical Interpretation* 9 (2001): 123-40.

———. "Foundations for a Jewish Theology of the Hebrew Bible: Prophets in Dialogue." Pages 161-186 in *Jewish Bible Theology: Perspectives and Case Studies*. Edited by Isaac Kalimi. Winona Lake, In.: Eisenbrauns, 2012.

———. *Tanak: A Theological and Critical Introduction to the Jewish Bible*. Minneapolis: Augsburg Fortress, 2011.

Thielman, Frank. *Theology of the New Testament: A Canonical and Synthetic Approach*. Grand Rapids, Zondervan, 2011.

Thiering, Barbara. "The Three and Half Years of Elijah." *Novum Testamentum* 23 (1981): 41-55.

Thiselton, Anthony. "Canon, Community and Theological Construction." Pages 1-30 in *Canon and Biblical Interpretation.* Scripture and Hermeneutics Series 7. Edited by Craig Bartholomew and Anthony Thiselton. Grand Rapids: Zondervan, 2006.
Tigchelaar, Eibert. "Aramaic Texts from Qumran and the Authoritativeness of Hebrew Scriptures: Preliminary Observations. Pages 155-71 in *Authoritative Scriptures in Ancient Judaism.* Supplements to the Journal for the Study of Judaism 141. Edited by M. Popovic. Leiden/Boston: Brill, 2010.
Torrance, Thomas F. *Reality & Evangelical Theology: The Realism of Christian Revelation.* Eugene: Wipf & Stock, 2003.
Treier, Daniel. *Introducing Theological Interpretation of Scripture: Recovering Christian Practice.* Grand Rapids: Baker Academic, 2008.
Trible, Phyllis. *Rhetorical Criticism: Context, Method and the Book of Jonah.* Minneapolis: Fortress, 1994.
Tull, Patricia. "The Rhetoric of Recollection." Pages 71-78 in *Congress Volume: Oslo 1998.* Edited by A. Lemaire. Supplements to Vetus Testamentum 80. Leiden: Brill, 1995.
Ulrich, Eugene. "The Evolutionary Composition of the Hebrew Bible." Pages 23-40 in *Editing the Bible: Assessing the Task Past and Present.* Edited by John Kloppenborg and Judith Newman. Atlanta: Society of Biblical Literature, 2012.
_____. "The Notion and Definition of Canon." Pages 21-35 in *The Canon Debate.* Edited by Lee McDonald. Peabody: Hendrickson, 2002.
VanderKam, James. "Enoch Traditions in Jubilees and Other Second-Century Sources," *Society of Biblical Literature Seminar Papers* 1 (1978): 229-51.
_____. "To What End? Functions of Scriptural Interpretation in Qumran Texts." Pages 302-20 in *From Revelation to Canon: Studies in the Hebrew Bible and Second Temple Literature.* Leiden: Brill, 2002.
Van der Kooij, A. "The Concept of Covenant (Bᵉrît) in the Book of Daniel." Pages 495-504 in *The Book of Daniel in Light of New Findings.* Bibliotheca ephemeridum theologicarum lovaniensium 106. Edited by A.S. Van der Woude. Leuven: Leuven University Press, 1993.
Van Deventer, Hans. "The End of the End Or, What is the Deuteronomist (Still) Doing in Daniel?" Pages 62-75 in *Past, Present, Future: The Deuteronomistic History and the Prophets.* Edited by Johannes C. De Moor and Harry van Rooy. Leiden: Brill, 2000.
VanGemeren, Willem, ed. *A Guide to Old Testament Theology and Exegesis: Introductory Articles.* Grand Rapids: Zondervan, 1999.
_____. *Interpreting the Prophetic Word: An Introduction to the Prophetic Literature of the Old Testament.* Grand Rapids: Zondervan, 1996.
_____. "Our Missional God: Redemptive-Historical Preaching and the *Missio Dei.*" Trinity Evangelical Divinity School, 2010. Forthcoming.
Vanhoozer, Kevin. *The Drama Of Doctrine: A Canonical-Linguistic Approach To Christian Theology.* Louisville: Westminster John Knox, 2005.
_____. "Lost in Interpretation: Truth, Scripture, and Hermeneutics." Pages 1-35 in *Whatever Happened to Truth?* Edited by Andreas Köstenberger. Wheaton: Crossway, 2005.
Vanonen, Hanna. "The Textual Connections Between 1QM 1 and the Book of Daniel." Pages 223-46 in *Changes in Scripture: Rewriting and Interpreting Au-*

thoritative Traditions in the Second Temple Period*. Edited by Hanne von Weissenberg and Juha Pakkala. Berlin/New York: De Gruyter, 2011.
Van Ruiten, Jacque. "Biblical Interpretation in the Book of Jubilees: The Case of the Early Abram (Jub. 11:14-12:15)." Pages 135-52 in *A Companion to Biblical Interpretation in Early Judaism*. Edited by Matthias Henze. Grand Rapids: Eerdmans, 2012.
Venter, Pieter M. "Constitualised Space in Daniel 9." *Hervormde Teologiese Studies* 60.1-2 (2004): 607-24.
_____. "Daniel 9: A Penitential Prayer in Apocalyptic Garb." Pages 33-49 in *Seeking the Favor of God: The Development of Penitential Prayer in Second Temple Judaism, Volume 2*. Edited by Mark J. Boda, Daniel K. Falk, and Rodney Alan Werline. Atlanta: Society of Biblical Literature, 2007.
_____. "Daniel and Enoch: Two Different Reactions" *Hervormde Teologiese Studies* 53.1-2 (1997): 68-91.
_____. "Intertextuality in the Book of Jubilees." *Hervormde Teologiese Studies* 63.2 (2007): 463-80.
_____. "Intertekstualiteit, Kontekstualiteit en Daniel 9." *In die Skriffig* 31.4 (1997): 327-46.
Vermes, Geza. "Biblical Proof-Texts in Qumran Literature." *Journal of Semitic Studies* 34 (1989): 493-508.
Vogel, Winfried. *The Cultic Motif in the Book of Daniel*. New York: Peter Lang, 2010.
Von Rad, Gerhard. *Wisdom in Israel*. Nashville: Abingdon, 1972.
Wacholder, Ben Zion. "The Calendar of Sabbath Years During the Second Temple Era: A Response." Pages 193-207 in *Origins of Judaism, Religion, History, and Literature in Late Antiquity, Volume 5, Part 2*. Edited by Jacob Neusner and William Scott Green. New York: Garland, 1990.
Wallace, Daniel. *Greek Grammar: Beyond the Basics, An Exegetical Syntax of the New Testament*. Grand Rapids: Zondervan, 1996.
Wallraff, Martin. *Julius Africanus Chronographie: The Extant Fragments*. Berlin: Walter de Gruyter, 2007.
Waltke, Bruce and M. O'Connor. *An Introduction to Biblical Hebrew Syntax*. Winona Lake, IN.: Eisenbrauns, 1990.
_____. *An Old Testament Theology: An Exegetical, Canonical and Thematic Approach*. Grand Rapids: Zondervan, 2011.
Walvoord, John. *Daniel: The Key to Prophetic Revelation*. Chicago: Moody Press, 1971.
Wambacq, Benjamin. "Les prières de Baruch (1,15-2,19) et de Daniel (9,5-19)." *Biblica* 40 (1959): 463-75.
Watson, Francis. "Gospel and Scripture: Rethinking Canonical Unity." *Tyndale Bulletin* 52.2 (2001): 161-182.
Watts, John. *How We Got Our Bible: Files from an Alttestamentler's Hard Drive*. Eugene: Wipf & Stock, 2011.
Webster, John. *Word and Church: Essays in Church Dogmatics*. Edinburgh/New York: Continuum, 2001.
Weeks, Noel. "The Ambiguity of Biblical 'Background.'" *Westminster Theological Journal* 72 (2010): 219-36.
Wellhausen, Julius. "Zur Apokalyptischen Literatur." *Skizzen und Vorarbeiten* 6 (1899): 225-34.
Wells, Samuel and George Sumner. *Esther-Daniel*. Grand Rapids: Brazos, 2013.

Werline, Rodney. "Prayer, Politics, and Social Vision in Daniel 9." Pages 17-32 in *Seeking the Favor of God, Volume 2: The Development of Penitential Prayer in Second Temple Judaism*. Edited by Mark Boda and Daniel Falk. Atlanta: Society of Biblical Literature, 2007.

Wesselius, Jan-Wim. "The Writing of Daniel." Pages 291-310 in *The Book of Daniel: Composition and Reception, Volume 2*. Edited by John Collins and Peter W. Flint. Leiden: Brill, 2001.

Westermann, Claus. "Struktur und Geschichte der Klage im Alten Testament." *Zeitschrift für die alttestamentliche Wissenschaft* 66 (1954): 44-80.

Wildeboer, Gerritt. *The Origin of the Canon of the Old Testament: An Historico-Critical Enquiry*. London: Luzac, 1895.

Willis, Amy C. Merrill. *Dissonance and the Drama of Divine Sovereignty in the Book of Daniel*. Old Testament Studies 520. New York: T&T Clark, 2010.

———. "The Plans of God in Jeremiah and Daniel." Paper presented at the annual meeting of the Society of Biblical Interpretation. San Francisco, Calif., November 22, 2011.

Willis, Lawrence. "Daniel." Pages 352-356 in *Jewish Study Bible*. Edited by Adele Berlin and Marc Brettler. Oxford: Oxford University Press, 2003.

Wilson, Gerald. "The Prayer of Daniel 9: Reflection on Jeremiah 29." *Journal for the Study of the Old Testament* 48 (1990): 91-99.

Wilson, Robert. "The Persian Period and the Shaping of the Prophetic Literature." Pages 107-120 in *Focusing Biblical Studies: The Crucial Nature of the Persian and Hellenistic Periods: Essays in Honor of Douglas A. Knight*. Edited by Jon Berquist and Alice Hunt. London: T&T Clark, 2012.

Wilson, Robert. *Studies in the Book of Daniel, Volume 2*. 1918. Reprint, Grand Rapids: Baker, 1972.

Wood, Leon. *A Commentary on Daniel*. Grand Rapids: Eerdmans, 1973.

Wolterstorff, Nicholas. *Divine Discourse: Philosophical Reflections on the Claim that God Speaks*. Cambridge: Cambridge University Press, 1995.

———. "The Unity Behind the Canon." Pages 217-32 in *One Scripture or Many? Canon from Biblical, Theological and Philosophical Perspectives*. Oxford: Oxford University Press, 2004.

Wright, Christopher. "What Happened Every Seven Years in Israel? Old Testament Sabbatical Institutions for Land, Debts and Slaves." *Evangelical Quarterly* 56 (1984): 129-38.

Yamauchi, Edwin M. "Hermeneutical Issues in the Book of Daniel." *Journal of the Evangelical Theological Society* 23.1 (1980): 13-21.

Zakovitch, Yair. "Inner-biblical Interpretation." Pages 27-63 in *A Companion to Biblical Interpretation in Early Judaism*. Edited by Matthias Henze. Grand Rapids: Eerdmans, 2011.

Zenger, Erich. *Einleitung in das Alte Testament*. Stuttgart: Verlag W. Kohlhammer, 1995.

Index of Authors

Aaron, D. 82, 123, 128
Abegg, M. 73, 74, 75
Abraham, W. 140
Adams, J. 57-58
Adler, W. 63, 79,95, 135
Albertz, R. 50, 61, 62, 63
Allert, C. 140, 141
Alter, R. 98
Anderson, G. 44, 45,51, 121, 139
Anderson, R. 95
Auwers, J. M. 11

Bailey, D. 110
Barker, K. 16, 17
Barr, J. 16, 18
Barrera J.T. 59
Barton, J. 12, 16, 18,25
Beal, T. 25
Beale, G. 24
Beckwith, R. 75, 76, 80, 119, 125, 154
Beferle, S. 5
Beldman, D. 98
Bergsma, J. 32, 72, 97
Berner, C. 52,62, 63, 68, 84, 96, 98, 104, 122
Bernstein, M. 5, 6
Blass, F. 136
Blenkinsopp, J. 20, 29, 30, 58, 60
Blomberg, C. 132, 133
Blowers, P. 140
Bockmuehl, M. 145
Boda, M. 34, 60
Boyarin, D. 27
Broyles, C. 15
Buhl, F. 12
Burer, M. 85

Caird G. B. 71, 83, 123, 128
Cargounis, C. 9
Carr, D. 13, 14, 115, 19, 25, 26, 30, 48, 55, 65, 81, 114
Chapman, S. 2, 12, 15, 20, 22, 26, 28, 30, 31, 34, 38, 55, 56, 58, 59, 60, 64
Charlesworth, J. 75
Chazon, E. 45
Childs, B. 3, 8 9, 10, 11, 13, 17-23, 25-30, 34, 35, 47, 48, 51, 56, 57, 65, 71, 81-85, 91, 97, 98, 100, 115, 116, 119, 120, 123-125, 127, 129-131, 134, 135, 139-141, 143, 145-149, 154
Clements, R. 29, 59, 60
Collins, A. 78, 79, 102
Collins, J. 33, 42, 50, 82, 86, 87, 88, 94, 100, 101, 106, 109, 110, 113, 114, 125, 135
Cornhill, C. H. 78
Crawford, S. 12

Davies, P. 13, 125
Debrunner, A. 136
De Jonge, H. J. 11
De Long, K. 32, 98
Dempster, S. 10, 18, 20, 28, 31, 60, 61
DiLella, A. 113, 153
Dimant, D. 3, 5, 45, 75, 76, 80, 86, 87
Doukhan, J. 54, 101, 107
Driver, D. 18, 30, 129, 130, 140, 141
Driver, G. R. 57
Drosnin, M. 124

Ellis, E. E. 12
Eshel, H. 95
Esher, E. 5

Index of Authors

Eslinger, L. 27
Evans, C. 131

Falk, D. 6
Farris, M. H. 124
Finn, L. 140
Fishbane, M. 8, 9, 15, 23, 25, 26, 28, 34, 36, 37, 43, 46, 48, 53, 68, 69
Fitzmeyer, J. 73, 80
Flint, P. 5, 6, 77

Gerstenberger, E. 130
Gibbs, J. 113
Gignilliat, M. 144
Gilbert, M. 34, 56
Ginsberg, H. 35
Goldingay, J. 4, 5, 37, 43, 47, 52, 56, 58, 63, 64, 70, 72, 77, 78, 80, 81, 82, 84, 85, 93, 96, 102, 106, 107, 108 114, 115
Goswell, G. 89, 90
Gunke,l H. 138
Gzella, H. 115

Hahn, S. 10
Halvorson-Taylor, M. A. 74, 113, 124
Hartman, L. 113, 153
Hasel, G. 95, 172
Helmer, C. 28, 130
Hehn, J. 72
Henze, M. 36, 37, 39, 40, 43, 46, 47, 48 52, 54, 57, 63, 65, 74, 78, 79, 119, 114, 115
Holladay, W. 50

Irenaeus 141, 142

Janowski, B. 59
Jeffrey, G. 124
Jeremiah, D. 1
Jerome 107
Johnston, R. 85

Kelsey, D. 140

Kline, M. 42, 111
Knibb, M. 5, 8
Koch, K. 5, 7, 8, 36, 46, 48, 63, 66, 69, 72, 77, 79, 92, 95, 101, 107, 114, 116, 139, 153
Koorevaar, H. 16
Kratz, R. 99
Kristeva, J. 7, 25

Lacocque, A. 36, 43, 54, 56, 58, 68, 72, 83
Landmesser, C. 16
Lang, B. 38, 99
Lange, A. 60
Laurentin, A. 37
Leiman, S. 12
Levine, B. 87
Lewis, C. S. 144
Lindsey, H. 1, 124
Liverani, M. 82
Luckenbill, D. 50
Lurie, D. 68
Lust, J. 113, 117
Lyons, W. J. 20

McDonald, L. 11
Mertens, A. 75
Metzger, B. 12
Miano, D. 76
Milgrom, J. 55
Miller, J. 60, 65
Montgomery, J. 1, 86, 94, 101, 113
Morgan, D. 28, 151
Morgan, T. 25
Moule, C. F. D. 136
Müller, H. 87

Naiman, H. 74
Newsom, C. 128
Nissinen, M. 49
Noble, P. 17
Nogalski, J. 24
Noth, M. 61

O'Connor, M. 69

Oegema, G. 91, 102, 103, 125, 126,
Olson, D. 128

Paul, S. 110
Porteous, N. 68, 112
Portier-Young, A. 13, 115, 116
Provan, I. 18
Poythress, V. 33, 69
Puech, E. 74

Radner, E. 40
Redditt, P. 32, 94
Rendtorff, R. 28
Ricouer, P. 128
Riffaterre, M. 127
Rigger, H. 36, 69
Rowe, C. K. 145
Rowley, H. H. 65
Ryle, H. 12

Sæbø, M. 58
Sailhamer, J. 15, 110, 153
Sanders, J. 10
Scalise, C. 10
Scheetz, J. 7
Schlenke, B. 32 51, 62, 69, 100
Schmid, K. 13, 34, 51, 54, 55, 62, 63,
    80, 82, 103, 104, 112
Schultz, R. 15
Seeligman, I. L. 15, 26
Seitz, C. 11, 17, 18, 21, 22, 23, 24, 28,
    29, 30, 61, 64, 65, 98124, 127, 131,
    138, 139, 141, 142
Shea, W. 90
Sheppard, G. 29, 60
Smith, T. C. 124
Sommer, B. 12, 26, 27
Steck, O. H. 49, 62
Steinberg, J. 15, 16, 28, 154
Steins, G. 15
Strickert, F. M. 91
Stone, M. 78
Stone, T. 15, 24, 59
Su, S. P. 123

Sumner, G. 40, 51, 52, 57, 65, 105,
    123, 126, 128, 134, 136, 137, 138,
    139, 144, 145, 146
Sundberg, A. 12
Swanson, T. 29
Sweeney, M. 38, 40, 46, 63, 67, 68,
    70, 88, 89, 92, 9396, 126, 130,
Thielman, F. 10
Thiering, B. 78
Thiselton, A. 123
Torrance, T. F. 126
Treier, D. 17, 18

Ulrich, E. 11, 12

Vanderkam, J. 5, 6, 7, 32, 74, 79, 80,
    81
Van Deventer, H. 62, 63
VanGemeren, W. 24, 105, 126, 146
Vanhoozer, K. 10, 16, 17, 24
Vanonen, H. 5
Van Ruiten, J. 73
Venter, P. 25
Vermes, G. 80
Vogel, W. 6, 43, 68, 72, 85, 88, 89, 90
Von Rad, G. 125

Wacholder, B. Z. 76
Wallace, D. 136
Wallraff, M. 68
Waltke, B. 10, 69
Walvoord, J. 124
Watson, F. 16
Watts, J. 56
Webster, J. 14, 19, 129, 141
Weigold, M. 60
Wellhausen, J. 130
Wells, S. 40, 52, 57, 65, 105, 123, 126,
    128, 134, 136, 137, 138, 139, 144,
    146
Werline, R. 13, 31, 36
Wesselius, J.W. 65
Westermann, C. 56, 87
Wildeboer, G. 12
Willis, A. M. 6, 34, 49, 62, 120, 128

Willis, L. 70
Wilson, G. 33, 34, 43
Wilson, R. 13, 46
Wolterstorff, N. 16

Zakovitch, Y. 26, 73
Zenger, E. 59

Index of Scripture

Old Testament

Genesis
1 138
1:11-12 43
1:26 43
1:27 43
1:28 43
1:29-30 43
2 71
2:1-3 41, 43, 125
2:2 85
2:3 85
3:17-19 43
9:11 107
29:27 70
41:7 70
41:22 70
41:36 107
50:3 70

Exodus
7:25 70
8:9 107
12:15 107
12:16 87
13:6 72
13:7 75
15:17-18 117
16:23 71
20:11 84
23:14-18 72
23:20-23 43
23:26 70
24:12 73
24:15-18 73
29:35 70
29:36 87
29:37 87
30:26 87
31:13 84
31:14 107
31:15 71, 85
31:16 84-85, 112
31:17 84
32:7 55
32:11-13 40
34:10 55
34:28 56
35:2 85

Leviticus
8:33 70
11:7 115
16:31 85
23:2 85
23:3 71
23:15 69, 71, 85
23:32 85
23:39 72
23:34-40 72
25 8, 41-42, 44, 148
25:1-55 76
25:1-11 82
25:1 43
25:2 43
25:2-7 72
25:3 43
25:4 43, 50, 85
25:5 43, 50
25:6 50
25:2-6 43
25:8 41, 43, 69, 71, 85
25:8-17 72
25:9 43
25:10-54 74
25:10 74
25:11 72, 74
25:23-24 44
25:55 55
26 34, 38, 42-44, 47
26:2 4
26:4 43
26:11 4
26:12-25 43
26:17-31 47
26:14-46 53
26:17 53
26:18 41, 44, 70, 118
26:19-20 44
26:20 118
26:21 41, 44-45, 70
26:22 44-45
26:23 44-45
26:24 41, 44-45, 70, 118
26:25 44
26:27 45
26:28 41, 45, 70, 118
26:24-27 9
26:27-38 45
26:27-45 9
26:31 4, 42, 45, 53, 82, 118
26:32 45, 82, 118
26:33 45, 82, 118
26:34 118
26:34-35 1-3, 24, 38-39, 42, 82, 112
26:36-40 2, 42
26:39-45 64
26:40 43, 45, 47, 51, 53, 63, 148
26:41 148
26:41-42 42, 45
26:43 44-45, 82
26:44 44-45
26:45 42, 44-45
26:46 42-43
27:17-24 74

Numbers
5:21 40
18:3 112
24:24 43
31:6 112
36:4 74

Deuteronomy
1:1 56
1:37 55
2:25 43
4:21 55
4:30 43
5:1 56
7:9 43
9:6-29 55
9:9 56
13:16 106
14:22 70
15:1-11 72
15:2 74
16:9 71
18:18 45-46, 49, 57
24:16 40
24:28 43, 51
24:37 117
24:15-68 43
24:53-57 106
29:19-26 43
29:20 40-41, 43
29:34 41
30:1-10 64
30:2-3 34
30:15 57
30:19 57
30:20 57
31:10 72
31:16-21 43
31:16 43
31:20 43
31:21 43
32 40, 47
32:9 53
32:13 53
32:28-29 40
32:29 58
32:27-43 47
32:47 57
34:5 43, 45
34:8 46
34:9 46
34:10 46
34:12 56
34:10-12 32, 55, 59

Joshua
1:1-2 60
1:2 60
1:7 60
1:8 57-58
1:13 45
6:19 112
7:20-21 37
8:31 45
8:32 40, 46
8:33 45
11:12 45
23:6 40

Judges
8:14 70
10:15 37
19:15-24 106

1 Samuel
2:33-36 107
15:24-25 37

2 Samuel
12:13 37
21:10 117

1 Kings
6:1 77
7:45-51 112
8:46-53 64
11:5 113
11:7 113
17:13 55
19:10 55

2 Kings
9:7 46
14:6 40
23:13 113
25:8-12 112
25: 13-21 112
25:27-30 38

Isaiah
1:10-15 112
2:2 47, 49, 110
2:4 108, 120
2:6 48
8:11 47
10:1-2 110
10:10-11 110
10:15-20 110
10:20 52, 110-111
10:21 52, 110-111
10:22-23 5, 39, 52, 57, 110-111, 117
10:23 110
10:24-27 52
10:32 49, 108
11:5 86
11:6-9 110
11:9 110
14:2-3 48
15:1 118
16:4 118
19:2 108, 133
26:16 106
26:19 110
26:20 110
27:13 49
28:22 117
29:2 106
29:7 106
30:25 49
31:4 108
33:6 106
33:20 108
40:1-12 49
41:15-16 110
42:1-4 54
42:5-7 54
44:18 57
45:1 112
45:1-6 54
45:4 54
45:17 86
52:7 74
52:13 54, 57
52:15 58
53:12 54, 57
54:10 49
55:12 49

58:14 53
59:14 106
59:20 108
60:14 108
64:9-10 114
66:12-16 119
66:24 110

Jeremiah
1:1-4 34
1:9 57
1:12 36
4:13 118
4:20 118
4:30 118
5:1 106
7:4 50
7:13 50
7:14 50
7:15 50
7:25 46, 55, 57
7:26 55
9:23 57
10:21 57
11:7-8 50
14:13 108, 120
14:15 108, 120
16:18 118
17:25 52
19:9 106
21:8 57
23:16 118
23:18 118
23:20 36
23:39 47
25 43, 52
25:1 49
25:2 53
25:1-9 33
25:4 55
25:5 46
25:8 35
25:9 53
25:10-12 1-2, 8-9, 24, 33-34, 38, 70
25:11 49-51, 63, 82, 84, 117, 125
25:12 49-50, 82, 84, 125

25:13 49, 125
25:8-14 2, 50, 54
25:13 38
25:14 35, 38, 125
25:18 52
25:34-38 50
26:19 41
27:7 50
27:17-22 2
29 34, 43
29:1 49
29:1-23 33
29:10 1-2, 24, 33, 35-36, 49-51, 63-64, 82, 84
29:11 49-50
29:11-14 2, 33-34, 36, 64
29:15 33
29:18 117
29:19 46, 49, 55
29:24-32 33
30:1-2 35
30:16 47
30:24 36
31:23 49
31:28 49
32:1-22 52
32:12-16 48
32:32 52
32:34-35 118
32:37-42 119
32:26-43 52
33:8 87
34:14 52
35:15 52
36:3 49
36:4 48
36:7 49
36:21 49
36:32 48
39:8 106
42:18 117
44:4 55
44:21 52-53
44:27 49
45:1 48
46:10 47
46:26-28 54
48:8 118

48:15 118
48:20 118
49:26 106
49:28 118
50 54
50:4 37
50:7 47
50:30 106
51 54
51:48 118
51:53 118
51:55 118
51:60-63 34

Ezekiel
1:1-3 48
1:7 48
1:13-14 48
1:16 48
1:26-27 48
2:1 48
3:22 55
3:23-24 48, 55
3:25 55
3:26 55
3:27 55
5:11 113
7:20 113
8:3 48
8:5 48
11:18 113
11:21 113
20:8 113
20:12 84
20:30 113
25:7 107
28:2 5, 57
28:8 46-47
28:14 5, 46, 57
28:16 46-47
28:17 5, 46-47
28:18 47
28:19 46
32:7-8 133
35:7 107
37:24-25 54
39:23 47
39:23-26 47, 53
48:12-13 119

Index of Scripture

Hosea
3:5 37
4:1-6 55
5:6 37

Amos
2:12 55
5:16 106
8:12 37

Micah
4:1 47, 110
4:3 108, 120

Habakkuk
2:3 46

Zephaniah
2:3 37

Zechariah
1:12 8, 69, 81-82
3:9 77
8:4-5 106
8:21 37

Malachi
3:22-24 59
4:4 60
4:4-6 32, 59

Psalms
1:1 47
12:7 77
106 37

Proverbs
1:20 106
15:24 57
22:13 106
26:13 106

Song of Songs
3:2 106

Lamentations
1:4 119
2:7 106
5:18 109, 119

Daniel
1:1 119
1:2 112
1:4 58, 78
1:17 58, 146
1:21 84
2:20 133
2:20-23 47, 116
2:31-45 47
2:34 47, 68
2:35 110
2:44 116, 125
2:45 125
2:47 1, 142
2:48 146
3:12 147
3:19 70
4:22 70
4:26-27 70
4:32 70
5:2-4 112
5:11-14 146
6:3 147
7 35, 65
7:8 58
7:12 115
7:11-12 115
7:13 131, 133, 136
7:14 133, 136
7:16 1
7:18 144
7:21-22 2
7:23 133
7:24 133
7:25 132
7:27 108, 120, 133
8 35
8:1-2 48
8:10 48
8:10-12 115
8:11-14 4
8:11 114
8:12 114
8:13 76, 114-115, 117, 130-132, 135
8:14 76, 83, 87, 114
8:15 48
8:17 48
8:18 48
8:19 116, 119
8:23 86, 108, 115
8:24 108, 115
8:25 58, 68, 108, 111, 115
8:26 1
8:27 117
8:9-27 115, 117
8:19-27 36
9:1 23, 32, 35
9:2 6, 8, 23, 32-38, 40-41, 43, 46, 49, 54, 56, 63, 65-66, 68-70, 82, 84, 86, 137
9:3 63, 147
9:2-7 54
9:3-19 1, 6, 8, 23, 28, 32, 33-35, 38-43, 46, 49, 51, 54-61, 63-66, 69, 71, 84, 86-87, 136, 147-148
9:3 36-37, 65
9:4 32, 36, 42-43, 53, 60, 65
9:5 33, 42-43, 60
9:6 34, 41-43, 45, 52-53, 55, 63, 87
9:7 42-43, 52-53, 56, 87
9:8 84
9:9 84, 87
9:10 34-35, 40-41, 43, 45, 51, 55, 84
9:11 34-35, 40-41, 43, 45, 51, 56, 60, 114, 117
9:11-19 54
9:12 43, 49, 133
9:13 34, 36, 40-43, 49, 51, 56, 58, 60
9:14 35-36, 49
9:15 37, 60
9:16-19 37, 42, 46-47
9:16 49, 53-54, 87, 108
9:17 4, 36, 41, 53-55, 67, 109, 113, 117-118
9:18 36, 42, 53, 108, 117, 147
9:19 41, 53, 111, 147

9:20 32, 37-38, 42, 49, 55-56, 58, 66, 111, 147
9:20-23 8, 35, 38, 65-66, 69, 71
9:22 36-37, 58, 133
9:23 1, 36, 49, 66, 133, 147
9:24 2, 5-6, 23-24, 38, 50, 54, 63, 65-73, 75-76, 82, 84, 86-87, 108-109, 111-112, 116, 118-119, 134, 136-137, 142
9:25 23, 33, 57-58, 67, 72-73, 86, 106, 108, 123-124, 133
9:25-26 1, 3, 54, 73, 83, 85, 87, 114, 142, 146
9:24-27 1-8, 23, 28, 32-33, 35, 38, 41-42, 49, 54, 58, 61, 63-67, 69, 72, 74-75, 77-79, 81-83, 108-112, 119-124, 127-144, 146-149
9:26 46, 57, 67, 77, 84, 86, 107-115, 117, 141
9:27 1, 4, 35, 46, 57, 67, 73, 76, 83-87, 107, 109-114, 116-119, 130-132, 135, 137, 146
10:1 36
10:2-3 70
10:2-21 147
10:5-6 48
10:7-9 147
10:11 147
10:12 146
10:14 36, 84
10:18-19 147
10:22 146
10:40 68
11 76, 109, 133
11:2-45 115, 117
11:8 112
11:10 109
11:14 111
11:17 108
11:19 108
11:20-25 111
11:21 114
11:22 107, 109-111
11:23 111
11:22-25 111
11:26 109
11:27 84
11:28 110
11:29 84
11:30 43, 110
11:31 76, 109, 113-114, 117-118, 130-132, 135
11:32 110
11:33 5, 58
11:33-36 132
11:35 5, 58, 84, 133
11:36 52, 110, 133
11:40 109
11:45 109
12:1 133, 136
12:2-13 54
12:2 57, 110-111, 133

12:3 5, 57-58, 111, 132-133, 147
12:3-10 134
12:4 1, 68, 111, 147
12:6 134
12:7 87
12:8 147
12:9 1, 146
12:10 5, 58, 132-133, 147
12:10-13 57, 75
12:11 76, 83, 113-114, 117
12:12 73, 83
12:13 73, 131-133, 147

Ezra
1:1 69, 81
3:12-13 109
4:12-13 106
4:16 106

Nehemiah
2:13 106
4:7 106
10:29 40

1 Chronicles
23:13 87

2 Chronicles
7:18 107
36:20-22 69, 81, 82
36:21 8-9, 69, 81-82
36:22 59

New Testament

Matthew
18:2 136
18:21-22 70
18:23 77
18:24 3, 77, 122, 133, 138
18:3 132, 134, 137
18:4 133
18:5 133-134
18:6 133, 137
18:7 133-134
18:4-9 132-133
18:10 132
18:11 132-133
18:12 132-133
18:13 131-133, 137
18:14 137
18:15 47, 130, 134-136
18:21 133, 136-137
18:22 132, 134
18:24 133
18:27 133-134, 142
18:29 133, 137
18:30 133, 136
18:36 134
18:42 133
18:43 133, 141-142

Index of Scripture

18:44 133
18:45 134
25 3
25:1-9 134
25:10-12 136
25:13 133
25:27-28 136
25:34 137
25:37 137
25:35-46 137

Mark
3:24 136
7:9 136
13 3, 122, 138
13:14 135
13:26 131
14 47
14:62 131

Luke
21 3, 122
21:20 136

John
8:3 136
19:31 71

Acts
7:60 136
22:30 136

Romans
3:23 144
3:31 136
10:3 136

1 Corinthians
1:2 144
2:7 141

Ephesians
1:8 141
1:17 141

Colossians
2:3 141

Hebrews
1:1 148
10:9 136

1 Peter
1:6-9 141

Revelation
12 138
13:9-10 141
16:5 142
17:9 77
21:2-3 142

Septuagint

Daniel
3:32 114

9:24 77-78
9:26-27 78

12:13 132

Josephus

Against Apion
1:38-40 34

Antiquities
3:38 29
4:302-304 29
5:61 29

10:267-268 47
12:253 114

Early Church

Irenaeus
Against Heresies
3:21.10-23.8 141

Rabbinic Sources

b. Nedarim 60-61 76

Apocrypha and Pseudapigrapha

Assumption of Moses
10:5 133

1 Esdras
1:33 34
1:42 34
5:49 34
7:6 34

2 Esdras
5:4 133
12:10 130

Jubilees
1:15-18 74
7:8-9 74
11:14 74
12:15 74
50:2 73

1 Enoch
10:20-22 87
80:4 133
89:59-77 75
91:17 75
93:1 75
93:3 75
95:10 75

Wisdom of Ben Sira
1:1 34
1:10 33
1:20 34
1:25 34
46:1 29
49:13 29

1 Maccabees
1:10 114
1:11 111
1:54 76, 114
4:36-59 76
4:38 109
4:52 114
6:7 114
6:53 76
14:25-49 14

2 Maccabees
3 55
4 108
6:1-2 114
6:2 114
6:7 115
6:12-15 121
10:1-8 76
15 55
15:9 34

4 Maccabees
18:10 34

CD
3:20 3
4:4 3
7:15-17 29, 34
16:3-4 76

Seventh Vision of Daniel
3:1 77
25:2 77

4QapocrJer 57

1QM
10:5-7 3

1QPHab
7:4-5 46, 79

1QIsa 54

1QS
1:2-3 29, 34
5:17 41
8:14 41
8:15-16 29
10:7-8 75

4QPs-Ezek 57

4Q174
3:18 3
4:4 3

2Q25 34

4Q177
10:1-2 77

4Q243 76-77
16:1 77

4Q504
6:4-8 45

4QFlor
2:3 41, 47
5 117
6 117

19 79
20 79

4QMMT
9-11 34

11QMelch 72

www.ingramcontent.com/pod-product-compliance
Lightning Source LLC
Chambersburg PA
CBHW030521080526
44586CB00011B/278